THE ENDLESS HOURS

THE ENDLESS HOURS

MY TWO AND A HALF YEARS AS A PRISONER OF THE CHINESE COMMUNISTS

by Wallace L. Brown

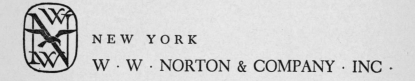

NEW YORK
W · W · NORTON & COMPANY · INC ·

To the ten members of the crew of
Stardust Four-Zero
who shared these endless hours, and
in memory of the three who died that cold January night.

THE ENDLESS HOURS

CHAPTER

ONE

"See those lights, Brownie?" My aircraft commander, Captain Eugene Vaadi, pointed up ahead and to the left where four long, slender fingers of light were sweeping back and forth across the clear night sky. They were enemy searchlights, probing the sky for planes of a bomber stream which we, in our lone B-29, were following. We were about fifteen minutes behind the last bomber. Our targets were different, but we could see their flares slowly floating toward the ground and the orange bursts of light as their bombs exploded.

This was my first combat mission—the night of January 12, 1953. It was cold and raining that afternoon when I kissed my wife good-bye and joined the rest of the crew for briefing at Yokota Air Base, Japan. It was still raining at dusk when we took off; but here, over North Korea, about three hours later, the skies were clear. Captain Vaadi was on his second Korean Mission. He had seen combat over Europe during World War II and had been shot down and held prisoner for a short time near the end of the war. As a combat veteran, he was making sure that I, his second-lieutenant co-pilot, saw all the signs of combat. None of us realized how much we would see before we arrived back in Japan—not six hours later, as planned, but after more than thirty-one months.

Our bomb bays were loaded with leaflet-filled bombs which we were to drop over six North Korean towns. News was printed on some of the leaflets, and "GET OUT—THIS TOWN IS GOING TO BE BOMBED" on others. Our first three drops were uneventful, with one minor exception. When Captain Vaadi opened the bomb-bay doors on our first target run, I was busy with the radio and didn't hear his warning. The doors flapped out into the slip stream, and as I felt the resulting shock on the airplane, I thought we had been hit by antiaircraft fire. Luckily, before I got too alarmed I saw the small amber light that indicated the doors were open, and I realized what had happened. This moment of alarm made me take stock of myself and my equipment. I made sure everything was secure. I removed my oxygen mask from its storage hook by my seat, and fastened it to my helmet so I could snap it on in a couple of seconds if necessary. I also made sure my survival kit was handy.

Shortly after leaving the third target, our tail gunner reported con-trails streaming out behind us. These long streaks of vapor caused by our engine exhausts were all the searchlight operators on the ground needed. They could sweep their lights back and forth until they spotted this trail and then follow it to the plane. A half-dozen lights were already sweeping the trail and moving closer. We began a hurried descent, hoping the temperature difference a few thousand feet lower would stop the formation of vapor. Two thousand feet down the trails disappeared, but not before the powerful beams had swept across our plane, lighting up the inside. Leveling off at 20,000 feet, we lost the lights and proceeded to our fourth and fifth targets.

The waist gunners and bombardier reported flak bursting wide and below us as we turned toward Cholson, North Korea, our last target for the night. We were now over what was called "Searchlight Alley," because of the large numbers of lights supposed to be concentrated in the area.

At first there were none visible in our immediate vicinity, but about one minute from our final target the night suddenly turned to day. Approximately twenty to thirty pairs of the giant lights snapped on at almost the same instant. We were caught in beam after beam and none of our evasive maneuvers could shake them. In what seemed like only seconds a stream of tracers raced by from the rear, followed by a Mig 15 which passed under our left wing and disappeared, climbing out of the lights in front of us. He hit our number two engine and left it a mass of flames. Vaadi had barely feathered it when we felt the vibration of our tail guns being fired. Two more Migs screamed by, one below and one above. The lower one hit our number four engine, which burst into flames. The third one loosed a salvo of rockets which passed just over the fuselage, missing us by only a few inches. We no sooner got number four feathered than the engineer reported loss of power and a small fire in number three. We didn't know whether it had been hit by antiaircraft fire from the ground or by a few shells from the last Mig, but we didn't feather it. We needed what little power we could get to keep control of our badly crippled and burning B-29.

While Vaadi gave the bail-out signal, I tried to make radio contact with the ground-radar station that was monitoring our flight path. I was unable to raise them on our assigned channel, so I changed to the standard emergency, or dog, channel. By now the nose gear had been lowered to make room for bailing out through the nose-wheel well. The bombardier climbed out of his seat in the nose, made his way back between the pilots' seats and disappeared through the hatch. He was followed by the two observers, one of whom was wounded in the leg. The navigator, who was also wounded, opened the door into the forward bomb bay, which was his emergency escape route; but he saw one of the big bay doors flapping in the breeze, making bail-out there dangerous. He turned around to the radio operator, who was neatly folding and stowing his mike cord and head set. He motioned him forward and they both disappeared down the nose-wheel well. By this time I had my radio tuned to the new frequency. I made a "Mayday" (distress) call and received an immediate answer. The voice said, "Go ahead Stardust four-zero." In the same breath he said, "Get a fix, George." This last remark was not meant for me, but for another operator on the ground who would make a radio fix of our position.

The plane was going out of control; I could see Captain Vaadi fighting to right it. I grabbed hold of my wheel to lend a hand and discovered that we had no aileron control: the wheel turned freely in my hands. Apparently the fires had burned through the cables. At that moment my throat mike came loose and dropped in my lap. The controls were useless; Vaadi bent down to put on his overshoes while I fumbled with my mike. Holding it to my throat, I got back on the radio and told the ground station that we had been hit by fighters, were on fire, and were bailing out. I didn't wait for an answer—our B-29 had already held together longer than it should have. As I climbed out of my seat, the daylight brightness suddenly dimmed to a flickering red. The searchlights had been turned off as if by a single switch, leaving only the flames from our burning engines to light up the cabin. By this time the aircraft was no longer flying; it was falling. I had to struggle to make my way the few feet from my seat to the bail-out hatch. I got to the hatch and noticed the engineer was still sitting at his panel. As I stopped and watched, he calmly, almost casually swung his legs over the side of his seat and disappeared through the hatch. Seconds later I followed him out into the forty-degree-below-zero darkness. Just as I dropped out of the burning plane, some part of it tore loose and hit me, ripping off my leather helmet, right glove, and the left leg of my heavy winter overpants. I was stunned, but the intense cold helped me keep my senses and dulled any pain. I heard a weird, high-pitched noise, which I guessed was our B-29 in its dying dive. I pulled my rip-cord and felt a world of relief as I received the opening shock.

I looked up at the parachute canopy just to be sure, and then looked down. Off to one side were two patches of flame separated by several hundred yards; one was much larger than the other. These were the remains of our B-29. The smaller patch of flame must have been one of the engines, or a wing that had burned and blown off just before it crashed. I noticed that I was still holding my D-ring, the parachute rip-cord's metal handle. I remembered from survival school that this could be a useful article, but my gloveless hand had grown numb, and I dropped the D-ring into the darkness below. I tried to put the hand in my jacket pocket, but my parachute harness was in the way, so I held it under my left armpit. All this had taken only a few seconds, but I could already see a mountain top rising nearby. I grabbed my risers and put my feet together in readiness to land. I could hear a dog barking below, and looking down again, I saw a small snow-covered field between two hills. The rows outlined in the snow looked very close together, giving me the impression that I was still some distance above the ground. A second later those same rows stopped my descent. Then I remembered: crops are planted much closer in the Orient than back home in Alabama.

I rolled instinctively as I landed in the snow, and the shock was much easier than I expected. I came down at the very edge of the small field; I could hear voices along with the barks. I could understand the barks better than the voices, but neither sounded very friendly. My parachute canopy settled over the top of some small scrubby trees at the edge of the field and became thoroughly tangled when I tried to pull it loose. I unbuckled the harness, grabbed my survival kit, and ducked back into the bushes, leaving the parachute. I was exhausted after moving a very few yards. This was a surprise, since I was in fair physical condition; but I still had to stop for rest. I began to feel a burning around my left eye and my left leg started to hurt. Although I had lost my helmet, my head was warm and my face felt flushed. I examined my face and leg and found them only bruised and scratched. I opened my survival kit to look for the hat and gloves I knew were supposed to be there. Instead I found an antimosquito head net and an oilcloth sun-rain hat, two items which had no place in a winter survival kit. I had been issued the kit just before the mission, and now I wished I had taken time to check to see if it was complete. I put the oilcloth hat on anyway, and took the leather shell off my left wool glove and put it on my right hand.

I could still hear activity across the field, so I crammed the articles back in the kit and started off again. I made my way a few yards further. This time the going was more difficult; it was up hill and through dense brush. I had to stop and rest again, but after a couple of minutes I started off and managed to go several dozen yards before stopping for more rest. I came to a small thicket where the pine needles underneath were almost bare of snow. After crawling well into the thicket, I stopped and began to rearrange my equipment for better traveling.

Inspecting the ripped leg of my overpants, I found the heavy zipper torn apart. I took a knife and cut some straps from my Mae West; after punching some holes, I then managed to lace my pants leg so it would offer some cover instead of dragging along behind. The oilcloth hat had frozen stiff as a board, providing very little protection, and I was beginning to feel the cold. I emptied the kit bag, and after I cut some eyeholes, put it on for a hood. Along with my survival kit, the bag contained a portable radio transmitter-receiver unit. Both articles were strapped to a vest, so I slipped them on over my jacket. The leather glove shell had also become stiff, giving little warmth to my hand, which began to ache and throb. I put the shell back on the other hand and examined my bare right hand to see what was causing the pain. I discovered that the little finger was broken in the last joint. There were no cuts, so I pulled the end to try to slip the bone back in place. Then I took an extra pair of socks from my pocket and substituted those for the missing glove.

Meanwhile I could feel other sore spots. My right foot and right shoulder felt as if they had been sprained. I found the reason when I discovered that a leather strap had been jerked off my right overshoe and a seam on the right sleeve of my nylon jacket had been pulled apart. Whatever hit me when I bailed out had given me quite a jolt, and my rapid tiring was probably caused by a state of near shock.

My strength was fast returning; so, making sure I left nothing behind, I started climbing the hill again. The hill wasn't high, but the snow made going rather difficult and I slid down continually.

The snow had soaked through my sock-glove and I tried to keep my hand in my pocket. This didn't contribute much to my efforts to walk without falling. When I reached the summit, which was clear of trees, I could see that my climb had been for nothing. I was on top of a very small hill completely surrounded by fields. An enemy search party would have no trouble flushing me out if I stayed there, especially since my parachute canopy, hanging in the trees, would show them exactly where to start looking.

I sat awhile, resting and looking at the flaming wreckage of our B-29 which was scattered over a large area on the side of a low hill less than a mile away. I could still hear an occasional bark from the house near where I had landed, but no voices. I hoped the people had gone back to bed. I heard a motor vehicle off in the distance, and from the sound I guessed it was a truck on a poor road. It seemed to be having a rough time. I could also hear other dogs, but none as close as the first. In the opposite direction from the burning wreckage I could see what looked like a fairly high mountain. I decided to tackle it, hoping it would give me a better hiding place.

Seeing that no matter how careful I was I still left an obvious trail in the snow, I took the easiest way down from my perch. One side was a straight slope to the field below and was bare except for small bushes. I chose this way and slid to the bottom, breaking my speed now and then by grabbing a passing bush. The trip down took a fraction of the time I had spent going up. I brushed myself off, checked my equipment, and then walked around the edge of the hill until I was opposite the mountain. As I walked across the field toward a grove of trees, I almost blundered into a small hut which was hidden from view by the darker shadows of the trees. I ducked quickly into the grove and breathed a thankful prayer that the occupants of this house did not have a dog.

At first, the going was easy. There was little underbrush and I found a small stream bed which I followed for a while. There was less snow to betray my tracks and most of what there was I could easily avoid. After I left the stream bed, which had some patches of ice here and there, the slope became steeper and trees fewer, but the underbrush much thicker. I finally had to crawl underneath the thick, bushy scrub oaks. Progress was very slow and tortuous but much safer, since my trail was better hidden. After some yards of travel in this manner, I came across a well-worn path, which led up the ridge and looked inviting, but I realized that if I followed it my tracks could probably be spotted easily. Resisting the temptation, I slid back into the underbrush and tried to erase the marks I had made on and near the path. Then I continued to crawl through the brush in a direction I guessed to be parallel to the path. Finally the bush grew less dense and soon disappeared completely. In its place I met big boulders. For the most part these were completely bare of snow; the wind apparently had cleared them. By carefully picking my way from rock to rock I was able to move without leaving any trail at all. The going got steeper, until eventually I was clinging to the face of a cliff. Darkness didn't help my climbing much, but at least I couldn't see what was below me. I climbed, groping from rock to rock, until I found a big boulder with a small hollow space behind it.

I slid into the cavelike hole—and only then did I realize just how tired I was. My bulky clothing, shoes, and equipment had not made the climb any easier. I took off the radio and survival vest and then my Mae West, which I decided to discard. Nor had I been able to wear the makeshift hood very long; it got stiff from the cold and the noise of bushes brushing against it made me feel as if my head was in a drum. In the semiprotection of the rock, I slipped it back on. Inflating the Mae West for a pillow, I curled up and dropped off to sleep.

I didn't check the time before going to sleep, but I couldn't have slept more than half an hour. I woke much refreshed, although I had grown very cold. I was still extremely sore, and my left eye had swollen almost completely shut. I started to light a cigarette, but thought better of taking a chance on the light being spotted. I could hear various noises around the countryside, one of which sounded like a motorcycle. I looked around, but couldn't tell how much higher I'd have to climb before reaching the top of the rocky cliff. Dropping the Mae West in a crevice behind a rock, I picked up the rest of my equipment and continued groping my way from rock to rock. I climbed on for some time—not always going up, for I often had to move along the face of the cliff looking for a way to continue upward.

I don't know how high the cliff was, but it took some effort to reach a ridge running along the top. Just before I got there, I saw a sort of cave made by two boulders leaning together. I climbed into the cave and once again curled up and went to sleep. As before, I awoke shivering, and chilled to the bone. This time I had only been asleep a few minutes. Making sure I had all my equipment, I climbed back to the ridge and proceeded uphill. Far to the southeast I could see a low range of mountains. Every few minutes, they were outlined by bombs or shells bursting beyond them. I could not hear the explosions, but I ruled out the possibility of flares because the lights were not sustained. Going along the ridge was fairly easy. The chilling wind was stronger, but there was still some snow on the ground. This didn't worry me at first. I reasoned that, although my parachute canopy hanging in the trees would surely be seen the next day, anyone trying to follow my trail from there would lose trace of me at the foot of the cliff if not before.

I soon found reason to worry, however, when a little further up the ridge I discovered that I was actually following a path—probably the same one I had found at the foot of the mountain. I continued up the path until I came to a broadening of the ridge. Here I found a huge rock in the shape of an almost perfect cube. I sat down on the sheltered side for a rest and considered using it as a hiding place. I thought it would be possible to lie flat on the top and not be seen, but looking uphill, I decided anyone up there could see me. After a few minutes I continued up the mountain.

I left the path and tried to make my way parallel to it by using

rocks, as much as possible, for stepping stones. This slowed my
progress considerably and it was beginning to get light when I
reached the top. Nearby stood another mountain, a little higher
and bare of vegetation. Seeing I would have to cross an open, snow-
covered valley to reach it, I decided to stay where I was. Some large
boulders off to one side furnished a fair hiding place and I got behind them and settled down to wait for daybreak.

I decided to risk a smoke and got out one of my five packs of
cigarettes. I had put these, along with some cigars and two extra
pairs of socks, in my flying-suit pocket before leaving Japan—just
in case. I got out a cigarette and looked for my lighter, but couldn't
find it in any of my pockets. Apparently I lost it when I bailed out.
I knew there was a fire-starting kit included in my survival equipment, but after getting it out I couldn't make it work. That made
me unhappy, but I still had my smoke because, in another of my
pockets, I had what I called my personal emergency survival kit.
It consisted of three aluminum cigarette cases containing a total of
fifty-seven articles, all carefully packed and sealed with wax. These
were kits I had made up of things I thought would be most
valuable to a person lost in a wilderness with nothing else. They
contained such items as small wire, fish hooks, a compass, a miniature pad and pencil, medicines, sugar, salt, pepper, and stick
matches—fifty of them, all individually coated with wax to water-
proof them. These worked.

As daylight came I lit another cigarette, got out my map, and
climbed back up to the very top of the mountain to try to orientate
myself. I could see a river, all frozen over and white, which wound
around another mountain and across a valley, and led to a fair-
sized town about fifteen miles away. There were other mountains
around, all of which looked as rocky and barren as the one I was
on, and none much higher. In the valleys below I could see four
houses—one right below that looked very tiny. People were beginning to stir; they too looked very small. My roost was higher
than I thought; I judged it to be at least two thousand feet above

the fields below.

I had little success locating myself on the map, although I already knew my approximate position. During our mission briefing in Japan, the intelligence officer had praised highly the map we were issued, especially for the amount of detail it showed. I discovered that this detail confused me more than anything else. Where I could see only the river and the stream bed I had discovered during the night, the map was covered with little blue lines indicating many streams of various sizes. What I could see on the ground didn't match anything shown on the small portion of the map which I knew included my position.

While I sat there looking around, I heard jet aircraft high overhead, but although the sky was clear, I couldn't see them. I scrambled back to my hiding place where I had left my equipment, grabbed the vest containing the radio and battery, and scrambled back to my perch. The radio was one piece of equipment that I knew would work; I had talked to Yokota tower over it from my room back in Japan. I quickly hooked the battery to the receiver-transmitter unit and pulled out the antenna. The radio was both UHF and VHF and would send either voice or code transmissions. I tried them all, but received no answer. After a few minutes the sound of the jets faded away.

I continued sitting there looking at the sky for several minutes, hoping the planes would return. At the intelligence briefing before the mission, we had been told that a large percentage of pilots downed in enemy territory were picked up by rescue helicopters. We had been told what to do to facilitate this rescue. I had followed those instructions as best I could and had gained an excellent position from which signaling and rescue could be accomplished. I was sure there would be other aircraft searching for us and believed the fix, taken from my brief radio message before bailout, would tell them where to look. I was highly confident that within a few hours, or minutes, I would be spotted and rescued. The only thing that gave me cause for worry was the possibility of the enemy finding my trail in the snow before help arrived.

People were becoming more numerous down in the valley and a train was making its way along the far side of the river, revealing the location of a railroad leading out of the town. Because of the distance I had not been able to spot the tracks before. Trying not to reveal myself to any observers below, I crawled cautiously back to my den and lit another cigarette. The other one had been forgotten in my mad scramble for the radio. Keeping the radio handy, I got out a signal mirror and flares so I would be prepared when the search planes returned. While waiting I remembered the railroad and got out my map to try again to locate my position. After close scrutiny I was still unable to match what I saw on the map with what I could see of the countryside.

I was beginning to feel hungry, but I decided to save my two tins of emergency rations. I contented myself with munching on a lump of sugar taken from the same small can that held my matches. The wind had grown calm and the sun was beginning to spread a little warmth, giving me some relief from the intense cold. My bruises continued to make themselves felt, especially my bent finger and swollen eye. I picked up my signal mirror from its place beside the radio and, using my good eye to look at the bad one, saw that I had some skin missing above and below it and that it was turning purple. A nice time for a shiner, I thought, but I was relieved that it looked no more serious. I was going to take a look at my leg, but decided the pain was not sufficient to warrant untying my patched overpants and separating the two flying suits and one pair of long johns from my leg. Locating a vial of mercurochrome, I applied some to my eye, then decided it was time to take another look around the mountain. Seeing nothing to indicate that I might be in danger, I settled down to wait for my rescue.

About eleven A.M. more jets came over and again I went to work with the radio. I could not see the planes, but I used my signal mirror on the slim chance that its flash might be seen. I was careful to keep it shielded from the houses below. This time the planes were around for several minutes and I got out a full dozen transmissions, with a pause between each as I listened for an answer. I could hear voices, but they were not loud enough to understand, nor could I even determine whether they were English. They disappeared along with the noise of the jets and I sat there somewhat dejected.

Looking down the mountain I saw even more reason for dejection. Coming up the trail were five black-clothed figures. They each carried a rifle and, much to my surprise and dismay, one carried my discarded Mae West. I wondered how they found that. It could only have been an accident, for I had dropped it in a deep crack behind a large rock.

My hopes revived for a moment when the men left the trail and began to gather twigs and branches from a patch of small bushes. They made these up into bundles which they carried to the trail. While this was happening I noticed quite a bit of activity all around. People were visible in nearly every direction, and now and then I could hear motor vehicles and shouting. I watched all this for perhaps half an hour or more, then one of the twig gatherers, who had climbed further up the hill, started shouting excitedly. His pals joined him and I rightly guessed they had just noticed my tracks. Before they had only been after twigs, but now they started up the trail chattering noisily. One of them stopped to shout down the mountain to someone I could not see.

The mild dismay I felt when I first saw the men now turned to the cold realization that I would soon be discovered if I didn't move from my position. The men didn't look like soldiers, but they were armed and I had no way of knowing what their attitude would be if they found me. Maybe they were friendly (there were supposed to be "friendlies" throughout North Korea), but I didn't want to risk it. Any direction I moved from my mountain top would have left a trail in the snow just as visible as the one they were following. To go ahead would make me visible from the fields below, so I decided to backtrack.

After making this decision I sat and watched another few minutes. When the five men disappeared up part of the trail that was not visible to me, I gathered up all my equipment and started walking backwards down the tracks I had made coming up. This was tedious, for I had to bend over to minimize the danger of being spotted from below. I moved in this manner for perhaps ten minutes, pausing many times to look around and inspect the trail I hoped I was not leaving. Finally I came to some small bare boulders beside the path and, using these as stepping-stones, I made my way off the path and down to some low bushes clinging to the side of the mountain. This perch was fairly precarious, but I couldn't look for a better one—I could already hear the voices coming up the trail.

I was only about fifteen feet from the path, and by raising my head slightly I was able to see the five men as they passed my position. They were dressed in black padded trousers and coats. The rifles they carried rattled as if they were about to fall apart. They were the size of American infantry carbines and I guessed them to be the twenty-five-caliber pieces that the Japanese used in World War II.

As they passed by I noticed that from my position I could see a stretch of path further up the mountain. That meant I would be in full view if any of the men happened to look back when they got there. As quietly as possible and, of necessity, very slowly, I moved along the face of the bushy cliff until I was out of sight of the path. While I waited a pair of small musk deer ran noisily through the bushes below, giving me quite a start.

After a few minutes I cautiously climbed back to the path and, not being able to see anyone up the trail, I started down. This time I didn't bother to walk backwards. The snow was well-trampled by the five men and I wanted to move in a hurry. I went some distance downhill, sometimes in a crouch and sometimes upright, depending on the cover. Just before reaching the place where my pursuers had left their bundles of twigs, I turned off the path and made my way down into some fairly dense brush. I crawled under these to a large rock which had an overhang barely high enough for me to squeeze under.

As I lay there hoping I had lost my pursuers, I heard a rifle discharged above—whether as a signal or at the deer I didn't know. But I decided they weren't shooting at me since I had not heard the bullet. Realizing that discovery was probably imminent, I started to take out my forty-five, but thinking it over, I decided to leave the weapon in my shoulder holster under my jacket. One pistol against five rifles would probably get me killed. I took off the vest containing my radio and battery and put them, along with the map, in a small hole and covered them with snow.

The men had more than time to reach the top of the mountain and the spot where my tracks ended. The next few minutes would determine whether my ruse had worked. Either they would search the top and continue down the other side or come back down this side. If they came back the way they went up, I felt I had little chance of escaping discovery, since I had inadvertently left some tracks. I knew I had done everything I could at the present—now all I could do was wait.

I didn't have to wait long. I had been lying under the rock perhaps twenty or thirty minutes when I heard voices coming from above. I could tell by their excited nature that the spot where I left the trail had been discovered. Soon bushes started rustling, indicating that at least one of the five was making his way toward my hiding place. As he came nearer I wriggled out and peeped over the rock. I could see four men standing along the path looking down and one man about two dozen feet away, following my tracks. So far no one had spotted me, but it was inevitable that they would. After watching a few seconds, I stood up and started toward them.

CHAPTER

TWO

My sudden appearance from behind the rock startled the man nearest me. At first he seemed on the verge of bolting, but with shouted encouragement from his four companions and quieter words from me, he calmed down enough to accept my surrender. I held my hands out to show I was unarmed, but he remained very cautious until we got to the path and joined the other four who were still chattering excitedly and waving their rifles.

The one carrying my Mae West pointed to it and then to me and said some unintelligible words. It was clear, however, that he wanted to know if the article was mine. I nodded yes, which satisfied him; then all five at once began to search me. They were cautious and timid at first, merely pointing at the article they wished to see. It was obvious they were looking for weapons. When I tried to tell them that it was useless to remove all the articles from the survival vest, they became insistent and began to take them out themselves.

Their timidity vanished completely as their excitement rose with each article they took from me. In addition to the dozen or so pockets of the survival vest, there were several more in my jacket and flying suit. Every one contained something—cigarettes, cigars, handkerchiefs, two pocket knives. I felt like a loaded Christmas tree being plucked clean by a bunch of kids. Some of the items, such as rations, were in sealed tins and each of these had to be opened. The first of these I wouldn't open, but after seeing the mess they made in opening it themselves I consented to open the others. The pockets of the vest, jacket, and those visible on my outside flying suit had about been emptied when one of the men discovered my shoulder holster strap. This led to the discovery of my pistol. I hoped this would go unnoticed and so had helped them empty the pockets near it. When they found the pistol, they temporarily forgot everything else.

No particular one of the five seemed to be in charge and there was some little argument about who would keep the pistol. Finally the one who discovered it took it and promptly pulled back the bolt, putting a round in the chamber. This he fired into the air. Now there was some further argument during which the loaded weapon was waved and pointed all around—not threateningly, but carelessly as the possessor gesticulated with both hands. I didn't know what the argument was about, but I expected to see myself or one of my captors accidentally shot at any moment.

No matter who was shot it would be bad for me, I thought, so I added the English language and a few gestures of my own to the argument. This only served to increase the gun-waving. Such stupidity angered me. I reached out and took the pistol, meeting with little resistance. Still mad and talking as if they could understand me, I tried to give them a lesson in handling firearms. Then I unloaded it, kept the round and clip, and gave it back. This seemed agreeable to them and, the original argument either settled or forgotten, they began to pick up all the many items and put them back in my pockets. On the survival vest, each pocket is made of a size to fit a special item, but this presented no problem to my captors. Their five pairs of hands put such things as small fishing kits into ration-can pockets and then forced the larger ration cans into small pockets. Everything was returned except the forty-five and a pack of Old Golds. They passed the open pack around, sniffing and commenting, but they wouldn't join me in a smoke. One, a friendly-seeming chap, kept the pack and each time I finished a cigarette, he insisted I take another. Then he lit it for me.

After the incident with the pistol, things got on a friendly basis.

My captors smiled, laughed, and showed concern about my black eye and the limp when I walked. I had not noticed the limp myself, but then my mind had been occupied with more serious matters. I tried to assure my captors that there was nothing seriously wrong—especially nothing that would be helped by their dirty fingers poking around my nearly closed eye.

Included in the equipment issued me in Japan were two small cans, each about twice the size of a pocket tobacco can. One of these contained trinkets for barter, the other contained the map I had tried unsuccessfully to use and a paper called a "blood chit." This paper had useful phrases in several Asian languages and a message which stated that anyone giving aid to the bearer would be rewarded by Uncle Sam at some future date. If there was ever a time for this to work, I thought, now is it. I pulled it out and tried to carry on a conversation. I pointed to such phrases as "Are there any Americans near?" and "Will you take me to the Americans?" I showed them the phrase and told them of the reward they would receive if they helped me escape. At first, to my joy and then to my suspicion, they heartily agreed to all the phrases.

One of them read the blood chit and told the others what it said. Then they all began to smile or laugh. To the questions about the Americans they pointed off to the south and nodded emphatically. No matter what I tried to say, they still nodded. They seemed anxious to start down the mountain so finally I gave up. Two of them wanted to help me as we went down the trail, but I convinced them I could make my way better without their overeager aid. I also convinced my "cigarette bearer and lighter" that I had had all the smokes I needed for a while.

Near the foot of the mountain we were met by two more black-clad, rifle-armed men. The youngest of these appeared to be in his teens, but he immediately took charge of the group and my forty-five. He was not smiles and grins, but all business, and he acted displeased with the friendliness the others displayed toward me. They in turn seemed to resent a punk kid ordering them around. He tried to make my "cigarette bearer" put the pack he held back in my pocket, but apparently he was overstepping his authority, for the fellow muttered a few words and ignored him. Maybe he was hoping to end up sole owner of the cigarettes, but I doubt it. None of them had dared take anything—not even the cheap barter watch from the blood-chit can.

The kid's attitude plainly showed he was no friend of mine, although he almost completely ignored me. When he finally did turn to me, it was to motion me brusquely down the path. Instead of complying, I showed him the blood chit, which he looked at and put in his pocket. That proved whose side he was on if I had had any doubt, and it looked as if I'd lost my paper interpreter. I asked for it back, but in reply he motioned me down the path. I shook my head and pointed to his pocket, insisting in English that he return my paper. One or two of the others spoke up, presumably in my behalf, so he impatiently took it from his pocket and gave it back.

We resumed our jaunt down the mountain toward a farmhouse perhaps half a mile away. We were joined by other peasants along the way until I had a sizable escort. I was led, and followed, through an opening in a sturdy mud-and-stick wall which surrounded the barnyard and houses. Here a donkey was trudging round and round a grain mill which was very similar to the cane mills I had known as a boy. A scrawny tree was growing near one of the three adobe buildings. The ground was hard-packed and bare.

I was led into the largest of the buildings. Inside, an aged peasant woman was tending a dirty, runny-nosed baby. One of my captors spoke to the woman and motioned me to join the baby on the "kang"—a raised platform built across one side of the house, which served as both a bed and a seat. The kang is built over a mud fire-box and is the warmest spot in a Korean hut. I did not realize how extremely cold I had been until I sat there a few minutes and began to thaw out. It was a painful process.

Judging from the woman's actions one would have thought it was a common event for captive American flyers to be brought into her house. Her face showed complete lack of interest as she handed me a bowl of steamed rice and a round cake of bread. I took the food, more from fear of offending than from hunger; my appetite had disappeared with my freedom. I was given a pair of chopsticks to eat the rice, but when she saw my inability to handle them, the woman brought me a tablespoon. The initials U.S.M.C. were stamped on the handle.

I had been followed into the house by my entire escort and more people were arriving every minute. The hut was soon overflowing. They just stood and stared with no readable expression on their faces. Now and then one of them urged me to eat more of the tasteless bread and rice or made some comment which drew a laugh from the otherwise silent mass of people.

I had been in the hut about twenty minutes when I heard a commotion outside. The peasants began to stir, making room for a comparatively large soldier and another person who appeared to be some kind of official. The soldier wore a khaki-colored padded uniform which exaggerated his size and gave him the appearance of a small giant. His hat was of the same material and had ear flaps tied together at the top. Above the short bill was a red star—he was one of Red China's "Volunteers." Strapped to his waist on a wide leather belt was a large pistol in a wooden holster. He kept his hand on the pistol, but otherwise said and did nothing.

His companion also wore padded clothes, but they were black and of a nicer cut. He was neat and clean, which was the main reason I took him for an official; the clothes worn by the peasants and soldiers were somewhat on the filthy side. A small red flag pinned over his right coat pocket gave further evidence of his ranking status. It was a miniature replica of the Chinese Communist flag. He looked me over and then questioned the men who had captured me. I gathered from their gestures that he was asking where I had been found and if they had searched me. My faithful cigarette-bearer showed him the pack of Old Golds and he took these. He also took my pistol from the kid who had been proudly wearing it stuck in his belt. After this he turned to me and indicated to me to empty my pockets. Then he helped me do so. He was thorough in his search, but he overlooked the fact that I wore another flying suit underneath. I had a compass and several other items in the pockets of that one which he didn't find.

I tried to keep the blood chit from being discovered by taking the other things out myself, but it didn't work. He searched that pocket also and found it. After looking it over he uttered a few unkind-sounding words and continued his search. Among the things he took was the whistle from my Mae West. I wanted to give it to the baby, but was not allowed to. All the things were put into the bag I had used as a hood the night before, then handed to the soldier.

The shakedown over, I was motioned outside and escorted about two miles to another mud hut. This one didn't have a wall around it. There were several soldiers inside—more volunteers. I, along with the bag, was left in their charge. Here again I was given a position on the kang. I was pretty tired, so I lay back on the warm platform and soon dozed off.

I had been asleep for several minutes when one of the guards woke me. In his hand he held a box that had been taken from my survival kit. Apparently he had been looking through the contents of the bag and this item aroused his curiosity. After seeing what it was, I couldn't blame him—I would have wondered too, except for the instructions on the box. It was part of the fishing kit which I knew I carried, but which I had never inspected. This particular part was a portable gig which, when assembled, more resembled a small harpoon than a gig. Its handle was in several short sections that could be screwed together, and the head was an assembly of blades and other complicated pieces of metal that formed a four-bladed spearhead about two inches across. I wondered what kind of fish I was supposed to spear with that thing. I tried to explain its use, but the soldier just stood with a puzzled expression. He took it away, but in a few minutes he came back and, by gestures, quite plainly and seriously asked if it was an instrument of torture. He indicated that he thought it could be used to hang people by the mouth. He seemed quite bitter. No doubt he believed the lies the Communists feed their troops about Americans torturing their prisoners. I tried to convince him that this was not true, but I'm not sure I was very successful.

My faithful cigarette-bearer, who had followed me and had been standing nearby while I rested, now asked me if I wanted more food. When I declined he indicated I should sleep some more. He did this by placing his hands to his cheek, palms together. I was about to comply with his suggestion when the official with the red flag-badge came in. I was told to get up and go with him.

As we left the hut I noticed, lying on the floor, a package of cigarette papers which had apparently fallen from the bag containing my belongings. This was another barter item from the blood-chit can and a highly prized article among the Asiatics. I picked up the pack and gave them to my cigarette bearer. Of course the official and soldiers had to see what I handed the peasant, but after their curiosity was satisfied, the peasant was allowed to keep them. By the look on his face I knew I had at least one friend in North Korea.

We left the hut and crossed a field. There was little snow on the ground, and I thought if only I had landed there instead of a few miles away, I would not have been tracked down and captured so easily. Thinking it over later I concluded that, snow or no snow, a person could not hope to evade capture long in a country so thickly populated. This was borne out by the fact that all of my fellow crew members were captured the same day, although most of them landed in an area that was bare of snow.

After crossing a field we walked down a gully that doubled as a road. A little way down the gully we joined another group of peasants and soldiers. There, leaning against the side of the gully, sat Tech. Sergeant Howard Brown, the flight engineer from the plane. We greeted each other and he asked how I got my black eye. Before I could answer we were hustled apart and warned not to talk. While pretending to talk to the official I asked the sergeant if he had seen any of the crew. He answered "no" with a shake of the head. The guards insisted I be quiet so I didn't press the issue, thinking I'd get a chance to compare notes with him later.

We were there only a few minutes when transportation arrived in the form of a cart pulled by two bullocks hitched in tandem. The sergeant and I climbed aboard and were made to sit back to back while several soldiers climbed on around us. The peasants and the soldiers who couldn't find room on the overloaded cart walked along above us on the banks of the gully. The ride lasted several minutes, during which we were met by a soldier-messenger on a motorcycle. He departed with a roar after a few words with the official, probably to report our capture.

Finally we arrived at a sort of crossroads where an American-made weapons carrier was waiting. After changing vehicles, all the soldiers piled on and, with the official in front by the driver, we started up the road leaving the peasants, including my cigarette bearer, behind. We rode half an hour, passing a few farm huts along the way. I noticed that most of them were enclosed by mud and stick fences. All the peasants wore the same style of padded pants and coats. Some stood and stared curiously as we drove by on the bumpy dirt road; others didn't give us a glance. We came to a group of six or eight huts and the driver stopped in front of one of them.

Howard Brown was led inside by two of the soldiers. When he was safely out of sight, I was led into the same building. In the central room of the hut I took a seat on the usual kang, while the soldiers stood around and stared at me. I could hear people in both the flanking rooms and knew the sergeant was in one of them. He was being questioned by someone who spoke English. The questioner didn't seem to be getting many answers.

While I was sitting there, the door to the room on the left opened and two soldiers led Airman Steve Kiba, our radio operator, out and into the yard. I spoke as he passed, but he was hurried away. A few minutes later he was brought back through. We spoke again—just a greeting.

Two men wearing brown wool uniforms came out of the other room. On their hats they displayed the same red star worn by the soldiers, but their uniforms were much different. They, like the soldiers, wore no rank insignia, but they appeared to be officers. One of them asked my name and then asked whom I had been talking to. He seemed a little perturbed when the guards told him I had seen Kiba, the radio operator. He asked about my eye and leg and if I thought I needed medical attention. When I told him "no" the two went into the room where the radio operator had been taken. After a few minutes they came out and left the building.

Several minutes later I was led outside and motioned into the weapons carrier. I was made to sit facing forward with my head down. Howard Brown and Kiba were led out and seated the same way. When I tried to raise my head a soldier pushed it back down. Another person got in behind and after a couple of whispers I recognized one of our scanners, Airman Benjamin. The soldiers covered us with a torn parachute canopy and kept our heads pushed down. We had been sitting there a few minutes when someone else was led up. I recognized Captain Vaadi's voice when he said, "Don't I get to keep these?" From the slight rattle I guessed he was being relieved of his identification tags. (Mine had been taken from me and I too had protested.) He was quickly hushed and loaded into the back. With soldiers crowding on the sides and in front, we were driven away.

It was almost dark when we left the small village. With the parachute canopy over my head, I was unable to see anything along the road. After several minutes we crossed a bridge. I could hear the guard posts go swish-swish and the roadway sounded as if it was made of wooden planks. Shortly after crossing the bridge we were again making short turns and stopped two or three times. I guessed, correctly, that we were in a town. We stopped and were taken off the weapons carrier one at a time. I was the last one off.

There were no lights, but I could see the outline of several buildings. The guards led me toward a fairly large one, still making me keep my head down. The town seemed very quiet. I could tell the streets were paved and the sidewalks were not. We entered the hallway of the building and went into a large lighted room.

I was given a seat at a long table while the guards stood around. All the windows were covered with blackout curtains. A chubby-looking woman in a padded uniform brought some food. I didn't particularly care for the look or taste of it, but ate a little anyway. I was too tired and weary to be very hungry. I was also given a cup of hot water to drink. People went busily in and out, and the official with the red flag-badge brought me a brown padded coat and hat to match. I welcomed these for the truck ride had been very chilling and there was no visible or feelable heat in the room. I had no idea where I was, but I was told some months later that the building was the police station in Antung, just over the North Korean border in Communist China.

CHAPTER

THREE

After sitting about two hours I was led outside to a waiting jeep. Two Volunteers and a civilian driver got in with me and we were soon leaving the town in the darkness. We rode perhaps half an hour over fairly good roads, stopping at the end of our journey in front of a two-story structure. The two soldiers climbed out, pulling me out behind them, and the jeep departed.

The street, or whatever we were standing in, was dark but not wholly deserted. More soldiers were waiting around. They led me into a building and up a flight of wooden stairs. The room we entered at the top of the stairs had an electric light bulb hanging from the ceiling and a straw mattress lying on the dirt- and dust-covered floor by a steam radiator. I didn't have to be encouraged to lie down. A soldier brought me a blanket and I was soon asleep.

In a few minutes, however, I was roused by a soldier who apparently was my guard. There were two other men standing by me. One wore the uniform I had earlier labeled as an officer's and the other was a civilian. The officer spoke English. He said he had brought the doctor to look at me. The civilian examined my black eye and, finding it nothing more than a bruise, indicated that it would be all right. He didn't bother to look at my leg; as I was standing on it, it was obviously not broken. The officer asked if I needed anything and told me the radiator didn't work, but some one would come to fix it. I was certainly aware that it didn't work. I was cold in spite of the heavy coat and blanket. My visitors left and I lay back down. The guard stood by the door. Before going to sleep I noticed he was armed with an American carbine.

When I awoke the next morning the same guard was still there.

I said "good morning" and he shook his head. I was inclined to agree with him, that under the circumstances it wasn't such a good morning, but he shook his head to everything I said. I decided he wasn't being disagreeable; he just didn't want me to talk.

I explored the room which was about sixteen feet square and at one time had been papered with plain brown paper. It now had large patches of wood showing where the paper had been peeled off. There were two sets of closets—at least I thought they were closets. I finally figured out that the shelves were actually bunks, three high and a little short by American standards. The floor was literally covered with trash and dirt. There were two windows along one side of the room, pasted over with newspaper.

One of the soldiers brought me a bowl of food and a spoon. When he opened the door, I saw there was another soldier at the foot of the stairs, also armed with a carbine. I took the bowl and ate the contents, not knowing what it was. It looked like some kind of coarse leaf cut into strips and boiled with a little meat and some small spongy-looking cubes. It was tasteless, but hot. After eating I was given a cup of hot water which also helped to warm me.

I wanted to use part of the water to bathe my eye and the scratches on my leg. My handkerchief had been taken from me, so I pulled a piece of cotton from a seam of the padded coat and used this. The guard, noticing what I was trying to do, took a small mirror from his pocket and handed it to me. My eye was feeling better, but was still swollen and blue. After bathing it, I took off my flying pants and boots and took a look at my leg. Dried blood had glued my long johns to the scratches, but with the use of a little water I separated the two. The scratches didn't look bad, but they were still plenty sore. I asked the guard for something to put on them, but he shook his head so I had to be satisfied with cleaning them.

Then I explored the room and found part of an old straw mattress. Using this, I made a broom and swept the trash and dirt into a pile. I did it in stages because of the dust it raised. When I attempted to open a window the guard stopped me. He did open the door, however, which helped a little.

While I was busy raising dust, the guard stayed outside the door on the stair landing. I took this opportunity to tear part of the paper off a window and look out. I could see soldiers outside and a row of four two-story wooden barracks facing the one I was in. They appeared to be deserted. Considering the state of the one I was in, I felt sure it had not been occupied either until I arrived. I wondered why such comparatively modern structures were not in use.

While peeping out the window I saw Howard Brown come out of a door below and, with a guard on each side, walk up the avenue between the barracks. It was comforting to see him although I was sure that he and the others I had seen after capture were being held in other rooms of the same building or in other buildings near by. I suspected he was being taken to a latrine and I was feeling an urge myself. I told my guard, hoping to be taken while Howard was still there. The guard called down the stairs and, after receiving an answer from below, said something that sounded like "*mamonte.*" Since he made no move to take me out, this obviously meant "later." In a few minutes I heard someone enter the room below and guessed Howard was back. My guard motioned me to tear some paper off the wall and follow him. I knew now what had happened to the wallpaper.

I took a piece and went down stairs. At the bottom landing the guard stopped, keeping me inside while he looked out and shouted up and down the avenue to make sure the way was clear. It seemed our captors didn't want any of the crew to see or communicate with each other.

One of the soldiers standing around outside joined us as we walked up a slope to a long, low, open building. There was no mistaking the function of the structure; the odor was terrible. Inside there was a long concrete slab with a row of rectangular chutes opening into a pit below. The chutes were about nine inches wide by thirty inches long, and midway on either side the concrete was slightly raised and formed into the shape and size of a shoe sole. When one assumed a squatting position with feet placed on these, there was little danger of missing the chute.

On the way back I got a chance to see the entire camp layout. There were two rows of four barracks each, facing each other across a dirt avenue. The avenue ran downhill with the latrine across the uphill end. At the opposite, or downhill end there were some single-story brick structures. These I took to be the administrative part of the camp—for camp it obviously was, although deserted for the most part. Off to the left and behind one row of barracks were a group of mud-brick huts. Behind these and some distance away stood a fairly impressive mountain, completely treeless and covered with large boulders. The country all around looked very bleak.

We went back to the building I was being kept in, the third one down the row. The guards tried to make me keep my head lowered but they were not entirely successful. I accentuated my limp, and, walking slowly, took a good look around. I saw that each barracks had four rooms, two upstairs and two below. Each second-story room had a separate set of stairs side by side in the center of the building but separated by a partition. A small hallway at the foot of each stairway gave access to the downstairs room. By counting the guards I concluded that at least nine and possibly ten members of the crew, including myself, were being held prisoners. A little later I asked my guard how many there were, but he only shook his head. He wouldn't talk to me.

That noon I received a bowl of rice—almost tasteless, or so I thought at the time. Later I learned to like it. I also received the usual cup of hot water. This too was tasteless, but as before, it served to warm me a bit. The afternoon was long, lonely, and boring. No one came and I went nowhere. The guards changed every two hours, but that wasn't very exciting. I swept the room again, then explored and re-explored it, finding some writing on the wall—in Korean or Chinese. I peeped out the windows every chance I got but didn't see anyone I knew. I heard someone go down the stairs of the next room, but I couldn't see them. They returned after awhile. A vehicle drove up outside and I got a peep at a couple of Chinese officers. Every now and then I casually tapped on the floor or wall to the rhythm of "shave and a haircut, two-bits." No one returned my taps. I could heard Howard Brown cough now and then in the room below. He had a very distinctive cough—quite different from that of the Chinese soldiers, who coughed constantly. Each time a different guard came on duty I would try to talk to him, but none would return the favor. Thus the day passed.

For supper I was given another bowl of the same kind of food I had eaten for breakfast. I ate it, still not knowing what it was. After supper I again felt the urge to relieve myself. I told the guard and he asked me, using gestures of the simplest kind, which I needed to do. When I indicated that I only needed to urinate, he led me down the stairs. After checking with the other guards he took me outside. He showed me a pile of rubbish in the avenue and waited for me. It was dark, but I could see a dim glow behind the paper-covered windows. I counted nine rooms with lights on inside, including mine. Now I was sure eight other members of the crew had been captured. That left five. I hoped they had been able to escape.

A little while after returning to my room, I was visited by an English-speaking Chinese in a soldier's uniform. He looked more intelligent than the guards, and his English was good. He asked about my health and appetite and commented that I was not used to the food they served. This was a prize understatement. He further stated that the local peasants were very poor and food was scarce, but I would soon be moved and would be fed better.

I asked why I was not allowed to open a window for fresh air. He replied that the people were very fierce and might come in and try to harm me if they saw me. For that reason I must keep the windows closed. I asked if the rest of the crew were okay, and was told that two were in the hospital and some had been killed in the crash. He then told me who the two were that had been taken to the hospital. One, he said, was in serious condition but would survive. They were the navigator, and the instructor pilot-observer, who had come along to check our crew's combat procedures.

My visitor then handed me a typed sheet of questions and a fountain pen. He explained that it was a form given to all POW's and said I should fill it out. I looked it over and filled in my name, rank, and serial number. The other questions concerning my unit, the mission we had been on, and my family I left blank. I gave back the paper and pen. He read what I had written and in a rather hurt manner said, "But you haven't answered all the questions." I replied that I was required to give only my name, rank, and serial number. At this he explained that all POW's filled out the form. He said the information was needed so that my family could be notified that I was a prisoner. I replied that my name, rank, and serial number was sufficient information for that. He argued some more and became highly indignant. He said all the rest of the crew had completed the form and I was being childish to refuse. I told him if he showed me a form completed by one of the other crew members, then I'd fill in mine. I was sure none had done so. This made him angrier still, but he left, saying I must think it over.

After he had gone I turned off the light to go to sleep. When the light went out my guard got rattled. He had a flashlight, but he couldn't decide whether to shine it on me or to use it to look for the light switch. He finally succeeded in turning on the light, all the while acting as if he was in a cage with a wild animal. With the light back on, he made it clear that it must stay that way. I lay down, turning my back to the light. I didn't get to sleep right away; I spent a good part of the night thinking, but not about the POW form. I tried to figure out who of the crew were prisoners and who could possibly have been killed. I knew every one in the front compartment of the plane had bailed out, and I knew the bail-out signal had been given to the men in the rear compartment. The inter-phone had been knocked out with the first pass of the Migs, so there was no way of being sure of the situation in the rear crew compartment. Bail-out from there, however, was much easier than from the front, and there were only six crew members in the rear compared to eight up front. The scanner I whispered to on the truck had been in the rear compartment, so I knew that at least one of the six had made it.

Of course there was the slim possibility that some of the crew were still hiding in the mountains without the enemy being aware of it. Maybe in saying that some had been killed, the Chinese were trying to find out how many men had been on the plane. I decided that if I were asked I would say there were eleven of us—the normal complement of a B-29. This would coincide with the nine men I believed to be in the three barracks, plus the two in the hospital. Still puzzling over the situation, I finally became lost in dreams.

The next day passed much as the last one. I made one trip up the hill. I heard jets come over on two different occasions. They were extremely low, but the guards didn't seem to pay any attention so I decided they must have been Chinese. I continued my previous efforts to talk to my guards, but had no success; they just were not communicative. They left me alone completely, and one even remained outside at the head of the stairs instead of inside as the others had done. This gave me the opportunity to look out the windows more often, but there was nothing new to be seen. Every time I heard someone enter or leave the rooms below I tried to get a glimpse of them, but I only saw Howard Brown, and him only once.

After supper that evening two more soldiers came into my room and, taking my straw mattress, escorted me downstairs into the lower room on the opposite end of the building. Some member of the crew had been moved, because the room was occupied the night before. There was a straw mattress on the floor by the radiator and the soldiers deposited mine on top of it. Really living! Two straw pads. The radiator worked and this really was something. The guards motioned me to bed and I was warm that night for the first time.

The next morning after a breakfast of rice soup I explored my new accommodations. The room was smaller, but was comparatively clean. This cleanliness, plus a stick of Dentyne chewing gum which I found on the floor by the mattress, confirmed my belief that the room had been occupied by one of the crew, probably my commanding officer, Colonel Arnold, since he would most likely be the first to be removed for interrogation. I expected that all of us would be interrogated soon and then sent to a POW camp. It never occurred to me that we would be kept separated more than a few days.

My new room had a small hallway outside, and the guard remained there, leaving the door closed between us. This gave me the chance to tear a corner of the paper covering on the window and look out whenever I pleased. I had to be careful that none of the soldiers outside saw me, but there was little danger since the hole I made was very small. I again saw Howard when he was taken outside. I cleared my throat and whispered as he walked by, and was cheered to hear him grunt in reply.

I also took advantage of my privacy to take inventory of the contents of my inner pockets—the ones that had not been found when I was searched. Of the items there, I considered the compass most important. It would prove invaluable if I managed to escape, I thought, so I put it in an inside leg pocket, hoping it would be overlooked in case of further shakedowns.

I had an extra pair of socks in one pocket, and in another I found one of the cigarette cases I had converted into a survival kit. This one contained salt, black pepper, sugar, powdered milk, coffee and tea. These items were in small, one-serving packages taken from K-rations. I had hot tea instead of hot water after my next meal. I also found I had a bottle of water-purification tablets. These, I thought, were needless as long as I was given steaming hot water to drink. But again, if I could escape, they might come in handy. I carefully put all the things back in my inside pockets, but for the next two days I treated myself to a cup of sugar water, coffee, tea, or hot milk whenever I was given water. I used these things sparingly, however. I wanted to make them last as long as possible and I hoped to get a chance, in a few days, to share my treasures. I wished later I had not been so conservative. I got to use only a small part of them before they were taken away.

That was my fourth day as a prisoner. It already seemed weeks. A deck of cards, I thought, would make the long hours more bearable. I wondered why I had not remembered cards when I was making my survival kit. This gave me an idea. I pulled some paper from the wall and then tore it into fifty-two small rectangular pieces. I found a piece of chalk on the floor and used this to mark the suit and number on the tissue-thin paper. But the paper was light in color and the chalk marks didn't stand out very clearly. I knocked on the door to get the guard. He loaned me his pen and I was in business. I soon had a very serviceable, though flimsy, deck of cards. The only difficulty came when I tried to shuffle. It was somewhat like trying to mix fifty-two squares of toilet tissue.

Late that afternoon I was again visited by the interrogator.

"How have you been today," he asked as he entered the room.

It was a question for which I had no ready answer, but I tried not to indicate how miserable I was; I answered, "Very well, I guess."

"Your eye is still bruised, but I think it is not serious," he said.

"No, I think not," I replied.

"Your new room is much warmer and comfortable, is it not," he said, continuing with petty conversation.

I knew he would sooner or later get around to the subject of the POW questionnaire and I had no desire to get friendly with him.

Still, I felt I should be civil. I made my answers short, but polite.
"Yes, I am warm enough," I replied.

"What have you thought about filling out the questionnaire,"
he asked, finally getting down to the purpose of his visit.

"I have not thought about it," I replied.

"Well, what have you been thinking of all day," he asked, ever
so slightly ruffled. "How have you passed your time?"

My deck of cards were out of sight, so I didn't bother to tell him
that I had passed most of the day playing solitaire.

Instead I replied, "I have been thinking of the rest of the crew.
When are we going to be put together?"

"You must not worry about them," he answered. "That is something you can do nothing about."

It wasn't quite clear what it was I could do nothing about, so I
persisted.

"How are the other members of the crew? When are you going
to send us to a POW camp?" I expected no sensible answers—I
was trying to steer the conversation away from the POW form. I
had no wish to get into an argument with him over it.

In answer to my last question he said, "I think that you will not
be sent to a POW camp. I think you might be shot instead."

He smiled when he said this and I hoped he was having a little
joke, but I could not be sure. He continued:

"You must be very cooperative. You must answer all questions.
This will be very good for you. You will see." With this he left and
I was glad to see him go. I was lonesome by myself, but I preferred
my own company to his.

After dark I told my guard I needed to relieve myself. I had
waited until then in order to be able to count the lighted windows
again. There were only eight. My first room was dark. This sup-
ported my theory that one member of the crew had been taken
somewhere else. Back in my room the radiator was still putting
forth a little heat, so I lay down and tried not to think about what
the interrogator had said about my being shot. I finally slipped

into troubled sleep.

My fifth day of captivity started much as the fourth, but by midmorning I had something new to occupy my mind. I was sitting on my straw mattress playing solitaire when the door opened and in walked a man in a Chinese officer's uniform. Speaking English, he asked, "What is your name?"

"Lieutenant Brown," I replied.

"What are you doing?" he asked, pointing to my cards lying on the floor. His queries were short and sharp.

"Playing cards—solitaire," I replied just as short, but less hostile.

"You should not waste time playing silly games," he said.

"I have nothing else to do with my time," I answered.

"You should use your time to think of ways to improve your position," he continued. "Your position is not very good."

I did not reply that I knew it and had spent much time doing just what he suggested—exploring escape possibilities. I didn't think he had that kind of improvement in mind.

Then he said, "You must find ways to atone for your crimes."

"Crimes! What crimes," I wondered. I didn't have to ask. When I said that I had committed no crimes he nearly exploded with wrath.

Shouting, he said, "You and your crew have flown your damn B-29 over Chinese territorial air. You have invaded the Chinese People's Republic. You have committed a most serious act of aggression against the peace-loving Chinese people. You must pay for this!"

I was completely taken aback. The accusations were certainly serious—as serious as they were false.

As he continued to rant and rave, mentioning such phrases as "American imperialist warmongers" and "saboteurs," a flood of thoughts swept through my mind. Was this a trick to try to scare me so interrogation would be easier? Or was it a propaganda move against the United States? Our last target had been close to the Yalu. Perhaps while trying to evade the Communists' fighters, we had accidentally crossed the border into Red China. But if that was the case, why had they waited so long to confront me with the accusation? Why did they suddenly consider me a criminal instead of a POW? The accusation and the tirade which followed it sounded rehearsed—so much so that my suspicions were aroused. Maybe they intended to take us into Communist China and then tell us we had flown across the Yalu. Then I remembered the bridge —the one we had crossed in the weapons carrier. We were already in China! Or were we? I couldn't be positive. I ruled out the possibility of having flown across the Yalu by accident. Cholson, our last target, was not close enough to the border so that the minute or two between the time the fighters attacked us and bail-out would have taken us over it.

When the officer stopped for breath, I told him I knew I had not flown into China, and that as far as I knew I was still in North Korea. This brought on a second fit of curses and accusations. Finally he gave up and departed, leaving me with a dire warning that I would soon change my attitude.

I was fed lunch as usual, but I didn't feel hungry. My mind was in a whirl trying to guess what my captors were up to. After lunch, when the guard came in to get my bowl, I tried to see if he would shed any light on the puzzle. With his pen and a piece of paper I drew a rough map of Korea and Manchuria, showing the Yalu River dividing the two. By pointing to myself and the room floor and then to the map, I hoped to learn from him if I was in China or Korea. I had no success. He nodded "yes" to everything I said. I tried to get him to do the pointing, but could make no sense out of it when he did. I gave up and went back to my straw mattress, where I sat and ran the incidents of the past few days through my mind again and again. I could be sure of only one thing—we had not flown into China.

After dark I heard a vehicle drive up outside. Taking a peek, I saw someone from the next barracks being hustled into a curtained jeep. Approximately forty minutes later the jeep was back. It made four trips that night and I expected to be taken each time it returned. I was keyed up and waiting for this unknown move, but after watching and listening over an hour, I decided that the fourth trip had been the last. I found myself feeling disappointed, but I finally dropped off to sleep.

Next morning when I made my trip to the top of the hill, I counted the guarded rooms. There were only four, including my own. This tallied with my previous counts. I felt that I could be reasonably sure of being moved soon, probably the following night. I hoped so. It could only be a change for the better. My first English-speaking visitor had told me that we would be taken to a POW camp—at least that's what I thought he meant. I was obviously not in a regular prison camp and I was looking forward to the company I would have in a prison camp. My visitor also said the food would be better at the next place, but this was of little concern to me. The poor quality and small quantity of the food didn't bother me nearly as much as the inaction and the suspense. These were getting on my nerves. I was thoroughly bored with my present accommodations and even more with myself. I wanted to compare notes with the other crew members, and I felt that prison life would not be so bad if I had someone to share it with. With several of us together, we could begin working on escape plans. But most of all, I was lonesome.

This day, my sixth in Communist hands, was long and dull, but completely uneventful. Waiting for the anticipated move only served to make it seem longer. I spent some time playing cards, walking back and forth around my room, peeping out the window, trying to make friends with my speechless guard, and thinking about my visitor of the day before. As night drew near I became even more restless. I had no idea where the expected move would take me or what to expect when I got there, but I was sure it would be an improvement.

I couldn't have been more mistaken.

CHAPTER
FOUR

That night the jeep made an appearance shortly after dark. I was taken out and shoved into the back seat, followed by two guards. Another person, who had been standing in the dark by the vehicle, got in front with the driver and we were off. The jeep was fully curtained, making it impossible to see out except straight ahead. The curtains did not keep out the bitterly cold air, however, and I sat and shivered. After driving about fifteen minutes we came to a deserted town. There were no lights and no people, and the few buildings I could see looked gaunt and ghostly. I guessed it to be the same town that I saw the first night after my capture. We stopped in front of a two-story building; I was taken up a flight of stairs to a room.

There were lights on inside, and several soldiers and civilians were milling around in the room. They stood staring at me while I sat on a bench and waited for their next move, whatever it was. The windows, I noticed, were well covered with heavy black paper. Blackout curtains. This meant that I was either in North Korea or, if in China, only just across the Yalu. One of my guards gave me a loaf of bread and a stick of sausage that he took from a bundle containing several more of each. He carried the rest into the next room, and I was sure more of the crew were being similarly fed. Both the bread and sausage were delicious. One of my guards indicated that I could have more of the bread if I liked, but no more sausage. I needed no more bread and, although I could have eaten several more of the sausages, I put half of what I had in my pocket, thinking it might come in handy if I could manage to escape.

After eating the bread I was given a cup of hot water; at least, I thought it was water until I tasted it. It was tea—weak and unsweetened, but tea nonetheless and very good. Things certainly seemed to be looking up, if food and drink were any indication. My hunger abated, I lay back on the bench and soon dozed off in spite of the noise of people going and coming and busily chattering over a telephone which sat on a table nearby. On the same table I saw my cargo pack, which contained the things that had been taken from me, and on the floor nearby there were bundles of paper leaflets. Apparently one of the containers in our leaflet bombs had not opened to scatter its contents to the winds.

Finally about 9:30 P.M. my guards woke me and motioned me up. I was escorted down the stairs and out into the dark street. We walked about three blocks, making one wrong turn and having to walk part way back. Finally the guards located a pair of steps leading up an embankment and into a rail depot. Here we boarded a crowded passenger coach and took seats near one end. I had picked up an extra guard in the building, so the four of us occupied a pair of facing seats. The coach was the size of American day-coaches, but its wooden seats were closer and smaller. The windows, I discovered as I moved one of the heavy red curtains, were coated with an inch or so of ice.

The coach, already overcrowded, was becoming more packed by the minute. The people were of both sexes and all ages. They were dressed in heavy padded clothes which added greatly to their size. Many wore long-eared, fur-lined hats which made them look like Mongolian herdsmen. Some wore gauze masks over their mouth and nose. Whether the masks were for protection against disease or frostbite I could not decide, but either reason was valid enough. There were soldiers carrying heavy packs and women carrying bundles on their backs. The bundles, upon closer inspection, became babies. The coach was a nightmare in sound. People were constantly jabbering, trying to be heard over each other, and someone near the opposite end of the coach had a wind-up record player which screeched out its eerie mixture of clanging cymbals and other strange instruments.

We sat there an hour, long enough for me to look over the teeming, squirming, squawking mass of passengers and determine that there were no other Americans aboard. Most of the passengers didn't notice me and of those that did, some stared and some didn't give me a second glance. A few soldiers sitting nearby saluted me in a friendly manner. One of them threw some pieces of candy to one of my guards who in turn gave it to me. I nodded thanks and put it in my pocket, eating only one piece and saving the rest.

Finally the train jerked and started to roll. A man standing in the doorway of the coach shouted something that must have been the local equivalent of "all aboard." We were on our way somewhere—I had no idea where. I spoke to my guards for the first time in an effort to learn our destination or, for that matter, our point of departure. Either they didn't understand or didn't care to—I strongly suspected the latter. The only answer I got was a waving of the hand across the face which obviously meant I should be seen and not heard.

The train picked up speed only to begin slowing almost immediately and coming to a jerky stop at the next station. There was added confusion to the already existing chaos as people climbed over others to get off and other people boarded to take their places. The little man who I assumed to be the conductor shouted, the train jerked, and we were off again. This was repeated throughout the night, with the coach becoming more crowded and more noisy at each stop. Every two or three hours the conductor forced his way through with a bucket of hot water or loaves of bread, sticks of sausages, and candy. These he sold to the passengers. Most of them, however, seemed to have brought along refreshments of their own. One of my guards purchased food for the four of us. Again a portion of it went into my pockets to be saved for less plentiful times.

So far escape had been impossible; I was too well guarded. After this ride, I thought, only God knew what might happen. I was being taken into China or, more probably, I was already there and being taken further inland. Another thought that crossed my mind was the possibility that I was being taken to Siberia. Whatever my destination, I knew my chances for escape grew slimmer with every passing mile. I decided to take advantage of even the slightest opportunity to get away.

I noticed that the toilet was at my end of the coach and the door between coaches stayed open. The conductor stood there at the exit. If the toilet had a window, it might be possible to get out of it. Or, once at the end of the coach, I might be able to push past the conductor and jump off. After trying to figure all the possibilities, I waited until the train was pulling away from a stop, but had not gained full speed. Then I told the guards I needed to relieve myself. At this, one of them went to the end of the coach and closed all doors, standing outside with the conductor. The other two led me to the toilet. One waited outside and the other came inside with me. They were taking no chances. The toilet had a window, but it was too small to get through even if I had the opportunity. That was the end of that.

Between stops I was able to get a few minutes sleep, and now and then one of my guards began to nod, but the other two woke him up. Every hour or so a man dressed in black with a red star on his hat came up, spoke to the guards and went into the next coach. I labeled him the chief honcho, the chief big wheel, of the prisoner movement. I was sure there were other members of the crew in other coaches. The honcho, I figured, was making periodic checks on each of us.

After sunrise, nine and a half hours from our point of departure, we made a final stop and everyone on board got off. The quietness that flowed into the coach as the people flowed out was a tremendous relief to my sound-tortured ears. The guards kept me sitting after everyone else had departed. Soon the chief honcho came in, bringing a piece of black cloth and a pair of handcuffs. They were snapped on my wrists and the cloth tied around my eyes. Then, with a guard supporting me on either side, I was taken off the train and put on a truck. Another American weapons carrier, I realized as I was pushed into the back.

The guards climbed in behind and away we went, down smooth and rough streets, around sharp turns and finally, from the sound of the motor, up a fairly steep hill, where we stopped. The train had been fairly warm except for the floor where my feet rested, but in the truck I was soon chilled to the bone again. I was taken from the truck and half led, half carried, into a building, through a corridor, and down a step into a room. Here my blindfold and handcuffs were removed and the guards departed.

Inspecting the room, I found it to be about twelve feet square with a high ceiling. The walls were masonry, covered with yellow, chalky plaster. There was one small transomlike window high up on the corridor side. The floor was square brick tiles. In the middle sat an iron cot with a straw mattress on top. The room was warm to the point of being uncomfortable, and a closer inspection revealed one of the side walls as the source of the heat. I later discovered that the partition between each pair of rooms or cells was actually a furnace which was stoked by the guards in the corridor. Because of this method of heating I came to think of this prison as the "hot box." My first prison I remembered as "the place with the crapper on the hill."

The door of my new quarters was of heavy wood construction with a massive iron bolt on the outside. It was painted dark green and had a slot cut at outside eye level. The slot was about one and a half by six inches and had a cloth flap over the outside. I discovered the purpose of the slot when I looked up and saw a pair of eyeballs peering through at me. The guard outside quietly raised the flap, stared awhile, and as quietly lowered it. In a very few seconds, however, the eyeballs appeared again. When this happened several times I decided I must be some sort of curiosity and, after the guards were satisfied, they would stop peering in so often. I was mistaken. As regularly as clock work, day and night, the eyeballs appeared every few seconds. This was highly annoying because it was so ridiculous. I was locked in a cell, alone, with one piece of furniture and the clothes I had on. I wondered why they had to watch me so closely.

I soon found out. I had been in the cell a couple of hours when I was visited by two people. One I presumed to be an officer although he displayed no rank insignia. He did, however, have a white patch with a red border covered with Chinese characters sewn above his left breast pocket. The guard, who had entered with them, had the same patch sewn above his pocket. None of the soldiers I had seen before wore the patch.

The officer spoke English and introduced his companion as the prison warden, who had something to say to me. The warden was dressed in a blue padded suit. This was a change. Everyone else was dressed in black or brown. The warden held a sheet of paper and read aloud from it. The words he spoke were as alien to me as the written characters. The officer translated for him, however, and thus I received the rules of the house, or prison as they called it. I learned that I could sit on the cot during the day, but must not lie down or sleep. I would receive three meals per day which I must eat and be thankful for—it was the same food the guards ate. I would receive hot water to drink. If I needed to go to the latrine I could tell the guard, otherwise I must not talk to him. I must not look at the guard and when outside I must not look up or around. I must obey the guards at all times. After they got through with their "musts" and "must nots," I asked where the rest of the crew were being held and where I was. He replied with another "must not"—I must not ask questions. Although I had little idea where I was, I was sure that the rest of the crew were in other cells nearby—simply because I could see no reason why I should be an exception.

When the two left, they went down the corridor a short way

and I heard another cell door open and close. After a while I heard them again and by peeping through the slot, holding the flap out a little with my finger, I saw the same two men walk by and heard them enter another cell further down the corridor. This confirmed my belief that I was not alone. Other members of the crew were being informed of the prison rules.

About then the guard walked up and opened the flap, leaving my finger sticking through the hole. I was caught peeping, but I remembered what I had just been told and pretended I was trying to attract his attention and needed to visit the latrine. This satisfied the dull-looking guard and, after shouting a warning down the corridor, he unlatched the door and let me out.

I took a quick look up and down the corridor, but could see nothing except more guards armed with pistols in wooden holsters, more green doors, and little iron doors where some of the guards were poking with iron rods. My guard was careless; he didn't make me bow my head as we walked down the corridor, around a corner and into a side room which was the latrine. I looked around as I pleased, but there was little to see. The latrine had half a dozen slots, and along one side was a knee-high concrete trough for urinating. This was past using, however, because it had frozen and was now a waist-high mound of solid urine. A couple of the slots were also frozen over. The others were open, but to use them I had to stand on a few inches of ice. Relieving oneself wasn't the safest occupation, I decided as I nearly slipped into one of the slots. But at worst I could only break a limb or two—the slots weren't wide enough to fall through.

Back in the cell I did some more exploring. I searched all the walls hoping to find writing scratched in the chalk by another prisoner. I found none, but left some for my successors. The chalk-painted walls were easily scratched and the scratches weren't visible except at close inspection. By making a few scratches immediately after the eyeballs disappeared from the peep hole I wrote my name, the date and my date of capture in a couple of places, high up so the average short Oriental would be less likely to notice it.

This operation took several minutes because of the frequency of eyeball appearances. I had barely completed it when my door was unlocked, admitting two soldiers and the warden. The warden picked up my coat and overpants, which I had discarded because of the heat, and proceeded to search all the pockets. He found nothing except the bread, candy and sausage I had hoarded. Leaving these, he turned to me and went through all my outside pockets thoroughly. But he, too, overlooked the fact that I was wearing two flying suits. Although wearing the second one made me uncomfortably hot, I had been able to save the few articles I still possessed. Through with his search, the warden handed me a magazine, a green enameled cup, a tube of toothpaste, a brush, and a hand towel. He showed me with gestures how to use these various articles and how to read the magazine, then the three of them departed.

Left alone, I looked over my newly acquired possessions. All except the magazine were welcome. The title of the magazine was "China Reconstructs." It contained several pictures and was printed in English. Seeing printed English for the first time suddenly made me very blue, and it took much mental effort to keep from brooding over my not too pleasant situation. I forced myself to think of things that had happened since I was shot down and, as a way of cheering myself up, to think of ways to get out of the country if I could escape.

In spite of the prison rules, I lay down to rest. I got little sleep during the train ride and, coupled with all the recent activity, I was pretty exhausted. I lay there only a few seconds, however. As soon as the eyeballs spotted me in the prone position, there came a rap-rap on the door. Then it was opened by the guard, who reminded me, with a combination of gestures and gibberish, that I could not sleep until night. He pointed to "China Reconstructs" and indicated that I should read it instead of sleeping.

I picked up the magazine and glanced at some of the articles,

THE ENDLESS HOURS 55

none of which looked very appealing. One was about an American female atomic scientist who had grown tired of her country's "aggressive" policy and had come to live in China. Another was about a "world peace rally" held in Peking which a number of Americans had attended. Anti-Americanism stuck out all through and I still didn't care to read it, but I got an idea. Holding the magazine open, I lay down and turned my back to the guard and to the door. If they wanted me to read it so much they wouldn't care if I read it lying down. It worked. The guard walked out and closed the door gently behind him. I promptly went to sleep holding the magazine in front of my face.

I awoke when the door opened and my evening chow was handed in. The food was much the same as at the last place—watery stew and unseasoned rice. After eating I was given a cup of hot water to drink, but I used it to take a sponge bath. Used conservatively, a cup of water will go a long way.

My black eye was no longer bothering me, but the hot, wet cloth made it feel even better as I held it against my face. I saved a little of the water and used it to brush my teeth, but I had nowhere to spit it out. I got the guard's attention and, with a mouthful of water and toothpaste, I tried to talk him into letting me outside to empty it. He impatiently pointed to a corner of the cell and slammed the door, leaving me with two choices. The toothpaste tasted like toothpaste should and my mouth felt considerably better.

That night I discovered that here, too, I would be forced to sleep with a light on. There was no switch in the cell and the light was fixed to the ceiling, far out of reach and covered with a heavy wire screen. I knocked on the door to attract the guard and, when the eyeballs appeared, I pointed at the light, trying to indicate that I would like it off. He muttered a few words that sounded like *pu shih, pu shih,* then the eyeballs disappeared. The light stayed on.

I occupied my eighth day in much the same way as the seventh.

After a sleepless night I decided not to nap anymore during the day, but I did continue to use "China Reconstructs" as an excuse to lie down whenever I liked. I didn't read any of the articles; they still made me nostalgic and I considered the book nothing more than poor propaganda. On the center spread, however, was a map of China and Korea which showed all the large towns and the railroads between them. It was a roughly drawn map, but I studied it for hours, trying to pinpoint the location of the prison in which I was being held. I also memorized the rail routes, just in case I ever needed to know.

Taking everything into consideration, including the rail routes on the map and my nine and a half hour train ride, I decided that I could be in either of two places—Antung or Mukden. I hoped it was Antung. My chances of winding up in a POW camp were much better if I was in Antung. If the Chinese had taken the precaution of moving us as far inland as Mukden after kidnapping us, it seemed unlikely that they had any intentions of treating us as POW's. Whatever their intentions, I doubted if they were good. I had long since decided that the move from the barracks had not been an improvement.

After dark on the eighth day the warden and three soldiers came into my cell brandishing handcuffs, leg shackles, and a black cloth. What next, I wondered, as the hardware was snapped on and my head tied up in the cloth. The foot of chain between the two ankle clamps made walking difficult as we started out of the cell, so two of the guards dragged me through the door and outside to a waiting vehicle. This one was some kind of sedan. I was shoved into the rear seat and a guard climbed in on either side of me. The doors slammed and off we drove.

Another train ride? Siberia? A firing squad? Many possibilities presented themselves as we rode along. My imagination ran wild. But there was one thing certain—if security of movement was any indication, then I could expect worse instead of better. They had called me a criminal and somebody must have believed it, for I was being treated like a most dangerous one.

The ride was fairly brief. The car made a couple of short turns, then stopped and I was dragged out. This was not a rail-yard, I decided—not the right smell or sounds. I was half-walked, half-dragged up a flight of stairs into a building, down another flight, through a door which had to be unlocked and down a narrow corridor, where I was shoved through another door. Here the blindfold and handcuffs were removed. The guards deposited my towel, magazine, and other things on the floor, then they left. I shouted, telling them they had forgotten something—the leg shackles—but they indicated I should be quiet and go to sleep. I heard a heavy bolt slide and a lock snap.

Then I looked over my new accommodations. This cell was larger than the last; it was about twelve by sixteen feet. Along one side there was a wooden platform raised about six inches above a cement tile floor. It was about six by twelve feet and was covered with straw pads. Opposite this "bed," high up near the ceiling, hung a steam radiator which I soon discovered was for decoration only. One end of the room had a large window with two glass shutters that opened inward and were covered with heavy black paper. Blackout curtains, I thought until I opened one and saw lights shining outside. Apparently I wasn't supposed to see out, for a guard rapped on the door and indicated to me to close the shutter and go to bed. The door, I noticed, was also of heavy wood construction. The peephole in it was about eight inches high by six inches wide—large enough for a whole face and not just a pair of eyes. This peephole had a hinged wooden cover which stayed closed except when the guard look in every minute or so.

The walls of the cell were plastered with white chalk and were about two feet thick. This was evident by the thickness of the window sill and door jamb. Around two sides of the room about eighteen inches off the floor ran an insulated steampipe leading to the radiator. In the center hung an electric cord with an American-made light bulb burning at the end. The socket had a switch and was within easy reach, so I decided I would sleep in the dark that night. The guard had other ideas, however, and raised quite a rumpus. He finally called for the corporal of the guard who apparently kept the key to my door. They came in and turned the light back on, then gave me a lecture about not turning out lights in prisons. This was all in Chinese, but the meaning was clear. I brought up the subject of leg shackles again, but to no avail. I asked what I was supposed to sleep under. It was rather chilly in my new room and I didn't relish the prospect of sleeping between dusty straw pads. The corporal of the guard left and returned a minute later with a heavy quilt.

This cell was the exact opposite of the "hot box," but by scientific use of the blanket, I soon had a snug little bed made on top of five straw pads. I slept warmly, but not very soundly. My mind was busy trying to make some sense out of this latest move. The size of the bed platform and the five straw pads gave me hope that some of the crew would soon be joining me in my new accommodations.

Next morning, the beginning of my ninth day of captivity, I was again searched. This time they found my second flying suit and went through most of the pockets in it. They found and confiscated the last of my possessions with one exception—my pocket compass. This they overlooked. They also took my watch, which until then I had been allowed to keep. I didn't mind losing it so much because I had already learned that knowing the time of day only seemed to make the hours pass more slowly. Later I devised a sort of sundial system to tell time by using a sunbeam that shone through a crack between the window-shutters. This wasn't calibrated to hours or minutes, but rather to mealtimes.

The search completed, I was given a breakfast of bread and some kind of hash. The bread, a roll about half the size of my pint water cup and nearly as heavy, tasted good although it contained no seasoning. There was only one piece of bread and just a few spoons of the hash. Pretty short rations, I thought, but I forgot about my hunger when I was given a pan full of hot water and a cake of soap. I felt like a millionaire as I scrubbed myself from one end to the other. I would have stripped completely in spite of the cold, but the shackles prevented it. I made that bath last as long as possible—much longer than the guard liked, but it was well worth the raps on the door and the impatient *kwai, kwai!* that followed each rap. I pretended not to understand what he wanted, but I had learned my second Chinese word. *Kwai, kwai* undoubtedly meant "hurry, hurry!" When my bath water became too cold to use, I dressed and let the extremely unhappy guard know I had finished.

The corporal of the guard unlocked my door and escorted me to a small latrine down the corridor. He had long since finished with the other prisoners and hurried me as much as he could. I emptied my pan of filthy water and then made use of the oriental-style water closet. It was quite a trick keeping my leg chains out of the way as I squatted over the chute. Here there was no frozen urine and there was even running water to flush the chute.

I didn't get to enjoy the luxury of this modern plumbing again, however. When I got back to my cell, the guard gave me an earthen jar of about two-gallon size with a four-inch mouth. That was my latrine for the rest of my stay in that prison. There was no wall-paper in the room so I was given small pieces of newspaper instead. Once every day or two I was allowed to empty my jar. During these short stints out of my cell, I was able to learn something of the make-up of the prison. I decided that it had not originally been a prison. The cells had been added by partitioning the basement of the building. A maze of narrow corridors divided the fifteen or twenty rows of cells. Each corridor was patrolled by a different guard.

During the first day in my new quarters, I went through the now routine search of the walls for any writing scratched there. Finding none, I made sure the next unlucky soul would have more success. After this I tried tapping code on the radiator pipe, thinking that some of the other crew members might be nearby. I received no response, but for the remainder of my stay there I continued to try every few hours, as much for something to do as anything else. I soon gave up hope of receiving any answering taps.

When noon came around I was given another roll and a small portion of something I thought was sea weed, but upon closer inspection turned out to be bean sprouts. As hungry as I was, it wasn't a very tasty dish. After lunch I took the liberty of opening my cell window and much to my surprise the guard let me keep it open. This gave me the opportunity to see what the prison grounds looked like. My window was at ground level since the cell was in the basement, and I could see the prison yard, which was surrounded by a brick wall with an iron gate at the far side. The wall was about seven feet high and probably could be climbed easily. Along the wall near the gate was a stack of firewood. As I watched a guard pace back and forth just outside the gate, I thought what a handy weapon a stick of the wood would make if I could only get out of my cell. I saw myself sneaking up to the stack of wood, grabbing a piece in my hand, pouncing on the guard, relieving him of his submachine-gun, and fleeing down the street outside. My dreams of escape and heroism were dispelled as my eyes focused on the bars in the window only a few inches away. I dropped my thoughts of escape and decided to give the window a closer look.

In addition to the wood and glass shutters which opened inward, there were two screens with wooden frames that covered the window. Outside the screens there were fancy scroll-work bars which appeared to be more ornamental than functional. Further inspection proved otherwise. The screen wire was old and rusty, so when the guard looked in my cell and moved on to the next, I tore a hole in one corner and reached through to the bars. They were solidly anchored top and bottom. The guard's return interrupted my exploration. I closed the shutter quickly to keep him from spotting the hole I had torn in the screen.

The guard had changed and, since the new one had the most

pleasant face I had seen since becoming a prisoner, I tried to strike up a conversation. All attempts with other guards in the past had failed, but much to my gratification this guard proved more congenial. Because of his cheerful, friendly nature I named him "Smiley." We got along famously. Each time he came on duty Smiley tapped lightly on my door to get my attention and we exchanged a few words. Smiley seemed more intelligent than any of the other guards and he never tired of learning words I taught him. After each new word I gave him, he paraded up and down the corridor repeating it to himself. Soon he stopped for another one. He was far more interested in learning English than in teaching me Chinese, but I soon made it clear that we would trade word for word or I wouldn't play. He taught me several useful words. I tried many times to get information from him about other members of the crew and about the location of the prison, but in this he was firmly silent. I showed him the map in the magazine and pointed to various likely places, hoping that I could determine by his expression when I had the right one. I could not. He was not dumb, and when I gave him the magazine so he could do the pointing, he smilingly refused.

I tried the magazine trick on my next guard, who nodded agreement to every place I indicated and to everything I said. That told me nothing, but shortly after he went off duty the warden came to my cell with a pen and piece of paper. He wanted me to write down everything I had asked the guard. Instead of doing so I made the mistake of trying to get the same information from him, via the map. When he saw the map he muttered a few unkind-sounding words, took the map, and left. Before he departed, however, I reminded him that they had forgotten to remove my leg chains. When he refused with an impatient gesture, I muttered a few unkind words of my own. Luckily for me he didn't understand English. My attempts at getting information had gained me nothing and had lost me the map. I didn't mind the loss so much; I had the map pretty well memorized, but the hostile attitude of the warden lowered my spirits considerably.

After the warden left and things were back to normal, I sat down on the bed boards and inspected my leg shackles. I hadn't done so previously for I had expected to have them removed momentarily. Now it looked as if they might be with me for awhile. They were painful, to say the least, and restricted walking. The clamps had already worn the tops off my socks and were beginning to work on my ankles. Even today I still have slight scars caused by the clamps.

After looking them over I decided they would be easy to open. I scouted around for something to serve as a substitute key, and I noticed that the insulation around the steampipe was held in place by metal bands half an inch wide. Making sure the guard wasn't near, I removed one of these and broke it into short pieces. I waited until the guard returned and left again, and then I inserted a piece of the band along the clamp. With just a little pressure the clamp opened. Not wanting the guard to know, I left the clamp on, but in the loosest notch. I then tried the same procedure on the other clamp. It wouldn't open. I worried it at least an hour, working a few seconds between each round of the guard. Then I discovered that the left clamp had a broken snap, otherwise the piece of metal would not have opened it. One loose clamp was almost as good as two; walking was much easier and less painful, so I gave up trying to loosen the other one.

For something to do, I decided to take another look outside. It was a pleasure just to see "free" people and blue sky. I climbed up and sat on the windowsill, but this didn't last long. The guard raised a rumpus, banging on the door and making wolfish noises through the peephole. When the corporal of the guard arrived and opened my cell door, I reluctantly gave up my perch and let him close the window shutters, but not before I saw a man entering the prison gate carrying a pan of rolls and rice. Pretty soon the same pan was brought to my cell door and I was given two rolls and some rice. The pan could have contained food for no more than four people, I guessed.

Shortly after I was fed, I could hear buckets and dishes rattle outside in the corridor. I peeped through the hole in the door and watched as the guards fed the other prisoners. I could see two other cell doors from my position, and when the food was passed in I got a brief glimpse of the occupants. They were Orientals. Their food was different from mine and they were all fed from the same big bucket. This led me to believe that the food in the pan had been for Americans—members of the crew. But why just four? What had happened to the others, I wondered? I could only guess that they were being held at the prison I had left the night before—the "hot box."

After supper I stood near my door, listening and peeping when I got the chance. I saw several Oriental prisoners as they were taken to the latrine, and heard others that I could not see. None of the walking was accompanied by the rattle of chains. I seemed to be the only prisoner in shackles. Night came. I had had a fairly active day. This, coupled with a lack of strength due to the highly inadequate diet and the steadily worsening cough and chest cold that I had contracted, left me pretty tired. I decided to get to bed early.

I was soon reminded that prisoners in Communist jails don't go to bed any time they feel like it. The guard happened to be away from my door when I rolled up in my blanket, but his normal rounds brought him back in a few seconds. Seeing his charge rolled up like a cocoon, he banged the door and let out a roar that scared me half out of my wits and all out of my sack.

Tired, sick, and now unnerved by the unexpected noise, I yelled at the guard as I threw my blanket aside and went to the door to see what was wrong. This only served to bring more coarse noises from the face in the peephole and another rap on the door. Shortly the corporal of the guard arrived and I told him that I didn't like being shouted at. He explained that I was not supposed to shout at the guards and that I was not supposed to lie down until the guard told me to. Holding up three fingers, he indicated that I was not to go to bed until then—whatever time that was.

I guessed the time to be about eight P.M. when the guard tapped lightly on the door and pointed at my bed. I was never sure of the connection between the guard's three fingers and eight P.M. The best guess I could make was that bedtime came three hours after sunset. After getting all covered up, I took the metal band and removed my left ankle clamp. That night I dreamed Smiley helped me escape.

CHAPTER

FIVE

My tenth day as a prisoner began with the guard rapping on the door at daylight. It was Smiley; he had a pan of hot water waiting for me. I quickly slipped the shackles back on and got up to take the water. I tried to talk to Smiley, but my throat was so sore all I could do was croak. My nose was becoming somewhat runny and I had no handkerchief. I indicated the predicament I was in, and Smiley replied with the now familiar *mamonte*.

After bathing I was given a roll, period, for breakfast. It didn't matter; I wasn't hungry anyway. After the cup of hot water my voice improved, but my feelings didn't. I asked Smiley for some medicine. He nodded yes and said *"mamonte."* I picked up a couple of new words and opened my window before Smiley went off duty. I was afraid my next guard might not let me.

Outside the world was waking up. Whistles were blowing and soldiers were strolling back and forth to the mess hall across the prison yard. Some walked around with their bowls of rice and chop sticks. I watched them hold guard mount and recognized a couple of the guards from the day before. A squad of soldiers marched out the gate and down the street. Maybe I was in Antung after all, I thought, for there should be no need for armed patrols as far in the interior as Mukden. Or was there? Maybe the Communists weren't as securely in power as they would have the world believe.

After Smiley went off duty and I still had no handkerchief, I thought about the pockets of my torn overpants. I picked them up and was in the process of removing a pocket when the guard rapped on the door. He had to see what I was doing, so I told him my needs. "*Mamonte*," he said and called the corporal of the guard to unlock my door. After a thorough search of all the seams in my pants, they were satisfied that I was not looking for a concealed weapon. They warned me, however, not to tear out the pocket. I still needed a handkerchief, so after the next guard change I removed the pocket, making sure I wasn't discovered while doing it. I now had a handkerchief, though a somewhat coarse and stiff one. Once I had the pocket torn out, I used it freely and none of the guards noticed. They never gave me the promised handkerchief.

About the middle of the morning my door was unlocked and I was escorted out by two armed soldiers. They took me out of the basement and up two flights of stairs. They stopped before a closed door and one of them gave a loud rap. At a word from inside he opened the door and I was led in and positioned before a large desk.

Behind the desk sat two men in officers' uniforms. There was another desk off to the side with a third officer behind it. None of the three wore any insignia. I took them to be officers because of their better clothing. Their hats, which they kept on, had the same red star pinned in front and they wore the same patch that the guards wore. Out of the corner of my eye I could see two armed guards standing in the rear. The men behind the desks sat and stared, trying to look impressive. I was impressed—not by them, but by the whole situation in which I found myself.

The room was large with a high ceiling. The walls, ceiling, and floor were of hardwood, although the floor was much the worse for wear. The large windows were covered with red cloth. The desks and chairs were huge and looked expensive, but they also showed signs of hard wear. One of the desks had a leg missing and was held on an even keel by a couple of bricks. An earthenware spittoon sat by the larger desk. The floor around it gave ample evidence that the Chinese were poor shots. On each desk sat a cup or two and a wicker-covered thermos jug. In a corner lay a broken chair. This must have been a nice office, I thought, until it had been "liberated" and turned over to the "people."

I had not had a shave or even a comb in my hair for ten days. My clothes were beginning to show and smell of continous wear. My legs were chained together and I was almost too feverish with cold to stand, but I did my best to present a military appearance while I waited for someone to say something. Finally the officer in front of me began to speak. The one beside him translated while the third one began to write. They asked my name, then told me I was standing before the "Chinese People's Military Court" which had been appointed to investigate my "case." They went on to explain how I should act before the court and how I should cooperate by telling all I knew. I was told it would be very "advantageous" to me if I did cooperate. They said I would have a "bright future" if I showed a good attitude. They patiently explained that they realized I was a young junior officer who had merely obeyed the orders given me by my "criminalistic" superiors who, in turn, had to obey orders from the imperialistic and aggressive American government. My punishment would be severe only if I failed to realize the truth, only if I refused to confess my crimes.

So that was it! Confess and all would be bright! I wondered if they really thought I was so stupid.

They continued in this manner for some time, making liberal use of such terms as "criminals," "warmongers," "aggressors," "Wall Street imperialists," and "peace-loving Chinese People." Before they finished I had a fair idea of their opinion of the United States.

Finally, the preliminaries over, they got down to the business of interrogation.

"Why did you fly your B-29 into the Chinese People's Republic?"

"I didn't."

"Then how did you get here? Walk?"

"I don't know that I am in China."

"Not in China! Then where are you? At home?"

I didn't bother to answer as they sat there snickering at their wisecrack.

"How can you say that you did not fly into China?" they continued. "How can you not know that you are in China? You wish to play games, perhaps? We don't play games! It is a fact that you are in China! How can you say you do not know this? You are deep into Chinese territory! How did you get here?"

"If this is China, as you say, I was brought here by train."

At this reply the interrogator and interpreter started cursing and said that unless I changed my attitude I would never leave China, except in a box. Then they switched their line of questioning and began to ask about my unit, the other crew members, and my personal history.

In reply I pointed out that according to the Geneva Convention, POW's had only to give their name, rank, and serial number.

They explained, a little less patiently now, that I was a prisoner of the People's Republic of China and as such the Geneva Convention rules did not apply to me. They hinted at death and worse for those "criminals" who continued to help the "American imperialists" by not cooperating. They repeated their questions, but did not press for answers. It was clear that the main purpose of the interview was not to get information from me, but rather to lecture me. I was dismissed after about an hour and a half and taken back to my basement cell.

I found evidence in the cell that the place had been searched during my absence. The straw pads and bedding were in disarray instead of the neat pile I had left them in, and my few toilet articles were strewn around. Straw from the pads was scattered on the floor and the place was in a general mess. Newly learned Chinese words which I had scratched on the wall by the door had been found and rubbed off. Something had been added, however. On the bed platform lay a pair of brown padded pants, much like those worn by the soldiers. I didn't know how I was expected to put these on with my legs chained together, but I decided they would make a good pillow.

The guard, who had been watching, tapped on the door and indicated I should put on the pants. I pointed to my chains and he scratched his head and looked puzzled. Then he said *"mamonte"* and left. He returned with the corporal of the guard who came in and after looking the situation over said *"mamonte"* and indicated I should use the pants—as a pillow.

Two great minds, I thought. Before he left, however, the guard inspected my shackles and, finding one somewhat loose, he proceeded to tighten it. I let this go without comment, for I knew I could loosen it as soon as he left. I asked him for a broom to clean up my room. He left and returned with a wet mop. Better than nothing, I thought, and went to work cleaning up the mess.

As soon as the guard left I took a piece of metal band from my pocket and reloosened my left ankle clamp. Then I decided to find a better hiding place for my "key." I hid two pieces in the straw mats and put a third inside the neck strap of my B-15 jacket. This piece I had rubbed against the floor and the radiator pipe until I had honed a fair edge along one side, making a reasonable substitute for a knife.

When my sundial indicated nearly noon, I began to keep a sharp eye out the window. I was looking for the man who brought the food. He soon appeared and entered the building. My window was only a few feet from the front entrance, and by watching closely I was able to count the rolls he carried. There were eight. At two each, that verified my supposition that only three of my crew members were being held there with me.

Along with the two rolls I was given a handful of salted peanuts. What a treat! One peanut and one bite of bread—the salt made up for the lack of seasoning in the roll. It was delicious! As good as it tasted and as starved for salt as I was, I put some of the peanuts and part of one roll in my pocket—just in case.

After lunch I decided to take a short nap, but as I expected, the guard had strong objections. He indicated I should sit, not lie down. I knew it was almost time for a guard change, so I sat and listened. When I heard the new guard enter the corridor and the old guard go to meet him, I crawled beneath my bed covers and turned my back to the door, hoping the new guard would think the old guard had given me permission to sleep. It worked. I was all ears as the new guard made his first round. He stood at my door for some time and I could imagine the conflict going on in his mind—to wake me or let me sleep. He left me alone and soon I was asleep.

I was awakened by the rattling of my door lock. The warden and an interpreter came in and told me to get up. Then they made me dress myself in the clothes I had on when I was captured. I already had most of them on except for the torn overpants, the oilcloth rain hat and the gloves. I added these articles, wondering what kind of trick they were up to. Maybe they were going to shoot me and didn't want to have me wearing clothes that would indicate I had been a prisoner. Their attitude reinforced my theory and, considering that the Chinese Reds had violated international law by sneaking me into China, I didn't think they would hesitate to dispose of me if it were to their advantage.

I didn't have long to wonder. After they were satisfied that I was dressed just as I had been when captured, except for the leg chains which I still wore, they escorted me out the basement and into the yard behind the building. I was stood up against the wall, but only to have my picture taken by a Chinese with a Canon camera. So I was to become a member of a Communist rogues' gallery! After several shots were made, I was returned to my cell. There the warden checked my shackles and finding one loose he gave them a closer inspection. He spoke a few words to the guard then left to return shortly with a new pair. He replaced the old ones with these. Then he had me take off my overshoes and shoes. After removing the strings from my shoes he gave them back and left.

I didn't need the shoestrings, the zippered overshoes held on my shoes, but I wondered why they were removed. Possibly the warden was afraid I might use the strings as a weapon, or possibly he figured if I wanted to make a dash for freedom I would be greatly hindered if I couldn't keep my shoes on. In any case I had more pressing worries now—the new shackles.

Careful not to let the guard see me, I went to work trying to open them. I soon found out that it was impossible to unlock the clamps with my small metal "key," so I looked around for something more suitable. I soon found it in the form of a small piece of wire which was used to tie the bands around the insulated steampipe. After bending this in an S-shape, I inserted one end in the key slot of the clamp. With just a little effort I unlocked and loosened both leg clamps. Not content with this, I continued to practice opening them until I could remove both clamps in a matter of seconds—just in case I ever needed to get out of them in a hurry. I concealed my new "key" in the hem of my jacket.

The rest of my tenth day was spent in walking back and forth to keep warm, in trying to talk to each new guard, and in inspecting the door and the bars over the window. By the end of the day the window screen had two more holes poked in it. In fact it was beginning to look pretty well mutilated. I was afraid the guards would notice it so I kept one of the shutters closed. My investigation of the bars revealed the possibility of getting through the window if I could remove one short connecting bar between two other curving pieces of ornamental iron. This bar was held in place by an iron pin in each end.

To discover this much had taken a great deal of time because I had only a few seconds between each round of the guard in which to work. I was beginning to get highly proficient at quiet movements, however. I was usually at the cell door when the guard looked in. When he went to the next cell, I peeped out to make sure he had left. Then holding the leg chain to keep it from rattling, I walked the length of the room to the window, opened the shutter, and worked ten or fifteen seconds, listening closely for the guard; then I climbed down, closed the shutter and quickly went back to the door or started a casual stroll as he checked in again. I had to be extremely careful, for about every half hour the corporal of the guard made his rounds and he could be very quiet in his approach.

For supper that day I had bread and (surprises never ceased in a Chinese jail) a whole fried fish—guts, head, and all. It was bait size, only about four inches long, but salty—which alone made it edible. After eating, and as usual saving part of the bread, I held up three fingers to the guard and pointed to the bed. He nodded yes, so after what I considered three fingers of time I crawled under the covers and removed my shackles. I must have guessed accurately for the guard did not protest. Again my afternoon nap had spoiled my desire for sleep, but covered up in bed I was warm at least and it was the only place where I could remove my chains.

As I lay there I tried to piece together the significance of all the happenings of the day—the interrogation, the picture-taking, the new padded pants, and the new shackles. They must all mean something, I thought, but what? I could only make wild guesses. Finally I went to sleep.

The eleventh day started out as usual. The guard woke me at the first signs of daylight. After putting on my leg chains under the cover, I opened the window for fresh air and a look outside. The guard soon made me close it, but at least I had seen the dawn sky. Next I took my sponge bath and washed my socks. Then came my one-roll breakfast.

My second appearance before the "court" came shortly after breakfast. Here I received a couple of hours of questions and lectures. The main theme this time concerned the place where our B-29 was shot out of the sky. Again it was obvious that the real purpose of the interrogation was not to get information from me. What they wanted and what they tried time after time to get was an admission that we had flown over China and had been shot down over Chinese territory.

If I had been unsure before that such was not the case, the interrogation would have convinced me. Had I actually been in China when I was captured, I doubted if they would worry about getting me to admit it. Certainly they would not spend so much time trying to convince me. They seemed to be trying to scare me —probably in preparation for future interrogations.

I was exhausted and disheartened after standing two hours before the interrogator. When I got back to my cell I was glad to sit and rest; I didn't have the strength or desire to go about my favorite pastime of strolling back and forth across the room. As I rested, I tried to figure out what the Communists were up to. I felt it was actually relatively simple. The crew and I were members of a new Air Force unit. No doubt the Communists were highly interested in it and therefore in us. For that reason, as soon as our identity was discovered, we were taken into Communist China where we could be more easily intimidated and interrogated, and where the Communists would have a freer hand with us. That was my line of reasoning; the more I thought about it the less I liked it. Where at first I had expected to be questioned a few days and then sent to a POW camp, I now began to doubt if I would ever be sent to one. The interrogator had said that I was not a prisoner of war—I was a war criminal. Things might get pretty bad. I knew that if I admitted having flown into China, I would give my captors a completely free hand and they could, without fear, do whatever they wished with me.

Some of the crew, I realized, had no way of knowing that we had not violated the Chinese border. No doubt this was one reason we were being kept apart. I could only wonder what their thoughts were when they were confronted with such an accusation. Having known most of the crew for well over a year, I knew that our captors would have their hands full trying to get a confession from any of them.

There were other reasons for keeping us in solitary, too. Interrogation would be much easier if the interrogator could play one of us against the other. None of us would be able to invent any stories and hope to have them stick. None of us would be able to tell for sure what our captors already knew about us and what they didn't. The thought also crossed my mind that should the Communists kill or harm any of the crew, they naturally would not want any other member to know it; thus the secrecy about who was a prisoner and who was not. The more I thought about this last theory the more convinced I became that it was the primary reason for the secrecy. Until they had finished with us they wanted no non-Communist witnesses to how many of the fourteen men on board Stardust 40 had survived. With this in mind I decided to remind them at the next interrogation that I had seen and had been seen by other members of the crew after bail-out and capture.

When my sun dial approached the noon mark, I took up my station near the window to watch for the chow-bearer. He was my only connection with fellow Americans—not that he was really a connection, but he was proof that I was not alone. Feeling as I did, blue and discouraged, I wanted to reassure myself that more of the crew were in the same building. This knowledge gave me a small measure of comfort. If any of the crew left—if there was any change in the number of Americans being held there—I was sure it would show up in the amount of food brought in. Soon the food arrived and I could detect no change.

The handful of salted peanuts and the bread tasted as good as they had the day before. Although the small ration did not come close to satisfying my hunger, I again saved a portion of it. My reserve supply was gradually increasing. I hid the bread, which soon turned hard as a rock, under the bed platform in a pile of straw pulled from the sleeping pads. The peanuts I kept in my jacket pocket. I was tempted at times to munch on my reserves, especially the peanuts, but I firmly resisted. To make resistance easier I moved the salted peanuts from my jacket pocket, where my hand constantly reminded me of their presence, to a pocket further out of reach.

That afternoon the warden and two guards came to my cell and escorted me out and down the corridor, through a pair of metal sheathed doors and into another part of the basement. I wondered if this part of the basement was also a jail, but there were no cells visible, only several large rooms. I was taken into one of these. Inside there was a young girl dressed in a white nurse's gown and wearing a gauze mask. She had a male assistant, similarly dressed. Spread out on a small table were various medical instruments.

The nurse motioned me to strip to my waist, then she proceeded to examine me. She tapped my chest and back, listened to my chest, took my pulse, my temperature, looked in my mouth, and then gave me a shot in the arm. This done she gave me some powders, a box of pills, and a bottle of cough medicine. She explained how and when I should take the medicine. Though she didn't speak English, she got her message across by reference to sleeping and eating time.

I was led back to my cell where the warden took out a large string of keys and proceeded to look for the one to my leg shackles. As he tried key after key I couldn't help smiling, knowing that I could unlock the clamps in a matter of seconds, without a key. I wondered what his reaction would be if I did so. After about the fifteenth key, I was almost tempted to find out.

He finally got them unlocked and motioned me to put on the pants I had been given a couple of days before. I thought my shackles were being removed permanently. I was quite disappointed when I discovered differently. I protested as he started to put them back on, but resistance was useless; I was outnumbered three to one. I was soon back where I had started, except that I was now clothed adequately and no longer needed to keep moving constantly to keep warm. As soon as I was alone in my cell I got out my "key" and proceeded to loosen the leg clamps to the last notch.

Remembering my medicine, I looked it over and wondered if, considering the circumstances, it was safe to take it. I was under interrogation, had been threatened with death and worse, and had no idea to what lengths my captors would go to accomplish their aims. Was the medicine part of their plans? After much thought I decided I was probably being foolish and overly cautious. I certainly needed medical attention. I was sure I had been running a temperature for the last two days, plus all the other discomforts associated with a cold and cough.

I took a swallow of the cough medicine. It had a winy taste. I took a couple more. Except for the salted peanuts and fish, it had more flavor than anything I had tasted since being captured. I took the other medicine as the nurse, or doctor, or whatever the girl was, had told me. The cough medicine brought almost immediate relief and the taste itself was a treat. After the first dose of powder and pills I felt no ill effects so I decided the medicine was on the level.

The change in routine plus the fact that I had received medical attention raised my spirits considerably. I began to whistle. Then I found out prisoners in Chinese jails don't whistle or sing. I had not intended to create an uproar, but the guard took such a dim view of my musical efforts that I was soon visited by the warden and an interpreter. The interpreter was the same one who had been in on my interrogations. They entered the cell and he asked what the matter was. Had my whistling been so bad the guard had mistaken it for cries of agony?

The humorless interpreter didn't catch the joke when I put my thoughts into words. He proceeded to tell me that I must not make noises. Thinking it useless to argue, I changed the subject by asking him the name of the town I was in. I was told I had no need to know. I asked about the crew and got the same runaround. He wanted to know why I worried about them. It would be better for me to worry about myself, he said. Telling him it was only natural for me to want to know how the others were, I asked about the two who had been wounded.

This caught him off guard, but he replied with the question, "Who was wounded?" I repeated what I had been told shortly after my capture. To this he replied that he did not know. I then asked him when they intended to send us to a POW camp. This was one question too many. He blew his stack and left, saying that if I did not change my attitude I would be shot. The tone of his voice and his expression of hate left no doubt that if he were in charge, I would be shot at the next sunrise. Down went my newly raised spirits.

I had no trouble putting aside part of my evening meal; my appetite wasn't what it usually was. I spent the remainder of the evening and a good part of the night trying once again to make sense out of my position only this time I had a second direct threat of death to include in my thoughts. I could arrive at no one certain theory, but in general I felt that my captors were still bluffing. I did not believe that they could carry out their threats without fear of a reprisal from Uncle Sam. There was one hitch to this last line of thinking, however. To my knowledge, Uncle Sam had no way of knowing that we—any or all of the crew—were not already dead.

Next morning, the beginning of my twelfth day as a prisoner, my cough and cold were much better. Wanting to keep it that way, I used more prudence than usual in taking my morning bath, exposing only small parts of my body to the cold air. A morning bath, no matter how limited the water, raised my spirits considerably. A razor would have given me an even greater boost, both physically and psychologically, but the guards refused to bring me one. I asked for paper and pen and wrote a note to the warden, telling him I had a razor in my personal belongings and would like to be allowed to use it. The note brought negative results. The reflection I saw each morning, as I bent over the pan of water, made me feel more like a criminal than an officer.

My breakfast, a piece of bread, was handed through the hole in the door as usual. Smiley was on duty and after eating my bread (I didn't put aside any of my breakfast since it consisted of only one roll), I asked him for more. I was expecting nothing more than the usual *mamonte*, which I got, but very shortly Smiley produced another roll. This was not the first time I had asked for more food, but it was the first time I got any.

I ate the extra roll, but began to wonder how the guard got it so fast. I hadn't seen the man bring in the food that morning, so I didn't know if he had brought more than usual or if one of the other prisoners had been taken away or was sick. I didn't have long to think about it, however, for my door was soon unlocked and I was escorted upstairs for my third chat with the interrogator.

The atmosphere of this interrogation was somewhat more hostile than before. The "court" showed a good deal of impatience with me. When I walked into the room and took my place before my questioners, I saw, lying on the desk, a survival radio like the one I had. The interrogator and interpreter sat and looked me over a few minutes and, after exchanging a few harsh-sounding words, presumably about my appearance, they began:

"How have you been thinking?"

"I don't understand what you mean."

"What do you do with your spare time?" A snicker here. "What do you think about back in your room?"

"I think of many things."

"Tell us some of them."

"I think about the crew. I wonder when you are going to start treating us as POW's. I . . ."

"Never mind! Have you not thought about yourself? Have you not decided to tell us all you know so the Chinese People will be lenient with you?"

"No."

"You will learn! Is this yours?"

He was holding the radio, and I saw little use in denying that it was. Although others of the crew had the same kind of radio, I knew mine had probably been found. Also it might be a good idea to let the interrogator think I had made contact with American forces before I was captured. This might make them more reluctant to dispose of me, if they were seriously considering it. I replied that it might be mine.

They asked, sarcastically, if I didn't know for sure. Then they followed up with several other equally silly questions to which they neither expected nor got answers. They cursed and raved about my bad attitude and said I would not even admit known facts. I protested when they called me an s.o.b., but it did no good.

They built quite a story around my radio. I was labeled a spy and a saboteur. That was ridiculous and they knew it. They continued, however, to harp about the radio and the fate of spies caught by the People's Republic of China. They reminded me I was completely out of reach of my government. My fate was entirely in the hands of the "Chinese People's Court" which would never show mercy to "imperialist spies."

When I could get a word in, I reminded them that it was 1953 and governments had long ago stopped shooting POW's. I men-
tioned the Geneva Convention and told them, stupidly, that I knew they were bluffing and trying to scare me into answering questions. Actually, I was far from being sure of my statements. They had already violated international law by taking me into China. Because of that, they might let me remain Missing in Action forever.

Their next statements confirmed this possibility. In effect they said that they could do with the crew as they pleased because the U.S. Air Force did not know we were alive and would never know what happened to us. Realizing that this might be only too true, I nevertheless tried to act surprised. I told them they were quite mistaken because I, personally, had radioed back that we were bailing out (this much was true) and had given our position. I added that by using my survival radio, like the one lying there on the desk, I had established contact with a U.S. Air Force jet fighter shortly before I was captured. This bit of news visibly interested my questioners, though they said, "We know all about you and your so-called survival radio."

I wondered what they meant by that. Had they intercepted my

broadcasts and, if so, did they know I had not been able to establish contact from the ground? There was no way they could be
sure, I decided, so when they began to question me concerning my
"supposed" contact, I made it sound as simple and plausible as
possible. I told them that after the fighter answered me, I gave the
pilot my name and our aircraft call sign and told him we had
bailed out. When asked what reply I received, I said the pilot had
repeated my message and left.

Next they wanted to know the range of my radio. I was concentrating on remembering my story, and to keep it as truthful as
possible, I gave them the actual range.

"Ten miles!" they shouted. "How could you establish contact
with your damn jets when you were deep in Chinese territory?"

Still concentrating on making my story sound plausible, I explained that ten miles was the ground-to-ground range of the
radio. I said the ground-to-air range would be much more. Then it
dawned on me that my last statement could be taken as an admission that I had been in China. I was about to add that the
ten-mile range was more than enough to reach an aircraft flying
overhead, and that I was not in China when I was captured. But
much to my surprise the "court" started off on another line of
questioning instead of taking advantage of my slip.

They asked how many other crew members I had seen after I was
captured. Since they could check my answers I told them the
truth. Each time I mentioned seeing one they asked if he had
also seen me. I took these questions to indicate that, at worst, they
were undecided about my story and possibly believed it. I realized
that I would have to be extremely careful not to contradict myself. I had already discovered how easy it was to come out on the
losing end of a battle of wits with them. They had all the advantages, plus being highly trained in the art of interrogation. I had
only been given a few hours' training in how to resist interrogation,
but I did have two big factors in my favor. I knew I was in the
right and they were wrong, and since security in my outfit had

been very good, there was little information of value they could get from me no matter how hard they tried.

After a few more questions about the crew members, I was dismissed with the reminder that I was in a very bad position. Not only my future, they said, but also my life was in grave danger. There was little hope for me, and they said I should go back to my cell and think about my crimes and try to find some way to repent. They sounded sincere enough, but something gave me the idea that they, too, would do some thinking after that interrogation.

Back in my cell I reviewed the proceedings just completed and then set about memorizing my story. Since everything said during the interrogation was recorded in writing, I wanted to be sure I could repeat my story exactly as I had given it, should they ever ask me again. Of course, I could not be sure my story was of any value to me or the other crew members, but I felt there was definitely a possibility that it was.

It was nearly lunchtime and, remembering the extra piece of bread I got for breakfast, I opened the window so I could see the food being brought in. I wanted to find out if there were still four of us or if, as I feared, someone had been taken away during the night.

My efforts to look out the window brought an unexpected reaction from the guard. This guard usually minded his own business and let me mind mine, so I was more than a little surprised when he rapped on the door and, with his face framed in the peephole, emitted some wolfish noises through the gauze mask he wore. I turned from the window and asked, in English, what was the matter, all the while strongly suspecting what he wanted. He uttered more growls and made an effort to repeat what I had said, as if to ridicule me. I continued to act ignorant of his meaning and turned back to the window.

Wham! This time he must have kicked the door. My already high-strung nerves reacted and I shouted at him. At this he stepped back from the door and began to give forth a tirade that sounded none too pleasant. Realizing the futility of the situation, I calmed my own nerves and, walking to the door, tried to reason with him. This was just as futile and I finally gave up, but not before I had been told, in sign language and no doubt verbally, that I was going to be shot.

That bit of verbiage was popping up more and more frequently, but right then I was more interested in getting back to the window to watch for the chow-bearer. I started strolling back and forth, turning around and looking out the window quickly. This didn't fool the guard at all. My would-be executioner was still unhappy, but he contented himself with standing and muttering what must have been Chinese curses. Some of them I recognized from the interrogations.

Finally, after damning my eighteen generations of ancestors, he left to make his rounds of the other cells. I was immediately back at the window and stayed there until I heard the guard return. When he looked in again, I was nowhere near the forbidden area, so he only paused a few seconds and then continued on his rounds. Back to the window I went and this time my vigilance was rewarded. The chow-bearer came in the gate, crossed the yard and entered the building carrying the usual amount of food.

This gave me a great feeling of relief. Apparently there were still four of us in the same prison. Just to make sure, I asked for extra food that noon. Although the guard got over his mad spell and went to get more, he returned empty-handed. I could easily have eaten several more rolls, but I was happy for once at not getting any.

That afternoon Smiley relieved my guard and, after making a round of the cells, returned to my window for another lesson in spoken English. After being told I was to be shot, I wasn't too interested in teaching my captors anything, not even Smiley, whose friendship I had cultivated until then. I indicated as much in a not very warm manner. This must have hurt his feelings, for he left my peephole. He was soon back, however, trying again, so I told him that since the Chinese were going to shoot me I had no friendship for them. He insisted that this was not true. He said that Americans tortured and killed Chinese prisoners, but the Chinese would never do this to their prisoners. I took up the challenge and finally persuaded him to say that Americans didn't kill prisoners. I couldn't be sure if he was convinced or just wanted to end the argument, but at least I had done a little bit to counter the malicious propaganda the Communists fed their soldiers.

We were back on friendly terms, and to prove his friendship, Smiley told me I could lie down and take a nap, in violation of prison rules. Though intending only to rest, I lay down and was soon dozing. When it was time for a guard change, Smiley gently tapped on the door and told me my siesta was over. I wondered which one of us was the most likely to be shot if Smiley were ever caught doing me favors.

The next guard's attitude was somewhat more hostile than normal. When I tried to make conversation with him, he snatched off his gauze mask and started jabbering away. For once I really had no idea what he wanted other than for me to shut up. Every time I spoke or moved he hit the door and muttered something. Finally he put his arm through the peephole and motioned me to sit down. This I did, but soon grew tired of it and, drawing more attention from the guard, I continued with my favorite pastime of strolling back and forth across the cell. The guard, after having the last say, continued with his endless pacing up and down the corridor.

Walking and thinking, I tried to tire my body so I would be able to lose my troubles in sound sleep when sunset plus three fingers of time had lapsed. Why had my guards suddenly turned sour— more sour than usual, that is. Many possibilities entered my mind. Maybe the guards believed I had done the things I was accused of doing. They certainly acted like it. Or maybe they had been instructed to get tough with me as a sort of preparation for further interrogations. I could only wonder, but why did the morbid subject of my being shot continue to pop up. Had the guards heard the officers discussing my "future" or had they merely been instructed to keep reminding me of it? Whatever the reason, I decided the guards were far too simple to be acting a part.

Were the interrogators serious, too, or were *they* acting? The Chinese Communists were capable of things much worse than shooting a few prisoners. As long as they were only issuing verbal threats and there was no physical violence, I felt I could count my life reasonably safe. Besides, things like that always happened to someone else, never to me. But that wasn't a very cheerful thought because I never figured I would be shot down. What could I do about it if their threats did show definite signs of being carried out? That was the big problem.

Escape had been on my mind almost constantly since my capture, but for the most part I had used it as a sort of entertainment, like building dream castles, and had not seriously planned a break. Quite obviously, escape was next to impossible. Nevertheless I continually planned what I would do should the opportunity ever arise.

During the past few years I had read several books written by people who had escaped World War II prison camps. Certainly these men had overcome almost insurmountable difficulties, but perhaps the Chinese authorities had read the same books. Even the slim opportunities that these prisoners took advantage of had not presented themselves to me, or so it seemed. Besides, I wondered if they had not been more than exceptionally gifted with that substance commonly known as guts.

My evening meal was served and devoured, except for the piece of bread I always saved for the future. Then I continued my walking and thinking. A course of action, indefinite to be sure, but nonetheless a sort of plan, began to take shape. The way I saw it, there were three possibilities. The first one required little preparation, since if and when the time came it would almost certainly end in my death. If my treatment became so rough that there could no longer be any doubt about my ultimate end, then and only then would I make an open break. This, I decided, would be better than being stood up against a wall.

As my second course of action I planned to watch for the first opportunity to part company with my captors by stealth. While waiting for a chance to fold my tent and silently steal away, there were many things I could do. I would continue to add to my reserve of bread and peanuts. I would try to learn more Chinese words. I would continue to try to get information from the guards about my location. I would somehow need to get a pair of shoestrings to replace those that had been taken from me, since I couldn't walk fast in my overshoes and besides they would leave obvious tracks. I would also need a gauze face mask like what most of the natives wore. With a mask to cover my shaggy face and wearing the clothes I had been given, I felt I would be able to move about with relative freedom, once I got outside the prison. Lastly, I decided to carry out further inspection of my window, hoping to find some way of removing one of the bars.

These were some of the things I decided to do. There seemed little possibility of accomplishing most of them because of the close observation I was under; but I was, with every passing day, becoming more and more wise in the art of stealth. During the next few days I proved every task possible—with one exception, the escape.

The third and last plan was not a course of action, but rather the only thing left if neither of the other plans were carried out. I would just have to wait and let events happen as they would. In reality this would be merely a continuation of the past twelve days.

It was late into the night before I finally fell asleep, but even then my brain would not rest. Actually, my ideas and plans were not new. I had considered most of them in the past week, but the difference was that I had, in a way, organized them and set myself a sort of schedule.

CHAPTER

SIX

Next morning I was awakened by a loud rap on the door. The guard was impatient to have me up, but I remembered to slip my shackles back on before rising. I greeted the guard with a smile and a cheerful word, but he was having none of it so I tried to ignore the presence of his face framed in the peephole. I walked over to open the window. The guard wasn't having any of that either and indicated as much with another rap on the door. I humored him and went about folding up my bedding.

As soon as he left I returned to the window and took a look out. It had snowed during the night and the yard, the wall, and all the surrounding buildings were under a mantle of white. The soldiers were beginning to stir and the same thing happened here that I'm sure would have happened in any country—a snow-ball fight developed. I closed the window before the guard returned and began to prepare for my morning sponge bath. Several minutes passed and no water appeared. Thinking he had forgotten it, I held my empty pan for the guard to see. Among the words he said was one that always seemed to appear when the reply was in the negative. "*Mei yo*," he kept repeating as I continued to question, argue, and ask for water.

My efforts were in vain. I couldn't even get a *mamonte* from the uncompromising guard. In fact he grew tired of my badgering and, turning his back on me, walked off. That was quite rude and unmannerly of him, I thought, so I continued to pester him each time he came by. This got me nowhere and only served to make the guard mad at me. Breakfast was late and I had about decided that I had pestered myself out of my food when finally it was handed in—the usual roll and then a cup of hot water which I used for more things than drinking.

I was expecting another interrogation so I reviewed my story a few times just to be sure I could repeat it the same way, if asked. While waiting I stood by the door peeping at my fellow prisoners as they passed by my cell on their way to and from the latrine. With the guards as an exception, I never tired of watching other people and peeped through the door whenever there was movement in the corridor. One prisoner's face was old and withered, another's was covered with hair even shaggier than mine. These prisoners were also in solitary and appeared to be completely subdued and spiritless. When walking down the corridor they did so hurriedly with lowered heads, never attempting to look around. The guards seldom had to speak to them; all orders were given by brisk motions of the hand. Although they were prisoners in their own country, I wondered whose lot was better, mine or theirs. Misery loves company, or so I'd heard, and I was able to forget a measure of my own troubles while I was occupied in watching other humans. I saw them only a few minutes each day, however.

During the few times I had been out of my cell, I was careful to observe the manner in which the door was secured. It was simple; a heavy iron bolt slid into an eye-ring made from a piece of iron strap. The two ends of the strap were driven through the door. Inside, the ends were spread apart, bent a second time, and driven back into the door. A heavy padlock was used to secure the bolt once it had been slid into the ring.

Although the peephole in the door was large enough to admit an arm, the lock was out of reach, even if I could have fashioned a key. With the little pieces of metal I had found I began to work on the inside of the door where the strap came through. For the rest of the morning I scratched away at the wood. Whenever the guard approached my door, I walked away and made a couple of turns around the cell. As soon as he left and I heard him check the second cell down, I got back to work. By noon I had a small trench worn into the door, in which I might be able to insert something to pry out the strap.

Noon came and went, but no food accompanied it. I wondered if this were some kind of holiday. It seemed I was not going to be interrogated, and if I was to get any lunch it was as late as my breakfast had been. While I wondered I continued with my work. I needed something to use as a lever in order to bend the strap. There were nails in the bedboards, but I had no way of pulling them. I remembered the useless steam radiator fixed to the wall high up near the ceiling. This had a handle which was held in place by a screw. The handle looked like just what I needed. Most of the afternoon was spent in removing it. Between rounds of the guard I pulled myself up the pipe until I could get one shoe on the edge of a coupling in the pipe. Then, holding myself with one hand, I worked on the screw which held the handle in place. Getting into a working position and down again was so tedious and time-consuming that I had only a few seconds between each trip of the guard to work at the screw. I had only the little pieces of metal band to use as a screwdriver, and these were rusted and kept bending, but finally the screw gave up its hold and I had the handle.

Except that it was made of brass and bent easily, the handle made an excellent tool to pry with. By mid-afternoon I had pulled one end of the strap out of the door far enough to get a grip on it with my fingers. I replaced the radiator handle, but not the screw. This only took one round of the guard. Just then I heard the rattle of food pans and soon my late lunch was handed in—a small bowl of rice and a smaller bowl of broth. It was midafternoon and I was hungry. The food was good, but it left me almost as hungry as before.

When I finished lunch I returned to the door and began working at the strap with bare fingers. It was made of heavy iron and I could hardly move the three-inch end which I had pried away from the wood. Little by little it weakened, and by night the constant bending back and forth caused it to snap at the bend where it passed through the door. All I needed was to break the other end at the same place, then one good pull on the door would open it.

Even if I could get through the door, I knew I would still have to get by the guard in the corridor and the one at the door out of the basement. But if I were forced to make an open break, I could take the corridor guard by surprise and arm myself with his pistol. The remainder of the evening was passed in walking back and forth and planning my next day's work. If possible I wanted to finish with the door and get to work on the bars in the window. While waiting for my supper I remembered the date. It was Sunday, the twenty-fifth of January, 1953. I wondered if I were going to receive a third meal or if two meals on Sundays was SOP in Communist prisons. After a few weeks I no longer wondered—I knew it was.

Before turning in for the night I carefully hid the end of the strap I had broken, saving it for possible use as a tool to work on the bars. After lying down I had little time to wonder why I had not been interrogated that day. My physical exertions had tired me greatly and I immediately dropped off to sleep. If nothing else came of my efforts, they had made the day pass more quickly; made sleep come sooner, and boosted my ego. I felt I was outsmarting my guards.

I slept more soundly that night than I had in some time, and no doubt would have slept late if the guard had not roused me with the usual rap on the door. I snapped on my shackles under the cover and got up. I had little dressing to do since I slept in all my clothes except the padded coat. Even with a blanket I needed all my clothes to keep warm. Besides, I could not have taken off my pants or flying suits without revealing the fact that I could remove my shackles.

I didn't risk antagonizing the guard by opening the window while he watched; I waited until he left my door before taking my morning look outside. I had noticed that every time I made a guard mad at me, he watched me twice as closely. I needed to avoid that if I was to finish the work I had started the day before.

I closed the window shutter and waited for the guard to return so I could get some bath water, but I was again disappointed. No bath, I was made to understand. Wondering about this and feeling somewhat downcast, I waited for breakfast and in the meantime took my morning stroll around the cell. Eleven steps and turn, eleven steps and turn. The steps were short and restricted because of the chain connecting my ankle clamps. I could not walk in a circle because of the bed platform along one side of the cell. My path described an "L" and the turns were tedious. If I pivoted, the ankle clamps turned on my ankles and wore away at the skin. So I made the turns with a series of short steps.

After a couple of rounds my unpredictable guard put his arm through the peephole and motioned me to open the window, apparently as a favor to make up for the lack of bath water. This I gladly did. Outside were several soldiers with shovels and boards, scraping the snow which had frozen during the night. They cleaned the prison yard down to bare earth and left the icy, dirty snow in mounds. This was before their breakfast. After they had eaten I witnessed another guard mount and the departure of a patrol through the prison gate.

As soon as my one-roll breakfast was served and consumed, I took the piece of iron strap from its hiding place in a straw pad and went to work on the door. When all the soldiers cleared out of the yard I moved my activities to the window, taking advantage of the guard's leniency in letting me have it open.

The screen between me and the bars was already noticeably mutilated, and I was afraid that to damage it further would invite almost certain discovery. The only alternative seemed to be complete removal of the screen. In order to get at the short bar which I wanted to remove, it was necessary to take out only one of the two screens. The screen frame was nailed to the window frame in four places and was a very tight fit. To make my job more difficult, the window frame was made of hardwood, which had a death grip on the nails. I had no tools with which to pull the nails, so my only hope was to pull on the screen frame, hoping the nails would give. To do this I had to tear two more hand-sized holes in the wire. I could only hope the guards would not notice even though they were usually observant of conditions in the cell. By leaving the window shutter half closed, the torn part of the wire would be out of view from my cell door. As to anyone walking around outside, I just had to risk it.

I made the hand-holds. The wire was old and rusty and this required little effort. Next I went to work trying to work the frame loose. To do this I had to step on the radiator pipe, risking damage to the insulation which covered it. My shackles would not allow the eighteen-inch step required to reach the pipe, so I had to pull myself up by the window shutters. Once standing on the pipe I could get a grip on the screen frame to work it back and forth.

At first it wouldn't move, but gradually it developed a fraction of an inch of play. This little bit of progress consumed the better part of an hour. To make matters worse, the next guard made me close the window shutter. That meant that before I could get into position to work I had to open the shutter and also have it closed again before the guard returned. This left only a few seconds to pull at the screen frame. I soon gave it up, hoping that the next guard would let me keep the shutter at least partly open.

The morning was passing; it seemed it would be another one without an interrogation. That was fine with me. I was becoming wholly occupied with my escape preparations and wanted no interruptions. Because of my work, time seemed to be passing much more quickly, and I realized that whether my plans succeeded or not, my efforts were of great value to my mental and physical well-being. My work made it easy to keep my mind off unpleasant subjects.

After taking a few dozen turns around the cell, I fell to work on the door again. There I had longer to work between rounds of the guard. I was in a position to hear him coming and could keep at my task until he was only a few steps away. By noon I had succeeded in digging away the wood along one side of the second iron strap. All that remained was to bend it so I could get a grip on it, and then work it back and forth until it broke.

This I did after lunch and by mid-afternoon my door project was complete. I camouflaged the scratches and marks I had made by rubbing dirt into them. This was so effective I felt it unlikely that anything less than a close inspection of the door would reveal that it had been tampered with; yet one good pull from inside would force the latch ring out of the door and the door would fly open. It amused me to think of the surprise the guard would get if I ever did so. If my situation became desperate enough to make the use of this method of escape worthwhile, I would have to take advantage of the guard's surprise to overpower him. The only things I possessed that could be used as a weapon were my leg chains or the earthenware jar which served as my privy. I decided the jar would be more effective and moved it nearer the door.

My lenient guard of the morning came back on duty, giving me the opportunity to work on the screen. I opened the shutter and once again was allowed to leave it open. The guard, however, seemed attracted to my cell and stood for long periods with his face framed in the peephole. His breath filled the cell with an almost overpowering odor of garlic and his presence interfered with my work. Thinking he might want to be friendly, I tried conversing with him. He proved somewhat timid at first, but soon warmed up. In answer to my leading questions, he replied "yes," there were three other Americans in the buildings. "Yes," they were not in my part of the building. "Yes," they were okay. "Yes," they had been shot. I could see I was getting nowhere so I started over. "No," there were no more Americans there. "No," there were none near by. "No," they had not been shot.

That sounded better, but I was still getting nowhere. I tried a different approach. Taking some straw from my mattress, I broke it into equal lengths. Holding one of these I indicated that it was to represent myself, then I laid it down on the bed platform. I laid a second one beside it and indicated that it was another one of "me," but in another cell. The guard nodded "yes" so I continued. When I started to place the fifth straw the guard shook his head. Apparently I was right; there were only four of us in the prison. But where were the others, and how many of them were there?

To find the answers to those questions, I used more straws. I put them in a different pile and indicated that they were not in the same building, but were nearby. Five more straws were placed on the platform before the guard shook his head again. A total of nine—the same number I thought had been in the barracks with the crapper on the hill. Not counting the two I believed to be in a hospital somewhere, there were three men missing. I still hoped that some had avoided capture and had been rescued by choppers, but I doubted it. I had been in a perfect position for pickup, but had not even seen a rescue aircraft. I remembered having been told that some of the crew had been killed the night we bailed out. Three? I wondered how and which ones.

Next I tried to get the guard to describe the three prisoners who were being held in the same building with me. The description he gave didn't fit anyone I knew. In fact I wasn't sure we were still talking about the same subject. When he put his hands to his chest, describing something unmistakably feminine, I knew we were not. How we got from the subject of my fellow crew members to the subject of women I couldn't imagine, but we had, and it would have been difficult to find a subject which held less interest for me at that time. When the guard hugged his arms to his chest and smacked his lips like a young calf, I decided he was telling me about his girl friend. I wanted to keep him friendly so I smiled and nodded agreement with all he said. Next he took his padded cap and, holding it like a baby, rocked his arms back and forth. He hardly seemed old enough to have a wife and baby, but I smiled and agreed with this too. That satisfied him, and he left to look in on the other prisoners whom he had neglected for the past fifteen or twenty minutes.

He soon returned and I tried to shift the topic of conversation back to one more pertinent. I taught him to say my name, hoping he would repeat it to any other Americans he might have the privilege of guarding and hoping, too, that they would reciprocate. With this I gave up my efforts at conversation and the guard resumed his rounds. It was quite a relief to have him go. The garlic odor had become almost unbearable. At the risk of having the torn screens discovered, I opened both shutters wide to air out the room.

It lacked several minutes before another guard change. Thinking I could probably get away with more with the friendly guard on duty, I went to work determined to get the screen out of the window. Instead of being careful not to make much noise while prying and pulling at the frame, I made what noise was necessary and covered up by stamping my feet, kicking my bedboards, and rattling my leg chains whenever the guard was nearby. I pretended I was doing it to keep warm—which, with the window open, took little pretending. Finally, after giving the guard time to get as far away as his rounds took him, I braced my legs against the windowsill and, holding onto the frame, I pulled as hard as I could. One side of the frame split and it was out. It made a lot of noise, but apparently was not noticed by the guard.

I quickly climbed down and slid the broken screen under my bedboards out of sight. Then I closed the window shutters so the guard could not see that one screen was missing. When he looked in again I was walking up and down the room still pretending to be cold, just as I had been when he left. The risk I ran and the success I had in getting the screen out made my heart pound excitedly. I decided I had done enough for one day. I loafed and tried to relax for the few hours until bedtime.

Next morning I was anxious to get a look at the bars. Smiley was on duty, which was a break. I knew he had no objections to my having the window open. I didn't think he would notice that there was a screen missing as long as I opened only one of the shutters. I hoped that anyone walking around outside would not notice either. Again I decided it unlikely, since the bars helped balance appearances on that side.

Smiley was more smiles than ever. He showed me a brand new hundred yuan bank note and said he was going on a three-day pass. I wished him well and would have broken off conversation in order to get to work, but he was in a talkative mood. I lost much open-window time, but picked up a few more Chinese words in exchange for some English.

Finally, a few minutes before the guard change, Smiley began normal rounds leaving me to my work. This didn't last long, however, for the next guard made me close the shutter and then proceeded to walk his rounds so fast I didn't have time to open it between trips. He was one of the most irritating guards I had. He would step up to the door, look in, walk to the next cell at an accelerated pace, look in it, and so on down the corridor. His fast-stepping had him back again in less than half a minute. The exasperating thing was that he was stupid enough to do it. I could see no earthly reason for it. Any self-respecting American GI would loaf a little, but not that guy. He kept up the pace a full two hours. I named him "Speedy" although I thought "Stupid" fitted just as well. One thing was certain—there would be no escaping with him on duty, at least not without tapping him over the head first.

I wondered if he was really seeing anything when he looked in the cell, or if it was just an automatic action gained from months or years of such duty. To find out, each time he left my door I opened the window a little. Leaving it until he passed again, I opened it a little more. He made half a dozen rounds before he noticed and made me close it. This confirmed my suspicion that he was acting wholly out of habit. To further test my theory I hid in a corner beside the door, just out of view of the peephole. Speedy made eleven rounds before he missed me and began rapping on the door. Curious to see what he would do, I stayed where I was, but he finally got one eyeball far enough through the peephole to spot me. This satisfied him and he resumed his normal pace.

I tried talking with him, hoping that would decrease his rpm, but except for an occasional *pu shih*, he ignored my attempts at conversation. Finally in desperation, I began mimicking his quick, short steps, stopping at imaginary peepholes around the cell. He noticed this and, muttering some of the same phrases used by the interrogator, continued walking. My leg chains soon caused me to give up that little game. The fast steps threatened my ankles with the same fate my socks had met. Giving up all hope of changing Speedy's routine, I sat down to wait for a new guard.

The next guard's rounds were at the normal rate—from one to two minutes per round—and I went back to work. First I tested the guard to see his reaction to an open window. It was bad, so I had to open and close it between each round. Nevertheless, with the screen gone, I could get at the bars easily.

As I had guessed, the removal of one small bar which connected two loops of the grillwork would leave a space large enough to squeeze through. One pin in each end of the bar was all that held it in place. The pins were less than the diameter of a pencil, but after twisting at the bar over an hour without any signs of movement, I knew they were stronger than they appeared.

After lunch I continued my efforts, always being extremely careful not to let a guard catch me. Some of the guards could walk very quietly. When one of the quiet ones was on duty, I had to count the seconds between each trip until I had established his rate of reappearance. Then I could go to work with reasonable safety, stopping a few seconds before he was due back. Luckily for me, the guards almost never varied their routine, although each was slightly different. I had some close calls on the rare occasions they did vary, but managed never to get caught. My sense of hearing had sharpened considerably over the past few days.

I had to stop work at dark. I was afraid that with the light on inside, the opening and closing of the window shutter would attract the attention of the guard at the gate outside. While waiting for bedtime I made a passable face mask using a pocket from my flying pants and a string from my straw mattress pad. This and the padded pants, coat, and hat would give me a reasonable chance to pass as a local inhabitant, I thought, as long as I was not observed too closely.

My efforts of the day had the same effect as those of the previous day. Time had been speeded up and my body was fatigued. I slept soundly. This was a big help. Wakeful nights, I had discovered, added greatly to the misery of prison life.

Next morning I started again. Wearing the shell of my surviving glove on one hand and the wool liner on the other to protect them from the extreme cold, I twisted away at the bar. By mid-morning it had loosened very little more. I was developing great patience, but this was too slow and I began to doubt that I could ever remove the bar. I decided to try another approach. My bed platform was made of six-foot-long boards nailed to two four-by-fours which lay on the floor. Thinking one of the boards would make a handy lever to force out the bar, I moved my theater of operations to them.

With much camouflaging of the noise I made, I managed to remove one of the looser boards under the straw bedding. Using it as a pry bar, I loosened a second board on the edge of the bed platform. To perform even that simple operation required some fast moving. I had to remove the bedding, take the loose board, pry at the other board for a few seconds, then replace the first board and the bedding, all in the minute or so between rounds of the guard. Each time the guard looked in I was innocently walking up and down the room making all the noise I could, within reason.

By noon I had the board at the edge of the bed loose, and the first one permanently back in place under the bedding. I could get the edge board quickly and easily without moving any of the straw bedding, but when I had loosened the board, the nails wouldn't fit back in the original holes. By pressing the nails on the floor, I forced them out of the board, then replaced them with smaller nails taken from the broken screen. That allowed the board to lie loosely while giving the appearance of being nailed in place. Most of the afternoon was required to complete that part of the job. I did, however, get a few tries at the bar with the board before dark. It worked much better than merely twisting by hand; I loosened the bar considerably. I went to bed with high hopes of success and began to make definite plans for my departure.

Next morning, my seventeenth day in prison, I resumed my work with a passion. Although the bar was loose, the pins in each end still held it in place. There was no way of pulling the pins out so I had to try breaking them.

I worked at the bar all day, often using the board as a battering-ram instead of a pry bar. That required more covering noise. By nightfall the bar was so loose that I was sure one more day's efforts would remove it. I had succeeded in removing more than the bar— I had also nearly removed the skin on my hands. They were spotted with blisters, a number of them open and painful. I considered the condition of my hands and glove as dangerously likely to give me away if any of the guards noticed the blisters. To counter this possibility I kept my hands in my pockets whenever the guard looked in.

During the afternoon the warden and a couple of strange officers entered my corridor and stood outside my door chattering and looking in at me. Their presence gave me quite a fright. I was afraid they would enter my cell. I knew a close inspection of the room would give me away. They left after a few minutes, but I still wasn't easy. They weren't looking me over just out of curiosity, and neither was it an inspection of the prison, since they paid no attention to any of the other cells. Whatever they were up to, they lent impetus to my escape plan. I decided to make an attempt the next night.

For the first time I was actually faced with the possibility of escape and, knowing the risks involved, I grew excited and nervous. I wondered if I had the guts to go through with it. Being caught in the act would probably bring severe punishment if it didn't get me shot, but that was the least of my worries. I didn't know where I was or which way to go once outside my cell. It was midwinter and extremely cold. I figured my chances of getting out of the country were about one in a million, but on the other hand I seemed to have nothing to lose.

My plans were completed. I would go to bed the next night as usual, but my pockets would contain the food I had carefully hoarded. In bed I would remove my overshoes and lace up my brogans with the strings I had made from my straw mat bindings. Late in the night, after most people outside were sure to be asleep, I intended to get up, unscrew the light bulb in my cell and insert a small piece of metal strap in the socket. By replacing the bulb, I hoped to blow the fuse in the prison switch-box. I had to have darkness inside the cell to keep from being silhouetted as I crawled out the window. I figured blowing the fuses would be better than merely turning off the light in my cell. The guard would be sure to notice my cell if it were the only one with a light out. Also by blowing the fuses I would not have the outside light, by the gate, to worry about. If all the lights were out they would probably spend several minutes looking elsewhere, and all I needed was one minute to be out of the cell and over the low prison wall. This I had calculated over and over again. I gave up the idea of pouncing on the gate guard and taking his weapon, reasoning that the less disturbance I caused, the better my chances would be. Once outside the prison wall I intended to make my way to the nearby rail-yards and stow away on the first train that passed. I considered this the fastest way to get out of the immediate vicinity. After that, I would have to trust to luck and play it by ear.

CHAPTER

SEVEN

I slept little that night. My excitement kept me awake and I went over my plans time after time, looking for flaws and trying to think of ways to improve my chances of succeeding. Next morning I tackled the bar again. I pried and banged at it until it was loose—not completely out, but only awaiting the *coup de grâce*. Then I left it and closed the window. That noon I ate all my food as sort of a celebration of my success so far. Also I wanted to build up my store of energy.

I was as restless and nervous as the proverbial cat all day. When my evening food was brought in I again ate it all. The hours dragged by more slowly than at any time since my capture. I reviewed my plans over and over. I walked back and forth, tried to talk to the guards, and set my privy pot directly under the peephole in the door so the guard would get full benefit of it. I did this in protest for not having been allowed to empty it for three days.

Late in the evening I transferred my store of food from its pantry under the bed boards to my pockets. Finally bedtime came and I crawled between my straw pad and blanket. Once covered, I removed my leg shackles and put them in my coat pocket. They were rather bulky; I decided to leave them behind. Next I slipped off my overshoes and laced up my shoes with the homemade shoestrings. I was all set and my nerves were settling down.

After the second guard change I decided I had waited long enough. The guard change brought me luck in the form of the slowest guard I had. Slipping out of bed just as he left my window, I made sure he had gone to the end of the corridor. Then I turned off my light and took the bulb out. Holding the socket upside down, I dropped in the piece of metal and replaced the bulb.

That was as far as my escape went. When I turned on the light switch, instead of blowing fuses as I had planned, I tripped a circuit breaker which made a lot of noise and, to make matters worse, only put out one light—mine. The other lights blinked, but stayed on. This attracted the guard's attention and he came running. Forgetting my plans to escape, I barely managed to get back under my blanket when a flashlight shone in through the hole in my cell door.

First the beam stopped on me then probed around the room and stopped on the light bulb. The guard rapped on the door several times. I pretended to be waking up while I slipped my shackles back on. The guard indicated I should get up and turn on the light. I did so gladly, since I was afraid he might come in and find the piece of metal I had put in the socket. Turning the switch I showed the guard the light wouldn't work. Next he wanted to see the bulb. Standing with my back to him, I removed the bulb, catching the piece of metal as it fell out. I walked to the door; the guard inspected the bulb; finding nothing wrong with it, he told me to put it back. When I did, it came on. I gave him a puzzled look. He gave me a puzzled look and then we parted. I went back to bed and he went back to his rounds. He kept a closer watch, however, and I decided I could do no more that night.

Sleep came late; I was too upset over the failure of my plans. I made up my mind to try again the following night. I decided I would have to leave the light on and risk being seen by the guard outside. It would not give me much head start, since I would surely be missed within a couple of minutes, but I could think of no other way.

During the night I removed the food from my pockets and hid it in my straw bedding. I didn't want to risk having the bulge of my pockets noticed the next day. In the morning, shortly after breakfast, I was visited by the warden. This visit scared me. I thought he might be investigating the cause of the light failure during the night. Instead of this, however, he gave me a bundle he had brought, containing new clothes—coat, pants, gloves, and a pair of shoes. The clothes and shoes were black, of the cut worn by the few civilians I had seen.

After removing my leg cuffs, the warden instructed me to put on the new clothes. The shoes were several sizes too small, so he left to exchange them. I took advantage of his temporary absence to remove the "key" from the hem of my old paddeds, putting it in my new ones. The warden returned shortly, bringing another pair of shoes only a little larger than the first pair. These would have to do, I was told, and my shoes, overshoes, and old clothes were taken away, but not before I had again been shackled.

I was trying to puzzle out the meaning of this when, about mid-morning, my cell was again unlocked and I was motioned out and led upstairs to a large room. Two guards stood by while I was fitted with a pair of handcuffs and then pushed into a chair. There I waited and wondered. I was fully dressed in black—a color I associated with executions. Although I had no doubt that my captors were fully capable of killing me, I didn't quite believe the time had come.

My thoughts were interrupted when the warden and two more guards entered. A pair of goggles with painted lenses were slipped over my eyes and a black stocking pulled over my head. No part of my body was left exposed to view and all my outside clothing was Chinese. Apparently the prison authorities wanted my identity and nationality kept secret. Was I to be moved and were they making sure that no one outside the prison knew I was not a native? Execution? Siberia? Some Chinese dungeon? I sat and waited for the unknown.

Blindfolded, chained, and handcuffed, I was led out of the building and down the front steps. I wondered if any of the prisoners who occupied the front cells were watching from their windows as I had so often done. In spite of my blindfold I could see out of the corner of my eye under the edge of the goggles and through the thin stocking. I was half led, half dragged by the impatient guards to a waiting Chrysler sedan and shoved into the rear seat, flanked by two guards. The warden got in front with the driver.

The rear and side windows of the car were heavily curtained and a piece of cloth was stretched above the back of the front seat, making it impossible to see in or out of the rear seat. Wherever I was being taken, they certainly wanted it secret. It didn't look like any change for the better, I thought, as we pulled out of the prison yard. The driver turned right into the street which ran south, but from there on I lost all sense of direction.

Several minutes later the car stopped. From the noises and odor I knew we were in a railyard. There I was dragged out of the car and, with a guard holding each arm, I was led, stumbling, along a line of passenger coaches which I could see out of the corner of my eye. The ground was covered with snow and slush, which soon soaked my cloth shoes and made my feet ice-cold.

I counted five coaches before we stopped. My shackles would not allow a long step, so the two guards, showing little respect for my legs and shins, pulled me up the steps into the sixth coach. Once I was inside and seated in the middle of the coach, my blindfold was removed. Three more soldiers entered and the two who had escorted me from the prison departed. The coach was similar to the one I had ridden in before, with the exception that it was much cleaner and had no ice coating on the windows. The seats were the same wooden affairs and were arranged the same as seats in American daycoaches. I had four of these to myself—the pair I sat in and the pair in front of me. Across the aisle a guard set sideways, facing me. Behind me another one sat facing my back; and in front of me, occupying one of the next group of four seats, sat the third. He, too, faced me, although the seat he occupied was turned in the opposite direction. All three had large, wooden-holstered pistols strapped to their waists, and each kept one hand on the grip. Further down the coach sat a man in a black uniform wearing a pistol in a shoulder holster. There were no other people in the coach; I hoped they would bring in the other members of my crew. There was plenty of room.

Looking over the inside of the coach, I noticed that the red window curtains were not only pulled all the way down, completely covering the window, they were *nailed* down. The nails were driven through the curtain cloth and in several cases had broken the window frames. The covered windows gave another indication of the secrecy of the movement.

I sat there for what seemed like an hour, expecting each minute to see some or all of the other crew members brought in. I was disappointed. Finally, after the usual jerks and indecision about which direction to go, the train started out and soon picked up speed. The guard across the aisle was wearing a watch, which I could see. We left wherever we had been at eleven A.M.

As we left the town I calculated our direction of travel by the sunbeams shining around the edges of the curtain. We were headed just north of west. In that direction lay nothing good, no matter what our starting-point, so I kept waiting and hoping for a change in direction. Now it was quite obvious that I was not to be joined for the trip by any of my fellow crew members. This was quite a disheartening blow. I knew, however, that there were at least five other coaches on the train, so I suspected that there were at least five more crew members on board. It seemed we were VIP's (P for prisoner). I was amazed at the elaborate proceedings taken to insure secrecy. The heavy guard I was under gave me more food for thought. The three guards still sat with hand on gun and eye on me. This seemed rather foolish, since I was cuffed and shackled. It was surely temporary, I thought.

I asked the guards to remove my cuffs, but it was no use. Their attitude was friendly enough—they smiled when they refused. After an hour or so a man, apparently the boss of the operation, came into the coach. He had a string of keys and, after trying several, found one that loosened my cuffs. He refused to take them off, however. I hoped it would not be a long trip, but I had no way of knowing. The guards smilingly refused to talk.

My feet, which had grown numb from cold, were beginning to thaw, but only after I propped them on the steampipe that ran along the edge of the seat. To help the process of thawing out, I was given a cup of hot water. Although at first I had not liked the national prison drink of China, I was now developing a taste for it. It hit the spot. I was also given a loaf of bread of a kind that I had seen only once before—on my first train ride. It was delicious, far better than anything else I had tasted since becoming a prisoner. To make matters even better, the loaf was so big that I could not eat it all at one sitting. For the first time in many days my appetite was satisfied.

The first couple of hours we headed generally north-northwest. Siberia and the salt mines, I thought. They don't dare shoot me, but now that they've kidnapped me they can't risk having the world know about it. That seemed to explain all the secrecy and the security precautions. If that were true, then I was probably done for. Other people had disappeared in the same direction before, never to be heard of again.

Wherever we were going, we were making good time. Around noon, the train began to turn and the slender rays of sunlight shifted. After a few more turns back and forth, I guessed we were headed nearly south. I began to feel easier. Visualizing the map I had seen in the magazine, I tried to guess our destination. Tientsin would be the first large city in this direction, but it was several hundred miles ahead. Peking was west of Tientsin. Just as a wild guess, I chose the capital as our destination.

So far my three guards had not taken their eyes off me. I wondered if their arms weren't tired from holding onto their pistols. In an effort to ignore them, I lay down on the seats. Aided by a full stomach, I was able to nap awhile. When I opened my eyes the guards were still there. The train, as I was quick to note, was still heading south.

The rest of the day went much the same. More food and water were brought in and at intervals a bucket was given me in which to relieve myself—this in spite of the toilet in the coach. The bucket was identical to the one my water was served from, but the water was scalding hot, so I didn't let it worry me.

After a few hours the man in black took a guard's place, letting him move down a few seats to take a nap. An hour or so later he relieved another and so on, until they all had a bit of sleep. At no time, however, were there less than three people looking directly at me. At no time was I allowed out of my seat.

By watching the conductor (the pin on his hat was the same as the figure stenciled on the coach curtains) as he passed through my coach, and taking note of the water and loaves of bread he carried, I grew more certain that I was not alone on the trip. Until dark I was able to tell our general direction. It remained toward the south. After dark I had no way of telling. When the train pulled to a final halt, fourteen hours after our departure, I concluded that we were probably in Tientsin or Peking—Tientsin if our departure point had been Antung, Peking if it had been Mukden. I arrived at this conclusion by guessing at the average speed of the train and the distance between these cities.

After sitting in the train several minutes longer, I was again blindfolded and then taken off the train and put into a jeep. We rode about twenty minutes. Near the end of the trip the jeep made a series of six stops with a short movement forward after each. I took this to be an indication that I was in a convoy and that my vehicle was the sixth in line, since I got off at the sixth stop. I could hear two other vehicles, one in front and one behind, going through the same series of stops, and I figured that each was unloading a passenger, or a prisoner, then pulling away to make room for the next.

When my turn came I climbed out of the jeep. After a few stumbling steps I was met by someone who grabbed the chain connecting my handcuffs and unceremoniously slung me over his shoulder. The iron bracelets bit into my wrists as I was carried away, feet dragging on the ground. I had to bite my lip to keep from screaming, the pain was so great. I tried to kick at the legs of the person carrying me, but my leg chains prevented it and the effort only made the cuffs cut deeper. One of the guards picked up my feet by the chain between them. Thus I was taken into my new home.

After dumping me onto a platform in a cell, the guards removed my blindfold and left, locking the door behind them. I looked around the cell. Compared to this one, my other cells had been mansions. It was somewhat less than four feet wide by about nine feet long. Six feet of one side were taken up by a bed platform that extended the full width of the cell and sat on sawhorses about thirty inches high. At one end of the cell there was a barred window with a wooden blind over the bottom half. At the other end was the door which contained the usual peephole, a narrow slit covered with a cloth flap which hung on the outside. The cloth was weighted down by a pencil-size piece of wood; I could hear the flaps drop as the guards walked up and down the corridor. Running across the cell near the ceiling was a stovepipe. It entered through one wall and continued into the next cell through the other wall. By standing on the bed I could reach the pipe. Placing my hands around it, I could feel a little warmth. Apparently it was connected to some kind of heater.

While inspecting my new quarters, I kept a close watch out of the corner of the peephole. I was rewarded by a glimpse of another prisoner as he was brought in. He, too, was slung over a guard's shoulder, feet dragging on the floor behind. I cursed the Communists for this painful and humiliating treatment. I heard a door slam shut down the corridor and then saw a guard approaching the flap where I was peeping out. I tapped on the door to get his attention, hoping to get my cuffs and shackles removed, and to cover up for any possible suspicions he might have about my peeping.

The guard opened my door, but when he found out what I wanted, he muttered a few curses and slammed it shut. A little later, however, he opened it again and motioned me out. I was led to a room nearby, but outside the corridor. As we crossed the corridor I noticed there were several guards on duty, each armed with a submachine-gun. I also saw the source of the warmth I had felt in the stove pipe. Spaced along the corridor were four small coal heaters with pipes going into four cells where they apparently turned to extend through several cells before emerging outside. The guards, walking up and down the corridor, got the benefit of the heaters, while the prisoners, sitting in cold, cramped cells with hardly room to move around, had to content themselves with what little warmth the pipes gave off.

The warden and another guard were waiting in the room where I was taken. Here I was searched from head to toe. They found my last and most treasured item—my compass, which had weathered three previous shakedowns. The only things that were not taken from me were the pieces of strap and bent wire I had hidden in the hem of my pants and in the chin strap of my jacket. Taken from me, along with the compass, was my newly contrived face mask and a pocketful of salted peanuts. This last loss was a bitter one. I remembered the many times I had been tempted to eat them; now I wished I had.

After completing their shakedown, the warden and guards led me back to my cell. In spite of my protests, they left without removing either the shackles or cuffs. A heavy blanket lay folded at the foot of the bed, so taking this, I covered up and tried to get some sleep. I was too weary to wonder what was in store for me next, but if the day's treatment was any indication, I had little to hope for. I finally fell into a restless and nightmarish sleep, but only for an hour or so.

Dawn came shortly, accompanied by a rap on the door. This was February the first—my twentieth day as guest of the Communists. I was in my fourth prison, and from all appearances it was by far the worst. Outside the window I could hear a guard walking back and forth. A few feet from the building I could see the top of a wall about fifteen feet high. Three strands of wire ran across it, each about a foot apart and insulated from iron posts set in top of the wall. An electrified fence! I seemed to be in a maximum-security prison. I knew now that I had missed my only possible chance to escape. I had been moved one day too soon.

I could hear activity in the corridor outside my door. There was the sound of running feet and the rattle of chains. Finding a crack between the door and jamb, I used it instead of the guard's peep-hole. I could see a row of figures running past. Each was dressed in black, including a skull cap, and each wore a pair of leg shackles. The chain connecting the leg clamps was lifted off the floor by a string which each prisoner held in his hand. The sight reminded me of stories I'd read about slave-trading days and did little to cheer my thoughts. As I watched, several groups of ten to twelve Orientals were herded by, each group returning before the next was taken out.

Then I heard the rattle of buckets; this, as I expected, was break-fast. I was given a bowl of bean sprouts, a pair of chopsticks, and a cup of water. Even without handcuffs I would have had trouble eating with the sticks. As it was, I had to rake the food into my mouth. The guard stood watching the entire operation, his eye-balls shining through the narrow opening. I was not in a very good humor and didn't like being stared at. I thought I could shame the guard into leaving by offering him some of my food, but when I held my bowl toward the door, all I got in reply were gruff words and a rap. He didn't leave.

I could hear doors opening and closing down the corridor as the other prisoners were fed. There were a lot of cells. I wondered how many of my fellow crew members were here. At least seven, I figured, since there were at least seven vehicles in the convoy which brought me from the train. Here the food gave me no further clue; I was fed from the same bucket as all the other prisoners. Gone were the days when non-Oriental prisoners received a special ration. I didn't mind; rations at the last prison had not been that special.

After eating I gave the cell walls a close inspection, hoping that the last occupant had left something of interest. I found nothing, but, as before, I made sure the next unfortunate would have better luck. In two places I scratched my name, the date I was captured, and the date I arrived at the prison. This writing was found later by one of the scanners from the crew; until then he had not known I was alive.

About the middle of the morning the local warden came in with a large ring of keys. They were a welcome sight. I was thoroughly tired of my cuffs and shackles. After looking suspiciously at the cuffs, which I had loosened to the last notch, he removed them. This took several minutes; my jailers never seemed to be able to find the right key. This one looked at the number on the cuff clamps, and then searched through the ring of keys for one to match. When he couldn't find one, he began trying keys at random. Again I was almost tempted to show him how fast I could unlock them with my piece of wire. After twenty-four hours in handcuffs it was a great relief to be able to move my arms freely again. I tried to persuade him to remove my leg chains, too, but to no avail. I also asked for a spoon in exchange for the chopsticks, but got another shake of the head.

Before leaving, the warden had a guard bring me a small wide-mouthed jar and a five-gallon paint can. The little jar, I was made to understand, was my privy pot. When it was full I was supposed to empty it into the bucket. I never did figure out why I couldn't use only the bucket. The guard also brought me a large sheet of coarse, pulpy paper. The warden took great pains to show me how to tear it into little squares. He also told me how many to use each time—three, he said, was the maximum. If, after looking at the second one, I didn't need more, then I should save the third. Toilet paper must not be wasted.

As soon as the warden left and I'd taken a few minutes to check the guard's routine and rate of appearance, I tried tapping code on both walls, but with no response. Thinking perhaps the thick masonry walls muffled the sound, I decided to use a more direct method of establishing contact with my neighbor. I dug a piece of plaster off the wall. Using it as a pencil, I wrote my name on a small piece of the paper. Next I rolled it tightly around the end of one of the chopsticks. Making sure the guard was not near, I stood on the bed platform and pushed the piece of paper through the hole by the stovepipe, letting it drop into the next cell.

My message brought almost immediate response. I heard the prisoner in the next cell tapping on his door to attract the guard. When they started talking in Chinese I knew I had made a mistake. A few moments later the guard came to my cell, opened the door and showed me the piece of paper. I was made to understand, in no uncertain terms, that messages would not be poked through walls in Chinese prisons. He closed the door, leaving me wondering why the prisoner next door had squealed on me. Although I was disappointed, I found out that the cell on the right did not contain any friend of mine.

My lunch was served and I ate it, without relish. It consisted of a piece of bread and a bowl of bean sprouts—tasteless and unappetizing. After a little practice I managed fairly well with the chopsticks. When I finished eating, the guard handed me a cup of water to rinse my bowl and sticks. These I was allowed to keep in the cell.

All afternoon I amused myself by scratching pictures on the chalk-coated walls. Between eyeball rounds, I drew boats, and daydreamed that I was on them. I drew a music staff and tried to memorize the lines and spaces. I drew faces and figures—anything to pass the time and to keep my mind and hands occupied. When I grew tired of drawing, I walked back and forth across my cell. By walking diagonally across the space between the end of the bed platform and the door, I had room to take two short steps, turn and take two steps back. My walking space was about three by four feet. I purposely tried not to think about myself and the predicament I was in. They were not pleasant thoughts; besides, there seemed to be little I could do to improve my situation.

Supper was another bowl of bean sprouts. I wished I had some of the bread I'd left hidden back at the last prison. The bean sprouts were as tasteless as any thing I'd ever eaten. Even my state of constant hunger didn't make them any better. After supper I was visited by the warden and a young girl dressed in a Chinese officer's uniform. She was less than five feet tall. I shortly discovered she spoke English. The warden opened the conversation, speaking in Chinese, and the girl translated.

"What is your name?" she asked.

I replied and this was translated into Chinese—all very formal. The warden said something else which was again repeated in English.

"The guard reports you have been sleeping and walking around your room without permission," she said.

I started to comment about the big space I had to walk in, but was cut short by the warden. "Never mind!" the girl said, copying the warden's curt manner. She tried to sound gruff, but had little success. She seemed slightly out of place, to say the least, and would have looked more natural in a schoolroom instead of a prison.

The warden then told me I was about to hear the prison rules. He began to read from a sheet of paper. When he had finished, the girl interpreter read from another sheet. I learned that everything in this particular prison was done on a schedule. It went something like this: seven A.M.—get out of bed; seven until seven-twenty—walk around; seven-twenty—eat breakfast; seven-twenty until eleven-forty—sit on the bed; eleven-forty until twelve—walk around; twelve—eat; twelve to twelve-twenty—walk around; twelve-twenty until five-forty—sit on the bed; five-forty until six—walk around; six—eat; after supper—empty the bucket then sit on the bed; eight P.M.—sleep.

Some schedule! An hour and twenty minutes to walk around and eleven and a half hours to sit on my bed! I asked how I was supposed to know the time of day in order to comply with the schedule. This was translated for the warden who replied that the guards would let me know. He also said that I must obey the guards at all times. Not to do so would bring severe punishment— as if the schedule itself was not punishment enough! I knew now why the guard had been angry with me during the day; I had not asked his permission to walk around.

When the warden and interpreter left, I listened carefully at the door. I heard them stop and open another door about four cells away. The girl interpreter spoke to someone saying, "What is your name?" The door closed and I could hear no more, but I knew there was at least a third American in the cell block with me. His cell was in the opposite direction from the cell of the other prisoner I had seen brought in over the guard's shoulder. I did not doubt that these other two Americans were fellow crew members.

I continued to listen at the door and after a few minutes I heard it open again. Looking through a crack, I saw the warden and the girl go toward the far end of the corridor. Just then the guard walked up and opened my door. I thought I had been caught peeping, but it was time to empty my bucket. He motioned me out and down the corridor. I glanced in the direction that the warden and the girl had taken. They were about to enter a cell near the end of the corridor. The guard hustled me away before they entered, but I knew which cell another one of the crew was in. This knowledge did me little good, but it gave me some comfort and removed part of my feeling of loneliness.

From the courtyard I could see something of the layout of the prison. The building was made in the shape of a U, the two prongs of which were cell blocks. The first story of the base appeared to be quarters for the soldiers; the second story looked like a watchtower. I was led across the courtyard into a low shed. It was the latrine, with the familiar mounds of frozen urine and ice-coated slits. Behind the latrine I could see a narrow pathway between the cell block and the wire-topped wall. It was patrolled by an armed guard. Crossing the courtyard again, I saw the prison gate, a break in the wall at the top of the U. Just outside the gate stood a guard-shack about the size of a telephone booth. It was manned by a tommy-gunner. Darkness blanked out the view beyond the gate.

Back in my cell I listened for the warden and girl, hoping to hear them enter several more cells which would indicate the presence of more of the crew. I listened in vain; apparently the two had left the corridor while I was in the latrine. Soon I was told by a guard to go to sleep. I lay down, but couldn't sleep. Across the corridor a group of Chinese began a song fest. The strange, fascinating sounds kept me awake for hours. I did not know if the singers were prisoners or soldiers, but I strongly suspected the latter. Communist prisoners rarely talk, much less sing. Still they may have been a group that had undergone a change of heart and earned a special privilege. Whoever it was, their singing was as bad as a nightmare.

Next morning started out on schedule. I was roused by a rap on the door. Sticking his finger through the peephole and wiggling it, the guard indicated that it was time to walk around my room. I gladly did so. I wanted the exercise.

While I exercised, the groups of prisoners were again herded by. I decided they were being taken to the latrine. Apparently they were confined in rooms across the corridor. The doors across the way, I had noticed, were about ten feet apart, indicating bigger cells. I counted the prisoners in each group; there were from nine to twelve. I could imagine how crowded those cells must be. But then I decided that theirs would be no more crowded than mine with just me in it. I would gladly have traded places with one of them, just to have the company. As they passed I tried to watch their faces. They looked scared and miserable—completely subdued. I felt a surge of pity which quickly disappeared when I remembered that they were among their own people and in their own country. My situation, I thought, was much worse than theirs.

Next on the schedule was breakfast, rice gruel and bread. Then the guard indicated it was time to sit, so I did that awhile. Twenty minutes of walking had tired me. A few minutes of sitting went a long way, however, and in spite of my padded clothes and the two flying suits and a jacket I wore underneath, I soon grew chilled and miserable. The stovepipe did little or nothing to heat the cell. I decided to ignore the prison schedule.

The first time the guard saw me walking he just stood and watched. Then he went on with his rounds. I walked until I was tired, then I sat again. This routine continued a couple of hours. I thought I was getting away with it until the warden appeared, brandishing handcuffs. He made it clear that I would obey the schedule or be cuffed. I quickly decided it would be easier to do my extra walking between guard rounds than to wear the brace-lets. The memory of my last bout with them was too fresh; my wrists were still sore and raw.

I said I'd sit, and after a few more words of chastisement, the warden left. For the rest of my stay in that prison, I got my exer-cise while the guard was away. It griped me to submit to such a senseless rule so, as a sort of face-saving maneuver, I teased the guard by changing my sitting position between each of his rounds. One time he would look in and I'd be sitting with my back to the left wall; the next time I'd be sitting with my back to the other wall. He mumbled curses, but since he had not seen me move, he did nothing about it. It became a sort of game to see how long I could walk without getting caught.

My window shutter, which hinged outward, was opened each morning by the outside patrol. This more than canceled the tiny efforts of the stovepipe. I guess the thoughtful guard considered the fresh air good enough for prisoners if it was good enough for him. By the end of each day my privy bucket had a layer of ice over it. The open window also let in outside noises. These, to a certain extent, made up for the unwanted fresh air. They gave me some measure of entertainment and something to think about. I tried to guess what the few vehicles were that I heard and what was being sold by the people who periodically passed by yelling like newsboys.

Two of the noises I heard puzzled me greatly. One was quite obviously a ship's foghorn. But what were ships doing in Tientsin or Peking, whichever it was? I knew of no rivers in the vicinity, but I had heard of some large canals. Maybe it was a barge on one of these. The other puzzling noise was a whistling sound— something like mud-grip tires speeding down a brick street. The object that made the noise appeared to be moving through the sky, which further puzzled me. After several stealthy peeks through my window I learned what it was. It was a bird—a pigeon to be exact. Over two years later I discovered how it made the sound. Someone had fastened a wind whistle to one of the bird's legs.

I spent four days in this prison, trying to keep my body and mind occupied in any way possible. There were no interrogations and no visits. Each day I put a mark under the date I had scratched on the wall, and each evening when I was taken out to empty my bucket, I tried to catch a glimpse of other members of the crew as they carried their buckets out. I was never successful. I named this prison the Dungeon. The small cells and the dreary, hopeless routine were reason enough.

CHAPTER

EIGHT

Near midnight of the fifth of February I was roused from a restless sleep by one of the guards and the warden. They slipped a pair of handcuffs around my wrists and tied a black cloth around my head. Here we go again, I thought. I was led outside through the prison gate and shoved into the back of a waiting jeep. Though I had not the least idea where we were headed, I was not sorry to leave the Dungeon. The usual thoughts that accompanied my transfers went through my mind. The ride lasted perhaps half an hour and, between the blindfold and the curtains around the jeep, I was able to see nothing of the area we passed through. Finally the driver made a jerky stop and we were at our destination.

My exit from the rear seat of the jeep was not very graceful. Hampered by the cuffs, shackles, and blindfold and aided by the ungentle hands of the guards, I was literally extracted from the vehicle. My quilted clothing was all that saved me from receiving multiple bruises. Once out of the jeep I was escorted through several corridors and finally into my fifth Communist hotel room.

Inside the cell, my blindfold, cuffs and, much to my relief, my shackles were removed. I wondered if someone was making a mistake. I had been in them nearly three weeks and they had begun to seem like part of my normal clothing. The removal of cuffs and chains took the usual amount of key-shuffling, but finally they were off and I immediately began to flex my legs and arms. I felt like a different person, but the guards soon reminded me that I was not. Pushing me into a sitting position on the cell's bed platform, they told me to stay that way. I was in no position to argue, so I sat while the guards and the warden completed the business of transferring me to my new keepers. A few words were exchanged between the guards who brought me and the new guards. My toilet articles, including the washpan and tooth brush which I had not been allowed to use for the past several days, were given to the new guards who put them just outside my cell door in a small desk. Meanwhile I looked over my new quarters.

The bed platform, a few boards nailed together to form a shelf about six feet long by thirty inches wide, was along one side of the wall. Folded up on the foot of the bed were two blankets and a thin quilted pad—my bedding. One of my new guards entered and motioned me up. He then spread the bedding and indicated that I should go to bed. After I lay down he carefully tucked me in. This seemed unusual and in sharp contrast to the treatment I had received from some of my former guards. There was a reason for it. The guard was merely showing me how prisoners were supposed to sleep in this particular Communist jail.

He made it clear that I was to lie on my left side with my back to the wall and head tilted so the guard, looking through the peephole in the door, could see my face. He further indicated that when I was lying down my eyes would be closed, and when I was sitting up they would be open—like a little girl's doll, I thought. Except for being on my left side, I was at attention, with legs straight. I thought he was being silly, but as time passed I learned that he was completely serious. Sleep at attention, stand at attention, and sit at attention were three positions that I came to learn well during the next few months. They took up more than twenty-three hours of each twenty-four and made the twenty-four seem like two hundred and forty.

I was also required to sleep with a light on inside the cell. This one was high up in a slot cut in the wall opposite my bunk, and when I was in the proper sleeping position, it shone full in my face. Obviously it had been placed there on purpose and I was not allowed to move it. I discovered during the following months that all the lights were placed in this manner. It was part of the over-all scheme to make a prisoner as miserable as possible without physically harming him. I later came to call this "Chinese human-ity," taking the expression from my interrogators, who were to use it often.

Another thing I took note of before going to sleep was the door of my new cell. It was not the heavy solid affair that all the others had been. This one had panels, like the front door of many houses, and four glass panes, which were now missing. Three of the open-ings were covered with paper. The fourth had a cloth flap which was kept open while I was lying down and closed otherwise, ex-cept when the guard looked in. The door had a house-type lock and the entire thing was of comparatively light construction—not at all like a prison door. Of course I felt sure there were heavier doors at the entrance to the corridor. The cloth-covered peephole was about nine by twelve inches—large enough to admit the entire face of the guard outside. The last thing I noticed before going to sleep was that the gauze-masked face of the guard had not moved from the peephole once since he had locked me in.

Next morning when I awoke the face was still there—the same face. When I got up, the flap closed and the face entered my cell. I was shown how to fold my bedding and how to use the wooden bucket which was in the corner of the cell by the door. Next came my toilet articles and a small pan of hot water. The sight of these things cheered me considerably. I was sorely in need of a bath, and although the water was in short supply, I didn't complain. I thought I would get the top layer of filth removed anyway. Things seemed to be looking up.

I started with my teeth and brushed away for four or five minutes, enjoying every second of it. Then I washed my face. The warm, wet towel felt wonderful, but I had hardly touched it to my face when the guard rapped on the door and told me to pour out the water and hand him my toilet articles. I couldn't see wasting the water so I tried to reason with him. He was persistent, so I tried ignoring him, all the while continuing with my bath, but somewhat more hurriedly now. Finally he entered my cell, took my toilet articles away and poured the water in my urine bucket.

My spirits began to decline, but I thought I could eventually convince the guard that I needed more time for my morning ablutions. The guard pointed to the end of my bed platform and indicated that I should sit there until breakfast. I wanted a little exercise. The argument that followed was resolved by the appearance of a chubby girl dressed in a blue padded uniform—the same uniform worn by jailers and wardens but different from the brown of the guards. She had a round face and two long black pigtails hanging down her back. In her hands she carried several gallon-size aluminum buckets. She entered my cell to give me one of these, but from the look on her face I could tell that she was prepared to make a speedy departure. I didn't blame her. I had seen my reflection in the pan of water and it was not a pleasant sight. Twenty-five days without a shave or even a comb through my hair, plus several days without bathing, made me look and smell more like something out of a tree than a civilized human being.

The aluminum bucket was a mess kit. It broke down into a round, deep pan, two half-moon pans, and the bucket. The lid also served as a shallow plate or bowl. On the side of the kit were slots for chopsticks which, much to me relief, contained a spoon instead. The girl jailer stood outside staring through the peep-hole after she had finished feeding the other prisoners. There was no curiosity or any other readable expression on her face as she watched me consume the piece of bread and start on the pint of rice soup which the kit contained. Both the bread and the soup were unseasoned; the latter looked exactly like liquid starch and didn't taste much different. Only one thing good could be said about the breakfast. It was hot.

Finally the girl left and I could hear her collecting mess kits from the other prisoners. Soon she was back after mine, but the rice starch was not cool enough for me to eat as quickly as she wanted me to. The guard came inside my cell to add his two-bits' worth of hurrying, and I tried to speed up, afraid he'd take away the food before I had finished. This still did not satisfy them, so I stopped eating and, in disgust, handed out the remainder of my food. This didn't please them either. They insisted that I finish my meal. A prisoner was just supposed to eat fast. I continued eating, but at my own speed, while the guard and the woman grumbled and griped.

After breakfast I started walking around the cell for exercise. I didn't know if I was supposed to operate by the same schedule as at the last prison, but I soon found out. My walking brought immediate response from the guard who still stood just outside my door. He gave the door a rap and pointed at my bed. Just to see what would happen, I pretended not to understand. He didn't like that either, and rapped some more. Finally he came into the cell to show me. I sat down, thinking I'd do the same thing that I had done at the Dungeon—walk when the guard was away. I noticed, however, that he never left my door, but I credited this to curiosity; I was probably the first American he had ever seen.

As the minutes went by, he remained at his place by the peephole. He either held the flap open and stared directly at me, or raised a corner and peeped every three or four seconds. Finally I gave up hope that the guard, who I named "Horseface" for his striking resemblance to that animal, would ever satisfy his curiosity. The next one, I felt sure, would be more normal.

While waiting for a guard change, I inspected my cell from where I sat. Its size I estimated to be about seven feet wide by nine feet long—considerably larger than the one I had recently left, but smaller than any of the others I had occupied. The walls were bare concrete to about thirty inches high. Above that they were whitewashed. The end opposite the door had a large window which was covered completely with paper and heavy wire mesh. Through the paper I could see the shadow of bars.

As I looked around the cell I noticed that Horseface seemed to be getting more and more unhappy. For once I didn't have to play ignorant; I really didn't know what was bothering him. I was sitting just where he had told me to and making no noise. I couldn't imagine what I was doing that he did not like. Just living, I decided, and tried to ignore him. Finally his relief came and, after a lengthy conference outside the door, both guards entered my cell.

They indicated that I was moving around too much. My head, they explained, was supposed to face the wall opposite where I sat and not turn left, right, up, or down. My feet were supposed to stay flat on the floor, side by side, and my hands were supposed to stay in my lap. I was supposed to sit at attention! This was ridiculous. I was locked in a cell, alone and under guard. I should have the freedom of my cell at least. That was my attitude, but the guards were insistent and even threatened me with handcuffs and leg chains. They finally left, and the new guard took up his post outside to watch me.

His curiosity, if curiosity it was, was just as great as Horseface's. Every few seconds he raised the flap to look at me. He never left me unobserved for more than five seconds at a time, and periods of that length were rare. I could hear another guard walking up and down the corridor looking in at the other prisoners. This indicated that, for some reason, I rated a guard all my own. I hoped it was only a temporary setup. Certainly there was no reason for it. After a period of time which seemed like many hours, my second guard was relieved. His successor was every bit as vigilant as the first two. This constant watching and the inactivity my watchers enforced made time drag as never before. I tried to ignore the guard's presence by occupying my mind with other things, but this was extremely difficult to do. I was up against the most nerve-racking situation I had ever encountered.

Lunch was brought in by the pigtailed woman guard. When she opened the door to hand it in, I tried to count the food buckets she carried. These appeared to be five or six. How many, I wondered, were for other crew members? I listened carefully to the opening and closing of the cell doors as the prisoners were fed. Only four were opened. That meant at least one of the cells contained two prisoners. Neither of the cells adjoining mine was opened. The cell directly across the corridor contained a female prisoner. She was Oriental and her voice sounded like that of a fairly young girl; I guessed her to be in her late teens. I could not hear any of the other prisoners speak, but Chubby (my name for the female guard) spoke to the occupants of two other cells so they had to be Chinese. That left only one cell which might possibly contain an American. I hoped that it did, but I had no way of telling.

The food consisted of steamed rice and about a cup of soup. Again Chubby and the guard were in a hurry for me to finish eating. During lunch there was another guard change. Horseface was back on duty and just as curious, or watchful, as before. My guards seemed to be working two hours on and four off.

There was another guard who came by at intervals of about half an hour. He checked all the occupied cells including mine. He usually contented himself with one short look and then moved on. He seldom spoke to my guard. He was the local corporal of the guard, I decided, and I wondered who he was really keeping tabs on—the prisoners or the guards?

Supper was more of what I had had for lunch, but at least it was a change from the bean sprouts I'd eaten at the Dungeon. The merest hint of salt or other seasoning would have greatly improved the flat tastelessness of the rice. The soup at least had some flavor, though I couldn't tell what it was made of. More often than not it contained what looked like tree or bush leaves.

After supper I could hear the other prisoners being taken out of their cells and down the corridor, one at a time. Soon my turn came and taking my bucket, I was led to the latrine, a cell at the end of the corridor. It contained the usual chutes and iced-over trough. The guard watched closely as I used one of the chutes.

He was impatient to have me through with this, too. When I finished, he showed me a brush to scrub out my bucket. He told me to use the content first to rinse out the bucket and then to flush the chute. This, I found, was the set procedure, if not the most sanitary one. Once every few weeks, however, I was given some fresh water to clean the inside of the bucket and, on a couple of occasions when I splattered myself while rinsing the bucket, I was given a pan of water to wash my hands.

The latrine cell had a window at one end which was not covered. Outside I could see a large eight-sided, two-story rotunda with a guard-tower on top. The guards on duty were armed with sub-machine-guns—this in contrast to the corridor guard and my private guard, who carried no visible arms. I also saw another wing of the prison through the window. It went off at an angle to the one I was in, forming a triangular patio. The guard-tower and a short stretch of wall formed the third side. In the patio, tied to a long, heavy chain, was a large monkey. I wondered what crime he was being held for.

Horseface did not approve of my looking out the latrine window, but I managed to see all there was to see. Walking back to my cell, I made him even more unhappy by looking around the corridor. One end was closed by a set of heavy and permanently bolted doors. At the other end there were a pair of heavy wooden doors with a sliding iron grill behind them. There were six cells on either side of the corridor, but only two guards—mine and the corridor guard. That meant that if any of my fellow crew members were being held in the corridor, they were not getting the individual treatment that I was. I could see no reason for being treated differently, so I lost hope of there being any of them nearby.

The guard finally had enough of my looking around. He began hitting me on the back of my head to make me keep it down and rushed me back into my cell. I could tell that Horseface and I weren't going to get along, but I tried to humor him, thinking that I would surely be given more freedom soon. The trip of about thirty feet to the latrine was the first time that I had been able to walk without shackles in nearly three weeks. It was a very real pleasure, but I kept thinking of the monkey that was chained around the neck. I knew, of course, that he was a pet or mascot, but I hated the Communists more for keeping him chained than for anything they had done to me. I wondered if they carried him inside at night or if he stayed outside in the bitter cold.

Back in my cell I was given a cup of hot water and told to sit until *shui chao* time. I had learned the word from Smiley; it meant sleep. Finally, after what seemed like hours, I heard a bell ring and my guard told me to go to bed. Sleep came easily, but did not continue uninterrupted. Several times during the night I was roused by a bang on the door. At first I didn't know why, but after the guard entered my cell and jerked my blanket back to show me, I remembered that I was supposed to sleep at attention, with my face back so the guard could see it at all times. The raps on the door came anytime I turned over or tried to move my face to keep it warm. For the next several months this rule of the prison or whim of the guards, I never learned which, was rigidly enforced. It cost me much *shui chao* time.

Next morning when I was given my toilet articles and water, I quickly brushed my teeth and managed to get my shoes off and my feet in the pan before the guard got impatient and took everything away. Chubby served my breakfast as usual. She was getting less skittish with each trip to my cell. She inspected my bedding and cell for bugs while I drank the rice starch. I wondered what kind of insects she thought could survive the extreme cold of the cell. I was insulted when it crossed my mind that she might think I brought bugs in with me.

About the middle of the morning I was taken out of my cell and through the wooden and iron doors at the end of the corridor, which opened into another eight-sided rotunda. A guard, armed with a submachine-gun of Russian design, kept his weapon trained on me as I was led through to another cell block. There appeared to be five cell blocks fanning out from the rotunda like spokes of a wheel.

The cell block we entered appeared to be empty. I was shown into a cell and was joined shortly by the local warden and a girl interpreter. The prison rules were read to me. The schedule here was much simpler than at the last prison. It included no time for walking. In fact, I was told that I would sit at all times except when sleeping, urinating, and going to the latrine. The day was divided into two equal parts—twelve hours for sleeping and twelve for sitting. I was told that I must ask the guard's permission anytime I wished to use the bucket in the corner of my room. I was warned that I must obey the guards and the prison "caretakers" at all times. By caretakers it was obvious they meant Chubby and the various other people I had seen who wore blue uniforms and who obviously were not guards. To disobey the guards and caretakers would bring severe punishment, I was told. When they had finished, I started to ask a few questions, but I was not too politely informed that my questions were out of order. The warden and interpreter left and I was escorted back to my cell.

The remainder of the day dragged by. I made a few attempts to walk around my cell, but the guards highly disapproved, so I decided to play along with the routine for a few days. This I thought better than forcing them to reapply the chains and cuffs. I couldn't see asking for permission to relieve myself every time I felt the urge, however, and I got up and used the bucket when I pleased. This was frowned upon also, but nothing was done about it that day.

The food was the same as the day before—unseasoned rice and watery soup. I discovered that I was the only American in the cell block. I had strongly suspected it anyway. I was able to hear Chubby talking to the prisoners in all the other cells. This confirmation of my belief was a great disappointment. Just to have known that another American was nearby would have meant a lot. At bedtime I was again glad to lie down. The long hours of sitting on bare boards had a painful effect on my rear. I lay awake for some time, thinking of home and family, of the crew, and of the Communists. I tried to make sense out of what had happened to me so far, and to figure out what might happen in the future. But all I could do was guess.

The following morning I awoke before it was time to get up and I realized that sleeping at attention was almost as painful as sitting. I got out of bed before the prison bell rang, thinking that surely there could be no objection to a prisoner rising early. I was wrong. Objections came in the form of a nerve-shattering bang on the door, followed by voiced noises that were even more irritating. At that moment the bell rang, saving me, or the guard, from losing face.

When my toilet articles were handed in, I immediately started stripping and was bare to the waist before the guard could stop me. At the rate I was going I figured I would have a complete bath in a few more days and could then spend some more time brushing my teeth. Breakfast was late, but was no different than usual when it finally arrived. When noon passed and my lunch had not appeared, I remembered that my last two-meal day fell on Sunday. I counted back and sure enough—this was another Sunday. The lack of the few additional minutes of physical occupation spent in eating, plus being more hungry than usual, made Sundays in a Chinese Communist prison pass more slowly than any other day. I have no doubt that it was meant to be that way, as part of the master plan.

Two days was enough time for me to figure out the guard routine. I had three personal guards—Horseface, Chickenshit Shorty, and Hot Shot. They worked two hours on and four off, around the clock. When on duty they never left my door except to escort me to the latrine. One of their duties was to make a written record of everything I did, even to the movement of an arm or finger. Another and very important duty was to watch my bowel movements, presumably to make sure that I was not using them as an excuse to get out of my cell and take the enjoyable hike to the latrine.

In performance of this duty they shone a flashlight down the chute so they could see the results—sometimes while I still squatted. I was allowed a minimum of time for this as for everything else except sitting, and quite often the guards were not satisfied. Two of the guards merely cursed and made an entry in their book, but Horseface was more sensitive. He went to great trouble to explain that I would either produce more or make fewer trips than the one per day allowed. Whenever he started this routine, I used it as an excuse to stay longer. This made him even madder and he went through the entire routine again. I understood him well enough, but I could be plenty dumb when I wanted to be. Anything that kept me out of my cell a little longer was to my advantage, even if I was in the latrine. There at least I could see some sky through the uncovered window, and I could see the friendliest face in the prison—the monkey's. I wondered if the guards, and especially Horseface, felt silly during our visits to the latrine. But after some reflection, I decided not—they took their duties too seriously.

As to my guard's nicknames, I gave Horseface his because it seemed so natural. Chickenshit Shorty was named for his size and for his constant attempts to browbeat me. Hot Shot got his name because of his haughty attitude. He seldom spoke; all his wishes were expressed by a quick movement of his hand or head.

During the afternoon, Chubby brought in my shoes and overshoes which had been taken from me before my last train ride. This was an unexpected and a welcome surprise. I had constantly complained that my prison-issue shoes were too small, which was an understatement if anything, but all I got was an impatient wave of the hand. Now my feet, though numb with cold, began to spread out to their normal size and shape. The overshoes did not keep them warm, but they were less cold than before and much less restricted. The fact that they were Capitalist and not Communist shoes gave my declining spirits a slight boost.

My second and last meal of the day arrived late in the afternoon and left me almost as hungry as before. After this there were several long hours of sitting until bedtime. The more I thought about it, the more painful my rear became and the more useless the sitting business seemed. I wanted some exercise. I got up and started to walk around my cell, but Shorty banged on the door and told me to sit down. I didn't expect to get away with it, but I went to the door and explained that I only wanted to walk around awhile; I wasn't going away. Shorty insisted that I sit and jabbered away in Chinese. I argued with him, although I knew he couldn't understand me. He grew almost hysterical and called another guard.

While they stood outside and discussed the situation, I proceeded to stroll around the cell. The other guard left at a fast pace and I knew what to expect. Shorty stayed at his post and glared at me through the hole in the door. I continued walking until, a few minutes later, two guards, the warden, and an officer came storming up.

They entered my cell and the guards pushed me onto the bed, brandishing the expected pair of handcuffs. I was feeling far from brave, but I had started my little revolt and figured I might as well find out what would happen. The sight of the cuffs and the absurdity of the whole situation lent me courage. I refused to be cuffed, although the guards could have easily overpowered me. Shaking their hands off me, I told them they'd have to kill me to do it. That was an extremely foolish statement, but right then I thought I meant it. The warden said something to the guards and they let me loose.

Then the officer spoke to me in English, asking what my trouble was. He seemed not the least upset over the situation and acted as if he had little time to waste on such piddling matters. I hadn't expected anyone who could understand me, but I took full advantage of the chance to voice my gripes. He let me have my say and I tried to point out how unreasonable their restrictions were. Finally I cooled off and tried to reason with him, but I might as well have saved myself the trouble. He told the warden what I had said, but without waiting for his reply, he gave me the word.

I was informed that I would obey the rules and the sooner the better. If it took cuffs and chains they would use them, and they would not kill me to do it. He talked as if he were explaining something to an unruly child, only once or twice getting heated. His tone was infuriating and left me feeling helpless.

When they left I sat down—not from fear, but because I was faced with a situation I didn't know how to handle. I was frustrated, to say the least. The Chinese had done their best to keep me confused and uncertain from the very beginning, and although I was fully aware of it, they had succeeded to a large extent. They were using a tried, perfected and proven plan and I was having to learn by trial and error. I was not in chains and cuffs, but I knew they had not been bluffing.

My short-lived revolt gave my aching backside a break, but it didn't last long. Shorty was now more watchful than ever. He protested every time I shifted my weight from one burning cheek to the other. His constant rapping on the door, accompanied by a barking shout, was enough to drive me insane. I felt I was close to being just that long before the prison bell rang signaling the prisoners into their beds.

Next morning I was given even less time than usual to make use of the pan of water Chubby brought. I had hardly finished washing my face and hands when the guard came in and removed the toilet articles. Next my breakfast of rice starch was handed in, and they were in their usual hurry.

Horseface was on duty and it was quite evident that he had been told about my revolt of the day before. He hounded me at every movement, no matter how small. He came rushing into the cell every few minutes and stood in front of me, yapping and gesturing. I wanted to smash my fist against his already flat nose. I found myself gritting my teeth in an effort to resist attacking him. Finally the guard changed, but Hot Shot was just as bad, so I put forth a supreme mental effort and tried to forget the guards.

This was the twenty-eighth day since my capture and every day my situation grew worse. They couldn't keep it up, I tried to convince myself. Surely they would tire of their game and at least remove my private guard. With him gone I would be able to move around my cell and exercise my aching muscles. I also told myself that they would end my solitary confinement before long. Four weeks, I thought, was enough for anybody.

They didn't let up that day or the next. The guards grew steadily more worrisome and irritating. Now they were trying to restrict the movement of my eyeballs. Hot Shot became unhappy when I looked around the cell, though I did so with only very slight movements of the head. He came rushing into the cell to give me a dressing-down and to demonstrate just how far away from front-center he would allow me to move my eyes. It was comical, but I wasn't in a laughing mood. I felt they had reached the limit. Again I had to suppress an urge to commit mayhem. I sat looking past him, giving no indication that I was aware of his presence. This infuriated him, but I continued to ignore him even when he moved his hand in front of my eyes to see if I had suddenly gone blind. He stormed out of the cell and slammed the door. Outside, after recording a report of my conduct, he took up his post at the peep-hole, muttering curses under his breath.

Horseface arrived to relieve him and Hot Shot gave him a full report. I recognized a word now and then and knew very well what they were discussing. Finally Horseface opened the door and stepped inside. He stood glaring at me until I looked up and asked what I could do for him. At that he broke into a tirade of words and gestures. I toyed with the idea of turning my urine bucket upside down over his pointed head. As I had guessed, he was concerned about the excess movement of my eyeballs and my "disrespect" for his comrade. To show me just how much he would allow me to move my eyes, he drew a rectangle on the wall in front of me, about one foot by two feet in size and at the level of my head. This, he indicated, was where I should look. Anywhere outside the lines was *pu hao*—not allowed, no good, or some such.

That did it. "Nuts to you," I said, and stood up. I'd had enough and I indicated it by showing Horseface the door and ordering him out. Hot Shot, standing outside, didn't know what to do, so he stood there and did nothing. Making noises like a lion tamer, Horseface tried to push me back onto the bunk. I gave him a shove. This sent Hot Shot down the corridor toward the guardroom. Horseface stepped outside, locked the door and then stood with his face in the peephole cursing me.

I sat down to wait for the warden and his mob. I heard the corridor door slam open and several pairs of rushing feet. My door flew open and in nothing flat I was in cuffs and leg chains. This time my hands were cuffed behind my back.

All that day I was a curiosity to every guard and jailer in the place. Every few minutes a new face appeared and the guard on duty explained what the bad *Mei Kuo* (American) had done. Chubby brought my noon meal, but after a consultation with my guard she decided I couldn't eat it and took it away. That afternoon I sat on my bed, chained hand and foot. I would have given anything, even my life, to get my hands around Horseface's neck. When my evening rice was brought in, a blue uniformed jailer came with the keys to my handcuffs. He unlocked one clamp and locked it again with my hands in front of me. My arms were so numb they were almost useless, but I managed to put away all of the food. This took much longer than usual, but for once Chubby didn't try to hurry me.

I went to bed that night fully expecting to have many more days in cuffs and shackles. With my hands cuffed in front I could get at my wire "key," which was concealed in the waist of my padded pants. But I decided not to make any rash moves, so I contented myself with merely loosening my cuffs and shackles. I slept fitfully, and late in the night I was awakened by blood-curdling screams coming from another part of the prison. I had heard the same thing the previous night, but I had talked myself into believing it was the wind blowing through the roof tiles. Now I knew they were screams, and sleep was scared away completely. I lay wide awake for what seemed like several hours.

The screams were not continuous. Between each outburst I could hear shouts, in Chinese, like those of an angry interrogator. They were followed by weaker replies, also in Chinese, then the screaming started again. I knew some poor devil was catching hell, but I was thankful not to hear any American voices. When the guard noticed I was awake, he had the corridor guard close the large wooden doors at the end of the cell block. This toned down the noise considerably, and after an age of time and many tortuous thoughts I again found sleep.

I was not given any water for bathing next morning, but much to my surprise the cuffs and chains were removed shortly after breakfast. It was done only after I received a stern warning about disobeying the guards. I accepted the warning without comment, but I knew I would be a little more tactful with future infractions of the prison rules.

I resumed my sitting with a determination to ignore the guard's presence and forget my unhappy predicament. There was only one way to do this—I had to keep my mind fully occupied with something else. During my month in prison I had already relived most of my life many times. My memory surprised me by producing incidents I thought I had forgotten long ago. Escape plans and hours of puzzling over my captors and their purpose had also kept my mind busy. These thoughts came more or less naturally as a result of being in prison. Most of my efforts to occupy myself, so far, had been of a physical rather than a mental nature. Now that practically all my physical movement was restricted, I had to look for another way of killing time.

I had once toyed with an idea for an improved record player. Remembering this, I set about mentally developing and perfecting the idea. At first I was only able to lose myself in mental activity for a few minutes at a time. Then my burning, aching backside would again reign supreme, demanding and getting all my attention. The guards were more vigilant than ever, making it more and more difficult for me to relieve the pain by stealthily shifting my weight or flexing my muscles.

Noontime brought a brief respite. I made the utmost use of the opportunity to move around. The guard was angry, but he satisfied himself with mumbled curses to let me know I wasn't putting anything over on him.

That afternoon I resumed my work on the record player. I designed gears, cams, shafts, and all sorts of parts, then mentally followed their movement after I had fitted them together. This took much patience and, at first, much determination. Time after time I lost track of a certain part and had to start all over from the beginning. I often discovered I had invented an impossible situation, such as the time I realized one end of a shaft turned counter to the other end. I didn't give up—I couldn't. My hatred of the ever-present, ever-staring, ever-hounding guards would have driven me insane if I had let myself dwell on it for long.

I was tempted at times to lose my grip, to do what impulse so often dictated. At these times it seemed easier to let myself go beserk than to continue as I was. I understood how it was possible for normal people to leap suddenly over the brink into madness. These moments of temptation were short and served to increase my determination to ignore my tormentors.

The day ended, the next one arrived and departed and I was still working on my record player. I was able to concentrate for longer and longer periods, ignoring the guards, the pain, and the cold, which kept my body chilled and my feet numb. I gradually became more and more absorbed in my project and no longer had to force myself to think about it. In a few days I had it in running order and knew every part of it so well I could remove or change parts without having to start over again. Then I mentally put a stack of records on the machine and played them, on both sides, one by one. My imagination was not vivid enough to allow me to hear the music as the records turned, nor was I interested in the sound component of the player. I ran the records through time and again, looking for and creating all sorts of malfunctions. Correcting these malfunctions by redesigning gears, cams, or shafts took many more hours of painstaking, pain-relieving thought. When I finally had it completed, I tried to calculate the cost of manufacturing my mental creation. I soon concluded that my phonograph would cost far too much to market, so I set about simplifying it. Thus I learned to pass the time in my cell.

CHAPTER

NINE

It was in the middle of my thirty-second day in prison that the usual routine of my life was interrupted by a not-unusual loud rap on my cell door. This rap, however, was followed by the entrance of a blue uniformed jailer who motioned me up and out. I quickly left my mental phonograph scattered all over the cell and started wondering where I was being taken.

I followed the jailer, a larger-than-average Oriental, and Hot Shot followed close behind me. When we came to the wooden and folding iron doors at the end of the corridor, we stopped while the jailer opened one of them slightly and shouted into the rotunda. Though I could not understand him, it was obvious that he was letting the other corridor guards and the rotunda guard know a prisoner was being brought through. The rotunda guard shouted a reply, though he was only a few feet away, and we continued through the doors, across the rotunda, and stopped at an identical set of doors on the other side.

The same shouting procedure cleared our way into another corridor. As we walked down this hall, Hot Shot tried to keep me from looking around by continually hitting the back of my head with the palm of his hand. Even with my head down I could see all there was to see. There were an even dozen cells on each side of the corridor and a total of three guards for the block. Unlike my own cell door, the doors to these cells were solid and the peephole in each was only a narrow slit, covered with a cloth flap.

We left the corridor through another set of heavy doors, which one of the guards locked behind us from inside. We continued a short distance through a large hallway, took a right turn into an-

other wing of the prison, and stopped before a closed door. Again
the jailer let out with a shout, but this time he knocked first. A
reply came from the other side of the door and we entered.

I was led over to a position in front of a desk. Behind it sat a
man and two girls, all in officers' uniforms. The male officer dismissed the jailer and Hot Shot, and then he spoke to me in Chinese. One of the female officers translated.

"What is your name?" he asked.

"Second Lieutenant Wallace L. Brown, United States Air
Force," I replied. I did not salute. There was no rank insignia
visible on any one of the three.

"Sit down," I was told; I made use of a low stool which was
behind me. Although I had been sitting for hours, I was ready to
sit again. The walk from my cell, more exercise than I had had in
many days, tired me.

The male officer began to speak again, and when his words were
translated I no longer wondered why I had been taken out of my
cell. This was another interrogation, or interview as they called it.
It was a sort of get-acquainted session, with most of the time spent
in telling me what they expected of me. I was told that I was in a
serious situation, and that my attitude must be as helpful as possible so that leniency could be shown toward me. It was expected,
they said, that I would be reluctant, at first, to answer questions.
That was understandable since they knew I had received training
in how to resist interrogation. But first I must understand that I
was not in a position to resist interrogation. I was not a prisoner of
war but a criminal, and as such I would be required to answer all
questions. They were not after information, they already knew
more than I did. The interrogations would be used to discover my
attitude toward the "peace-loving Chinese people." If I failed to
realize this, if I did not believe that they were trying to help me,
then it would be bad for me. In any case, sooner or later I would
come to realize the truth of their words, and the sooner the better.
If I tried to be stubborn, I would find out that they had lots of

time.

That was what they expected of me. They tried to make it sound simple, but I had a feeling it wouldn't be. It was not an unpleasant interview. The interrogator asked a few personal questions, no voices were raised, no one cursed me when I refused to answer, and no threats were made. It was a pleasure to hear spoken English again, although I had little interest in what was said.

The interview lasted about an hour, and then the jailer and guard were called in and I was dismissed. Back in my cell, I sat and pondered this latest event in my prison life. It was some time before I mentally gathered up the scattered parts of my record player. That night I was again awakened by screams which sounded through the thin cell door. They were a terrifying reminder that my own interrogations had started again. I got out of bed on the pretense of using the bucket in the corner. The guard did just as I had hoped; he sent the corridor guard to close the big doors which normally stood open at night. As before, the volume of the unwelcome noise was reduced considerably. Back in bed I wanted to cover my head to muffle the sound of the screams, even though I knew it was against the prison rules. But I decided not to; I didn't want the guard to know that I was afraid. During the sleepless hours that followed I worked some more on my phonograph, but found concentration not so easy. I wondered how I would act, or react, if they used that kind of treatment on me. I didn't know, but I remembered my decision to try to escape, no matter how slim my chances, if it came to that.

Next morning I divided my time between formulating escape plans and perfecting my phonograph. That afternoon I heard the corridor doors open and a heavy-footed step approach. I correctly guessed that it was the big jailer (Big Stoop, I later named him), coming to take me to another interrogation.

This question session was in the same room as the one the day before. The room was about fourteen by sixteen feet and had two tall windows on one side, covered with blue cloth, as were the desk and ceiling. I had no way of knowing what was outside the windows or if it would be possible to break through them, but as this was a prison I presumed that there were bars. The room was lighted by two bulbs hanging from the ceiling—one over the desk, the other in front of the stool I sat on. In one corner of the room there was the ever-present spittoon, and on the desk were a small china teapot and three cups.

The interview was a continuation of the one the day before. The same things were explained and more inquiries into my personal history were made. Again it was conducted on a more or less pleasant level, and some concern was expressed for my personal well-being. When I was asked what I thought of my situation, I took the opportunity to put forth a few gripes. I asked why I was not allowed to exercise or even move, and I was told that he, the interrogator, had nothing to do with that. That was the responsibility of the prison authorities, he said. He pretended to know nothing of my prison life. I wondered if he expected me to believe that. If so, he must have thought I was pretty stupid. That was just fine with me; I pretended to believe him.

Before I left I was told that there would be more interviews in the near future and that I should be more cooperative. "After all," the interrogator said, "we do not expect a lowly second lieutenant to have any valuable information. All we want to do is test your attitude so we can decide what to do with you."

Back in my cell, I was served my evening rice by a new female "caretaker." This one was somewhat taller than Chubby and instead of pigtails, she had her hair cut square just above her shoulders. The most noticeable difference, however, was her clothes. Instead of the blue padded coat and pants worn by Chubby, she wore a skirt. The fact that she did not try to hurry me was appreciated more than her appearance, however. It was a real treat. Since eating was one of the very few pleasures my prison life afforded, I liked to enjoy it as long as possible. I named my new caretaker Mabel, for the lack of anything more suitable. For the next few months she and Chubby took turns bringing the chow and doing other menial tasks around the cell block.

With my thirty-third day in China nearing an end, I went to bed in fair spirits. The interrogation had given some variety to an otherwise dull day. It had been an easy interview and I was almost glad to have them start questioning me again. I had been sitting so long that any activity was welcome. I went to bed on schedule, and if there was any screaming during the night it didn't wake me.

Next morning was Sunday, a two-meal day. My high spirits of the night before were short-lived. In fact, they vanished shortly after dawn when the boards of my bunk began to make themselves felt through the seat of my pants and I realized there would be only two breaks in the day unless I was taken in for another interview.

My mid-morning breakfast came and was devoured with relish, although it consisted only of rice starch, a piece of bread and a few small pieces of something I took to be pickled and dried turnips. They were the only part of the meal that had real taste so I ate them one at a time.

As the day crawled by, it was obvious that there would not be an interview to break up the painful, monotonous sitting routine. During the afternoon the girl occupant of the cell across from mine was taken out for a couple of hours. When she was brought back I managed to catch a glimpse of her. This was the first time I had seen another prisoner in this prison and it didn't happen entirely by chance. I recognized Chubby's walk as she escorted the girl prisoner back to her cell. Choosing the instant they reached her door, I made a noise with my foot. On hearing this the guard jerked open the flap over the peephole. Realizing he had been tricked, he jerked the flap down almost immediately, but not before I got a look at the girl across the corridor.

As soon as she was safely in her cell, my guard jerked the flap open again to see what I had done to make the noise. Then he unlocked the door and rushed into my cell to chastise me. Holding his arms behind him, wrists together, he indicated what would happen if I did it again. He knew he had been tricked and it visibly irritated him. To make up for it, he stood by the peephole jerking the flap up and down every second or so for the remainder of his tour. This was extremely annoying, but at least the dull routine had been broken and I had seen a human being other than my tormenters. I judged the girl prisoner to be in her early twenties. She wore a black padded coat and was rather pretty. I wondered what "crime" she had committed.

After what seemed like ages, Chubby brought in the evening meal, the usual steamed rice, but instead of the usual cup of soup there was bean curd. At least this was different although it had little or no flavor. While I ate, and for some time afterward, Chubby talked with the girl prisoner across the hall. The girl sounded desperate, but meek. Chubby apparently was reading her the riot act. She kept it up until the girl began to moan—"*Mei-yo banfa, mei-yo banfa.*" This I knew to mean "no way" or probably in this case "no hope." She continued to moan and cry until after bedtime. It was pitiful and put me in a depressed, dejected mood, but it took my mind off my own troubles. It also created a great desire to stuff Chubby's pigtails down her throat.

The next couple of days passed in the usual slow and uneventful way. I still hoped with each new day that my permanant guard would be removed, giving me more freedom in my cell. But every day the usual faces watched me almost constantly and made the usual protests whenever I moved. The girl across the corridor was taken out every day for a couple of hours. I wondered if she were being interrogated or perhaps being indoctrinated by the Communists. She hadn't cried any more after the first day, and Chubby used a more pleasant tone when talking with her.

I expected to be taken out for another interview and found myself a little disappointed when I was not. I didn't want to be interrogated, but the last two interviews had been a welcome break in the dull prison routine. I felt I could easily handle the interrogators without giving any information, and I hoped that after a few more sessions they would give up and put all the crew back together.

My guards were beginning to look for other ways to hound me. Hot Shot all of a sudden decided that I used the urine bucket too often. To make sure I was not using it as an excuse to stretch and move around, he came inside the cell and watched me as I relieved myself. He made me nervous and on more than one occasion I was unable to urinate, thus confirming Hot Shot's suspicions. As a result the next time I asked, he made me wait until just before he went off duty. Then he let me use the bucket, acting as if he were giving me a million dollars.

To counter this trick, I told each guard, within a few minutes after he came on duty and again just before his two hour shift was up, that I needed to urinate. This gave me more than enough visits to the bucket and a little exercise too. It also kept the guards from being suspicious—or so I thought. It didn't work long, because each guard kept a record and passed it on to his relief. Finally after a couple of days, Hot Shot informed me that I would be allowed to use the bucket five times a day and no more: once when I got up in the morning, once before each meal, and once before going to bed at night.

I had heard of Communist thought control, but this! I wondered how long it took his measly little brain to figure out such a convenient schedule. He stuck to it, however, and received the fullest cooperation from the other two guards. To a person physically occupied this schedule would probably cause no discomfort, but to me, completely idle, five trips a day were not sufficient.

There were many times when I needed to relieve myself and was extremely uncomfortable because I was not allowed to. I was often tempted to use the floor, but I could never make myself show such lack of self-control before the Chinese guards. Consequently I waited and suffered this, in addition to the tremendous pain caused by sitting—a pain which had not lessened, but rather had increased and spread.

At first it was only my rear that protested so violently. Now my feet, which always felt as if they were turning into ice, were giving me their full share of complaints. I was not allowed to move them; according to my guards, they must stay flat on the floor and side by side. Although I did not comply completely with the rules, I was forced to restrict the movement of my feet and legs. Eventually the constant contact of my feet with the soles of my shoes caused an acute pain. I wondered at times if the two were not growing together.

The three pains—my rear, my feet, and holding back on the call of nature—were like fiery hell. I could do little to keep my mind from focusing on them during the hours, days, and weeks they had to be constantly endured. Periodically I reached the saturation point and the handcuffs and leg shackles were brought in. The only remedies for easing the pain were my efforts to keep my mind busy on some mental project and to exercise by very slight movements which the guards were becoming ever more adept at detecting. I finished my record player and after "playing" several dozen records to make sure it would work without fault, I directed my mental efforts toward designing a strawberry-picking machine, an invention that would make a fortune if I ever got back to the States. I thought for dozens of hours and attacked the problem from many angles. But finally I had to admit defeat, deciding that nature had produced something that man could only harvest by hand.

I turned my mental activities toward architecture. The only knowledge I had in this field I had picked up from my father, who had been a carpenter, and some things I had learned from reading various home magazines. This was sufficient to get me started, and I had plenty of spare time to figure out anything else I needed to know.

I designed everything from economy houses to mansions. I remembered some particularly pretty spot of ground I'd seen somewhere and then designed a house to fit it. I tried to make all measurements correct to a fraction of an inch. This gave me no end of trouble, especially when I designed split-levels with winding stairs. A pencil and piece of paper would have been invaluable, but these I didn't have. After I completed several designs I decided to build them. This was even more tedious than designing.

First I drew up a bill of materials. This required numerous mental computations, and much time was consumed in reviewing my high-school mathematics. I often had to start over again when I forgot measurements or previously compiled figures. I computed the cost of building from the bill of materials and then I started construction. Mentally I dug each foundation trench, laid each brick, drove every nail, and hung every door. If I discovered I had put a roof on without rafters or made some similar error in construction, I started all over again. As I did each job, I computed the time required so I could add this to the total estimated cost.

I didn't design or build a house in a day. My dream house took several weeks to perfect. It was the first one I designed and I probably put more than two hundred hours of thought in it. Each time I completed one of my houses I furnished it and then lived in it a while just to see how good a job I had done.

This was all extremely time-consuming; that was my purpose in doing it. Sometimes I sat for hours completely absorbed, and at other times I found it almost impossible to keep my mind off the pain and the guards, who were becoming more repulsive and sneaky with each passing day.

CHAPTER
TEN

The next interrogation came about a week after my last "friendly" interview. During the night, shortly after I had gone to sleep, Horseface banged on the door and motioned me up. It was not unusual for the guards to wake me by banging on the door. Any time I turned so they couldn't see my eyes, they woke me and made me move. This time, however, he quite plainly wanted me up. What now, I wondered? I made a correct guess when I saw Big Stoop.

We went down the corridor, passed the tommy-gunner in the rotunda, and continued through the next corridor. Since it was night and all the prisoners were lying down, the corridor guards had the peephole covers open. As we passed through they hurriedly closed them to make sure I didn't get a glimpse of anyone or vice versa. For some reason the guards and jailers always took great pains to keep prisoners from seeing each other.

Horseface periodically shoved the back of my head to keep me from looking around. This never failed to make me mad and once when he was particularly brisk with his head shoving I turned around and told him to keep his hands off me. This startled him, not because of anything I could do, but because I had spoken out loud in a place where other prisoners could hear me. I hoped they had—especially if any were Americans. I was hustled out of the corridor after that incident, and thereafter when Horseface escorted me through that corridor, he told me I should not look around, rather than pushing my head. I felt I had won a minor victory.

I was led into the Blue Room to stand before the same interrogator and two female interpreters. The guard and jailer were dismissed and left the room, but I knew they didn't go far. I could hear them walking back and forth just outside the door. The interrogation began with the usual opening question, "What is your name?" I felt like reminding them that I had already given my name, twice, just a few days before, but instead I told them my name, rank, and serial number. After this I was invited to take a seat on the small stool behind me.

They asked about my health and wanted to know what I had been thinking about during the past weeks and how I occupied myself. I refused to give them the satisfaction of hearing me complain again about my living conditions and lack of exercise. Instead I told them I was quite happy building houses. This reply seemed to puzzle them, and they chatted back and forth, in Chinese, for a couple of minutes before they said, "You mean you build dream castles?" I didn't see any need to explain, so I said "Yes," and let it go at that. This brought on a short lecture. I was told that I should face realities and not waste my time in fairyland dreams. I should, they said, try to find ways to atone for my crimes against the People's Republic of China.

I'd heard that line before and replied that I had never committed any crimes. That put an end to the pleasant formalities and brought on harsher words. The interrogator worked himself into a fury and the girl who was translating tried to mimic his anger. Her efforts to sound mad and ferocious were somewhat comical at first. She got her curses mixed and called me a son of a bastard, tried again and labeled me a bitch's son, then finally got it straight. My poor attitude, I was told, was going to be very bad for me. They said the first thing the Chinese People required of a criminal was that he confess his crimes. Therefore, only after I had confessed could my future be decided. Then they changed their tone and the girl said, "Never mind, leave it for now."

The other interpreter sat looking fierce during all this, adding only a comment or two. Now she took over the translating. A few of her questions were sensitive, but most concerned matters of common knowledge. Some of these I answered because it seemed silly not to, but only those to which the answer was obvious. A few weeks earlier I would not have answered even those, which indicated the progress my captors were making in lowering my resistance. To most questions, however, I still answered, "I don't know."

Once or twice during the interrogation there was a knock on the door and a young boy in a blue uniform brought in a pot of hot water so the interrogator and interpreters could have tea. While they made their tea, they chatted and now and then let out a chuckle or a curse word. This, I guessed, was for my benefit, so I ignored them. After about two hours the guard was called in and I was dismissed. I was taken back to my cell and went to bed.

The next night, again after I had gone to sleep, I was taken to the Blue Room. The same three people were there and this time they skipped the formalities. They told me to sit down, and began their questioning. A few questions later the interrogator used my "I don't know" as an excuse to start ranting and raving.

"Stand up," he shouted. I stood up.

"Stand at attention," he shouted and I stiffened my muscles. After a few minutes of shouted questions and curses, I relaxed my stance. He noticed and lit in again, but after about half an hour he calmed down and told me to sit. I did so gladly. It was not a pleasant experience, in my weakened condition, to stand at attention for so long. The light hanging a few inches from my eyes didn't help matters either. I didn't stay seated long, however, before he was again shouting curses and demanding that I stand at attention. I stood until I was dismissed.

This session, like the last, had lasted approximately two hours. I could judge time fairly accurately by the guard changes and by glancing at a clock hanging in the rotunda which we passed going to and from the Blue Room. At night, when the prison was quiet, I could hear this clock striking the hours and half hours.

The next two days and nights were a repeat of the last one. I was getting weary of being questioned, of being shouted and cursed at, and of standing at attention an hour or two during each session. The questions they asked now were military, but they were always interspersed with "enlightening" lectures.

"Why have you come to China? Why do you wish to make war on the peace-loving peoples of Asia? Have we ever attacked your America? For centuries Asia has been under the yoke of western countries. We have thrown off that yoke. We are no longer slaves. The Chinese have risen and soon all the peace-loving peoples of the world will greet us as brothers-in-arms. We will come to the aid of all the enslaved peoples of the world just as our glorious Volunteers have gone to the aid of the tiny Korean People's Republic. . . .

"Your imperialistic government wishes to destroy our new-found freedom. They have unceasingly followed a policy of aggression, attacking innocent civilians, killing thousands of women and children, torturing and killing thousands of prisoners. . . .

"Your damned airplanes have constantly provoked the peace-loving Chinese people by intruding across our borders, dropping germ bombs and attacking hospitals and schools. . . .

"These are well-known facts and cannot be denied! How can you say you do not believe this! You, who by your belligerent attitude, are one of the worst criminals! You have been a part of these atrocious crimes! The Chinese people will have recompense! Do you think your war-mongering government can protect you here? Your God cannot help you. . . .

"How many men in your goddamn spy wing?"

I tried to ignore the lectures, but some of the accusations scared me. To make things worse, the guards, who stood outside the Blue Room during each interrogation, apparently believed everything the interrogator said about me. They took advantage of any excuse to hound me, and tried in devious ways to catch me moving in my cell during the day.

In an effort to trick me, Horseface often cleared his throat, then stamped his feet, pretending to walk away from my cell door to use a spittoon nearby. He thought I would take advantage of his absence to make some unlawful movement, and he stayed by the door and jerked open the peephole cover to catch me in the act. He never did. During my weeks of inactivity, I had developed an abnormally keen sense of hearing and could detect the slightest movements out of the corner of my eye. After each of these ruses, Horseface disappointedly closed the flap and then made a wild dash to the spittoon to do what he had already pretended to do. This gave me a few welcome seconds of freedom which I used to flex some of my stiff and aching muscles.

Another favorite trick of his also involved the spittoon. He had another guard sneak up on tiptoe, and while he peeped in the side of the flap, Horseface made a great show of clearing his throat and walking away to the spittoon. My hearing was so sensitive that I could tell whether he had hit or missed the spittoon. He usually missed. He and the other guard never caught me this way either.

Shorty's favorite trick was even more stupid. One night when he thought I was asleep, he made a tiny hole in the paper which covered part of the door. The next day, leaving the flap closed for long periods, he used the pinhole to peep through, not realizing his shadow was plainly visible through the paper covering. His stupidity exasperated me, but his patience was amazing. He stood without moving, twenty to thirty minutes at the time, never taking his eye from the pinhole. Apparently he thought that, since he wasn't looking through the flap every few seconds, I would think he had left. The ruse was so obvious I felt almost insulted, and each time he tried it, I developed a consuming urge to jump up and slam my fist through the paper into his face. At times I involuntarily clenched my fist and had to grit my teeth to control myself. Of course Shorty saw my fist and began to raise hell, no doubt thinking he had tricked me.

Shorty spread the word of his supposed success at the peephole, and for several days the other guards also made use of it. Each time the relief guard or corporal of the guard came in the corridor, they sneaked up on tiptoe to peek through the pinhole before looking through the normal opening. Their efforts were comical; their heavy shoes made a squeaking noise when they tiptoed that was more noticeable than a normal step. But they never tired of this cat-and-mouse game; they played it day after day with only slight variations.

Another trick the guards used constantly was just as exasperating. After raising the flap to look in my cell, they closed it gently, then immediately jerked it open again hoping to catch me in some unlawful act. I knew each time they intended to take a second quick look because otherwise they let the flap drop after the first look. Although these ridiculous tricks got on my nerves to the point of making me want to scream, the need to outsmart the guards became an obsession. I took great pride in making the smallest movement without being caught. It helped occupy the endless hours.

I had almost welcomed my first interrogations, but now I hoped the interrogator would lay off. He had other ideas. The next night brought my fifth interrogation in a row. This one started like the others, with the exception that the guard stayed inside the room with me. I soon discovered why. Within a few minutes after the questioning started, the interrogator was again ranting and raving and I was standing at attention. The guard was there to see that I didn't relax. The stool was removed and the interrogation continued. Two hours later I was still standing. The interrogation was brought to an end, but I was not taken back to my cell. When he left, the interrogator advised me to think over the questions he had asked. He would be back after a while to hear the results of my thinking. He gave instructions to the guard, then departed with the two interpreters.

As they left, another guard joined the one already standing beside me. The two of them set about enforcing the interrogator's instructions. When I tried to move a foot or leg, they gave the guilty part a kick—not especially hard, at first, but hard enough. If I moved an arm or my head they used their hands. If I slouched they poked the relaxed muscle.

This continued for another two hours and I became aware of another form of torture, infinitely more painful than sitting. Every joint in my body cried out and the soles of my feet cried loudest of all. Any G.I. who has stood at attention during a drawn-out inspection knows how painful his feet become. I stood at attention on an ice-cold concrete floor. The soles of my feet were in hell. The light which hung just in front of my face made my eyes ache, but if I closed them I got hit across the face or thumped on the eyeballs. This was as painful as the burning in my feet, but a little less permanent.

To make things worse, I was reasonably sure my interrogator already knew the answers to most of the questions I refused to answer. This, I realized, was part of their interrogation technique, part of their plan to confuse and baffle me after having starved and weakened me and reduced me to a filthy, smelly, shaggy lump of humanity. They intended to create a conflict in my mind. They were forcing me to decide whether I would continue to suffer the steadily increasing pain or give them information which they already knew. This, of course, was the catch. There was no way I could be sure of what they knew and what they wanted to know. This was the decision they were trying to force me to make at a time when the pain in my body demanded all my attention. I realized what they were doing, and I realized that their methods, when applied to several people simultaneously, could be very effective. This realization helped to boost my resistance—a resistance that was becoming more difficult to maintain.

Sometime after midnight the interrogation team returned. After taking their places behind the desk and looking me over they began:

"How have you been thinking?" My reply that I had not been

thinking brought on a shower of curses.

"You are shitting, perhaps," said the interpreter, in a poor attempt to use an American G. I. expression. I told them I found it rather difficult to think while standing at attention. This brought more curses and I was informed that "time will prove that contrary to fact."

The shouting, cursing, and questions continued—talk, talk, talk, seemingly endless strings of questions and lectures. The pain in my joints and the burning in the soles of my feet grew steadily worse and I silently cursed the long-windedness of the interrogator. I had no desire to hear what he had to say and tried to blank out his voice by thinking of other things. He rumbled on, high and low, cursing and reasoning.

His reason was no reason at all. His logic was not logical, but I could not pick out his errors. It was impossible, in my physical and mental state, to keep track of all the contradictions in his speech and his questions. They came too fast and the subject changed too often. Too much was assumed.

"What is the mission of your wing? Why did your B-29 fly over the Chinese People's Republic? Can you deny that you were trained to drop spies? God damn your leaflets! You don't need training to drop leaflets! What have spies to do with leaflets? Why did you fly into China? Why did you want to kill innocent women and children? Has China ever invaded America? Does the Chinese People's air force fly over America? Does China claim territory that does not belong to her? Have we shelled and bombed your cities? Your schools? Your hospitals? Did your wife want you to go to war against women and children? Did your wife want you to leave her at home, alone and unsupported, while you made war against peace-loving people? Don't you know there has been a terrible depression in the United States? Don't you think maybe your family is starving?

"Why did your country and its running dogs attack the peace-loving Korean People's Republic? Have you not seen the terror and ruins left by your damned bombers and fighters in North Korea? I tell you there is not a city, a village, a road, a railroad that has not been bombed! I have seen. Thousands of civilians— women, children, and old men—have been killed by such as you! Millions are homeless! Have we ever bombed your home? Did we ever cross the ocean to invade you?

"Can you deny that your government started this war? You can not deny this well-known fact! We will not allow you to deny it! We will hear you admit it! You cannot deny that your imperialist government has committed act after act of open aggression against the peace-loving people of the world!

"Do you think such is the will of the American working man? The American working man is a slave! He has no say in his government! He is powerless to stop the aggressive policy of Wall Street and its mouthpieces in Washington! They will revolt someday, and we will help them. They will seek their freedom and look to the Soviet Union and the other people's governments for leadership. This day will come!

"Why did you fly into China?"

And so on for another two hours.

Finally they brought the interrogation to a close by repeating some questions which I was supposed to "think over and be prepared to answer" at my next interrogation.

They motioned the guards to take me out. I attempted to take a step and nearly screamed from the pain. My legs refused to obey. With the help of the guards I managed to get out of the room. Now that the shouting and cursing was over, for that night anyway, the guards were less severe and almost patiently helped me along. With each painful movement my muscles slowly relaxed, and after a few yards I was able to walk alone. Even so it took several minutes to cover the sixty yards back to my cell. I fell onto my bed platform and soon found relief in sleep brought on by exhaustion.

The patience and consideration of the guards disappeared with the night. I was roused at the normal time, but it took more than the usual amount of door-banging to do it. This day was different from the preceding ones only in the fact that the guards had more difficulty in keeping me awake. They banged on the door and when that lost its effectiveness they came storming into my cell to berate me, in Chinese, for daring to close my eyes even for a few seconds. Finally my hate for them overcame my drowsiness and I sat thinking of things I'd do to them if I had the chance.

When at last the bell rang for bedtime, I lay down, whispering a silent prayer that there would be no interrogation that night. My faith was not strong enough. I was awakened from a sound sleep and, for the sixth night in a row, was ushered to the Blue Room.

I was allowed to sit on the low stool while the interrogator asked for the results of my thinking about the questions he had given me the night before. At the considerable risk of starting him off on a tantrum, I told him I had not thought about them. Much to my surprise he remained calm and said only that I would learn. I replied that if I didn't know something, no amount of thinking would change it. I told him that if he insisted on having answers, I would try to make up a few, but I could do no more than that. He warned me against doing so, saying, "We want none of your fabrications." I had no intentions of inventing answers anyway; I was just stalling. He proceeded with a lecture.

He realized, he said, that I could not know much of value to them. Of course they would welcome this little bit, but the real purpose of the interrogations was not to get information, but only to test my attitude. This was getting to be a boring subject. I wondered if they really thought my attitude would be anything other than reticent.

"Your crew members," he went on to say, "have long ago come to realize that we speak the truth. They have told us all they know and they are well off, while you, you damn fool, are still trying to support your capitalist, warmongering, reactionary government. You are being very foolish. . . ."

Surely he doesn't expect me to believe that one, I thought. His job had not been quite so easy, I was sure.

Finally he gave me some more questions to "think over," then dismissed me. I returned to my cell, relieved at having gotten through the session so easily. Maybe my prayers had not been in vain after all.

My next interrogation was not so easy. It came the following night, and as I walked into the Blue Room for the seventh straight night, I was confronted with six faces instead of the usual three. The three extra people were male officers, dressed in the same brown wool uniforms as my interrogator and the two interpreters. The six sat looking me over and making comments as I stood before them. Finally they began.

"How have you been thinking?" said the one who had been conducting my previous interrogations.

"I don't understand what you mean," I replied.

"You know well enough what I mean," he said. "What have you thought about answering the questions I instructed you to think over? We are waiting to hear your answers."

I made the foolish mistake of saying that I didn't remember the questions. This was true, for I had been asked many questions during the last few nights and I promptly ignored or forgot as many as possible. Thinking over their questions while sitting in my cell was the furthest thing from my mind. I told them that I could find far better things to occupy my thoughts—but this was a truth that would have been better left unsaid. They used it as an excuse to begin their loud and irksome efforts to "freshen" my memory. This process involved standing at attention with all the accompanying discomforts. I was already standing; they had not invited me to take a seat. Of course, they would have found an excuse anyway, but I cursed myself for making it so easy for them.

My reply had an immediate effect. The number one interrogator jumped up, slammed his fist on the desk, and then started shouting curses. My nerves, not at their best anyway, caused me to jerk involuntarily at this sudden outburst. The guards must have thought I was about to attempt to run, and they held me firmly by each arm and went about their duty of prompting my relaxed muscles. The interpreter, by now standing also, was hard-pressed to keep up with all that was being said. She made a noble effort, however, and generated a tremendous desire in me to do a little face-slapping, so foul were the adjectives she translated.

After the number one interrogator was out of breath, one of the new faces took over. He was a small, anemic, evil-looking man whom I already thought of as the "executioner." He dispensed with the interpreter, speaking directly to me in English. He used a low tone, but put a great deal of feeling into his voice. He reiterated much I had been told before. While he droned on, the guards released me and were doing their best to make me stand at rigid attention. The other two visitors—observers, interrogators, or whatever they were—added comments now and then. They spoke only in Chinese and no one bothered to translate. I didn't mind. I knew I wasn't missing anything important. It occurred to me that they were all thoroughly enjoying themselves at my expense. I stood pretending to listen; I did not want to throw more fuel than necessary on the fire. But I was actually trying to do some mental calculations in connection with the house I was currently building. This was a trick I used to help ease the physical and mental pain caused by the drawn-out interrogation. It wasn't easy to do.

After about three hours my tormentors grew weary and brought the session to a close, but they left me standing with the guards to keep me company. This was becoming an unpleasant habit, but I could see nothing to be done about it. My number one interrogator, accompanied by the two interpreters, returned after a couple of interminable hours and got down to some serious questioning. Most of their questions concerned the aircraft I had been flying. They asked things that were common knowledge, but which I had refused, on principle, to answer before. There was nothing classified about our B-29, so I answered their questions, hoping to avoid being asked more sensitive ones. This worked, temporarily, and they gave up after I had been standing well over six hours.

As they brought the interrogation to a close, I was again told to think over certain questions when I got back to my cell. Just before leaving, the interrogator asked me to repeat the questions I was supposed to think over. I did not know; I hadn't been listening.

As I stood, hesitating, he grew impatient and said, "Well, we are waiting. What are the questions I told you to be prepared to answer when you come back?"

All I could say was "I don't know." At these words the interrogator jumped up so fast he knocked over his chair. He bounded straight over the top of his desk, shouting curses in English, which until then he had pretended not to know. He stopped a few inches in front of me and I had no doubt that his anger was genuine. One of the girl interpreters spoke to him in low, anxious tones. From all appearances he did not hear her. He had been smoking a cigarette and now he waved it, threateningly, in front of my eyes—so close I could feel its heat.

The two guards had grabbed my arms, but although I was so weak and sore from standing I could barely move, the urgency of the situation gave me new strength. I stood perfectly still and waited, knowing that if the interrogator so much as touched me with the cigarette I would somehow manage to get my hands around his neck and kill him. I knew what that would mean for me, but I didn't care in the least. I almost hoped he would force me to make a move that would put an end to the whole tiresome business. On the other hand, I also knew I would not do anything drastic as long as I had hope of staying alive.

As he threatened me with words and the cigarette, one of the guards spoke to him and, from his tone, I knew he was cautioning him. This particular guard was not one of the soldiers who normally guarded me. He wore the blue uniform of a jailer, but I guessed he had a little more authority than the soldiers. At any rate, his few words took effect, and the interrogator backed off and stormed out the door, shouting that I would stand there until I remembered, even if I died.

With the encouragement of the two guards, I stood until nearly daybreak. Then, finally, someone came to the door and spoke to the guards. I was led back to my cell, where I stretched out without bothering to cover up. After barely an hour's sleep I was made to get up. The hours that followed were even more of an eternity than usual. My weary, aching body felt as if it would soon collapse completely. I had only more interrogations, more terrible hours of standing, and more long days of sitting to look forward to.

I amused myself that day by planning ways to escape. By giving myself every possible break and several times the strength I possessed, I planned an escape which I would accomplish by overpowering a guard and using his submachine-gun to make the interrogation team escort me out of the prison to the local airport. Once there, I would commandeer a plane and with the use of superior navigation and luck I would soon be a free man. I didn't even know where I was, much less the location of the local airport, but I had to think about something. These thoughts gave me pleasure, so I let my imagination run wild.

Night came. Bedtime followed, and then the footsteps I had learned to recognize and dread—Big Stoop coming to escort me to the Blue Room. My stint that night was relatively short—only about two and a half hours. I didn't think I could have stood much longer, even with the help of the guards. I had much to learn.

I was somewhat more attentive during this interrogation; I didn't want to risk a recurrence of the last night's episode. The interrogator did not command all my thoughts, however. As I stood there I worked out a problem that had been troubling me for some time—how to wash my socks.

In the past I had tried periodically to wash them, but it was not allowed. In fact, I had not had them off my feet for nearly a month. Each time I started taking my shoes off, the guard stopped me.

The only articles of clothing I was ever allowed to remove were my hat, coat and overshoes—when I went to bed. I had tried several times to slip my shoes and socks off while still under the cover, just before getting up. This had not worked either. The hawk-eyed guards detected the movement under the blanket and came rushing into the cell, jerking up the blankets to see what I was doing.

After returning to my cell from my eighth consecutive interrogation, I executed the first part of "Operation Sock Wash." I pulled off my overshoes as usual and rolled up in my blanket. In doing this, I made a great play at getting the cover wrapped tightly around my legs. Actually I was pulling off my shoes. This was not very difficult since they had no laces to untie. I succeeded in getting them off without arousing the guard's suspicions. That completed the first part of my plan.

Next morning when I got up, I chose just the right moment to slip out of bed and put my stocking feet, minus shoes, into my overshoes. This also went unnoticed. I folded my shoes up inside the bedding, smoothing out the bumps as much as possible. When my morning pan of water was handed in, I put the last part of my plan into effect. I quickly set the pan on the floor, and slipping my feet out of the loose-fitting overshoes, I put them, socks and all, into the water.

It was a wonderful, luxurious feeling as the hot water covered my feet—feet that had not been warm for weeks! Of course, after a couple of seconds the guard realized what I had done, but it was too late to stop me. I slipped the filthy socks off and stirred them around in the water with my feet, enjoying every second of it.

The three or four minutes I was allowed to keep the pan of water passed all too quickly. When they came for the pan I also gave them the socks which they took somewhere to dry. Then, while the unhappy guard watched, I reached in my roll of bedding, took out my shoes and put them on my feet. I did it openly so the guard would know that I had outfoxed him. He muttered a few curses, which only served to boost my ego. Later in the day my socks were brought back. They were far from clean, but at least they had had an airing. The guard who threw them in to me made it plainly understood that the water I was given each morning was for washing my face and hands only—not my socks or feet.

"Operation Sock Wash" gave me much pleasure and was made even more satisfying by the knowledge that I had pulled a fast one on the guard. Even so, I decided that things had reached a poor state when a man had to resort to intricate planning to wash his socks. The guard, of course, made an entry in his notebook, no doubt to the effect that I had violated a prison rule. He also exhibited his displeasure in other small ways during the day.

The following night I made my ninth consecutive visit to the Blue Room. Some of these sessions had lasted several hours, others only two or three. They were getting some information from me each night, but I had not told them anything of real importance. There were dozens of questions which I still refused to answer and many others to which I did not know the answers. I was glad I did not, even though I had no choice but to bear pain and torment until they grew tired of asking.

The interrogators, I discovered, listened to anything I said and carefully wrote it all down. These notes, I was sure, would be compared with notes taken during the interrogations of my fellow crew members. This comparing and piecing together of small bits of information would enable them to figure out much more than they were actually told by any one person. I had no way of knowing how often the crew had been interrogated or when their interrogations had started, but I was sure our captors had not been wasting any time.

From the questions they asked me I could tell they already had a fair history of our crew and our wing. Some of their information must have come through agents working in or near our base; some came from members of the crew, just as some came from me. The interrogators had all the physical and psychological advantages.

I knew the crew were doing their best, as I did mine, but even time was on the enemy's side. As they pointed out over and over, they had all the time they needed. I was not going anywhere. I witnessed plenty of evidence that, as they boasted, the Chinese had a great deal of patience, especially when it was the prisoner who had to suffer for it.

As I stood before my number one interrogator and his two girl interpreters this ninth night in a row, I was asked one question. They wanted to know, as they put it, "What unusual discovery did your crew make while on a training mission from the Philippines?" I knew immediately that they were referring to an unidentified submarine we had sighted while on a flight from Clark Air Force Base. It was obvious, from the way they phrased the question, that they already knew all about it. I wondered what possible value this bit of information could have to them, but since a single member of our crew had made the original sighting, I was afraid this might in some way implicate him. I was determined not to verify their information, no matter what.

This interrogation started about nine P.M. Fourteen hours later I was taken back to my cell—a miserable, tormented mass of swollen human flesh. The physical violence they used—kicks, jabs, slaps—was incidental; standing for this length of time was the real torture. My hands, arms, feet, and legs had swollen to nearly twice their normal size. I could not close my hands. After the first four or five hours, I could not bend a joint except with the slowest of movements. Every part of my body was racked with pain more intense than I would have thought it humanly possible to endure.

During this fourteen hours of eternity, the interrogation team questioned and lectured me in two- to three-hour stretches, with two hours off in between while they left the guards to keep me standing. They made a special effort to let me know they were resting, sleeping, and eating between interrogations while I had to remain there. They assured me each time that I could be doing the same if I answered their simple questions. This had little effect on me; I was too occupied trying to find ways to ease my pain. The soles of my feet were giving me the most trouble. To counter the pain, I constantly shifted my weight from one foot to the other and from heel to toe. This made the pain slightly more bearable, but also brought on kicks and blows from the guards.

During the several interrogations throughout the night and the next morning, I was asked other questions, some of which I answered, but their primary concern was with the submarine. I held firm on this, saying that we had never discovered anything unusual on any of our flights. I was lying. They knew I was lying and I knew they knew I was lying, but I placed a great deal of importance on not letting them get this information from me.

Shortly before noon the next morning they gave up. They did so by saying, "You stupid son of bitch, you have stood here over twelve hours, refusing to tell us something which we know better than you. We know your goddamn crew sighted a submarine off Luzon Island on one of your training missions. We know that your Navy did not claim this submarine and that your intelligence was much interested in this sighting. Now why have you, you damn fool, tried to keep this information from us? We made it plain that we already know this, but you have refused to understand. We have told you repeatedly that we need no information from you. We know more than you. Much more. We only wanted to test your attitude toward the peace-loving Chinese People. You have proved yourself to be the worst of reactionaries! You are the most stupid person we have ever seen!"

I didn't bother to thank him, but I considered that to be the highest compliment he could pay me. I hoped he really did think I was stupid; that was the impression I wished to give. Thus ended the ninth and, so far, the longest session in the Blue Room.

When I got back to my cell, my bucket of food was sitting on the bed. I had missed breakfast and my noon rice was cold. I was not the least bit hungry, but I forced myself to eat some of the food, a process made slow and painful by my stiff, swollen, and aching muscles. The guard did not rush me.

I had to sit the rest of the day and the guard saw to it that I didn't sleep. For once I didn't mind sitting. It was a pleasure after the hours of standing. My joints and muscles slowly eased, but I doubted if they would ever be normal again. My feet, which were supposed to remain flat on the floor even when I was sitting, continued to revolt. They had hurt before; the cold and the constant pressure caused by the weight of my body made them ache and burn. Now, after so many hours of standing, the pain was multiplied many times and the tiny movements that had given me a small measure of relief no longer helped. Thus the periods of interrogation and the long hours of standing had a lasting effect which gave me no freedom from misery, except in sleep, which was more and more scarce and was becoming more and more tortured by unpleasant dreams. The whole process was calculated to destroy my will to resist. It was working—it had worked on stronger men than I and, I am fully convinced, will work on the strongest. Time is the killing factor.

There was no interrogation for me that night, at least not physically. But I had come to dread them so much that they found their way into my sleep. I was beginning to dream about interrogations and these dreams were so vivid that they were almost as bad as the real thing.

CHAPTER
ELEVEN

During the next three weeks I visited the Blue Room almost nightly. There was one three-night period during which I was not interrogated. This was like a reprieve from hell. There were a couple of other one-night vacations, but to make up for them I was interrogated twice during the day. The interrogation I received the night of the fifth of March left me somewhat puzzled. The interrogation itself was no different from the others, but one of the girl interpreters cried during the entire proceedings. The interrogator and the other interpreter were solemn, but I could detect a certain amount of irritation in the glances they gave the crying girl. Over two years later I learned the cause of the girl's tears— that was the date of Stalin's death. The girl had been proving herself a good Communist.

These interrogations followed the same pattern as those in the past. They lasted from two to sixteen hours each. Once in the Blue Room I never knew how long I would have to stay there, standing in pain and misery. Two different interrogation teams were working on me. When I received several interrogations in a single night they alternated.

During this period I was given two more private guards and Horseface got a day off—his first in over a month. A few days later Hot Shot and Shorty also had a day off. They had worked two on and four off without break since I had arrived at the prison. Not for a single instant had they grown lax or careless. I wondered what stimulant their superiors used to get this kind of result. Probably fear, I decided, fear of finding themselves on the other side of the slots in the doors if they were caught loafing. I named my two new guards "Biggum" and "Rags." They were added to my private escort force because two guards had to be on duty during the interrogations.

Biggum was a comparatively large, dirty, ignorant-looking soldier who appeared to have had fewer baths in the last two months than I. He was just as mean as he was filthy. One of his peculiarities was a fear that someone would slip something to me—a message, poison, or a weapon—buried in my food. To make sure this did not happen, he thoroughly inspected my food, using his filthy fingers to poke around in the rice and look at the occasional piece of bread. If he found any specks or bits of stick or straw, he dug them out with his fingernails. My rice often had small sticks, rocks, snails, or worms in it. The first time Biggum saw me toss one of these on the floor he got very excited. Banging on the door, he rushed into my cell to see what it was. I tried to tell him it was only a small rock, but he spent ten minutes looking for it. He found it at last, and after inspecting it closely, he threw it back on the floor. He made me understand that anything I found in my food should be given to him. To make sure I did this, he stayed in my cell while I ate, squatting a few inches from me and staring intently at each spoonful of food I took. This irritated me no end. I got some relief by pretending to think he was hungry and offering him each spoon of food before eating it myself. This shamed him a little and he moved back a foot or so, but he continued to watch closely.

Rags, my other new guard, lasted less than two days. His face and the way he wore his hat, which was three sizes too large, reminded me of some comic-strip character whose name I could not remember. His padded uniform trousers were too long and the bottoms were worn and ragged where he had walked on them. Thus the name Rags.

He was one of the two Chinese soldiers I saw who appeared to possess human kindness. (The other was Smiley.) Although Rags was dirty, ragged and probably illiterate, he had a friendly look.

This proved to be more than just a look. He was one of my guards during a long interrogation, and he made no attempt to force me to stand at attention. Not once did he speak to me in a harsh tone, and not once did he touch me except to keep me from falling when I became dizzy from pain. The other guard during this interrogation was one of the jailers, who appeared insulted at having to perform such menial duty. Between questioning periods, during the absence of the interrogation team, he found business outside the room every few minutes. I guessed he was slipping out to have a smoke. Each time he left, Rags looked at me and made a slight movement of his head. I knew by his look and motion that I could relax. He let me shuffle back and forth, moving my arms, fingers, neck, and legs to relieve the pain. When we heard the other guard returning, Rags glanced at me and I stopped. I stopped willingly because I had no desire to get Rags into trouble. He was voluntarily easing my hours of pain and torment. He pulled three shifts at my cell door after that interrogation and there we had the same silent agreement.

These few little favors endeared Rags to me, but it was too good to last. I never knew if his friendliness had been discovered or why he had been relieved, but after two interrogations and the one day at my cell door, I never saw him again.

Rags was replaced by "Babyface," a temperamental, unpredictable Oriental. He was the only one of the blue-uniformed jailers to pull duty at my cell door. He appeared to be filling in for the missing Rags. Babyface first made his appearance during one of my long stands in the Blue Room. I had developed a coughing spell and was spitting up blood. This rattled the guards and one of them took off out the door and returned a few minutes later with Babyface. He looked me over, but appeared to view the blood I was coughing up with little concern and left me standing. After that, however, he checked in periodically during all my long interrogations. He was probably the prison medic, but when he showed up as a door guard, he had little of the human kindness usually associated with those in the medical profession. He was as strict as any of my other guards.

Throughout these long, endless weeks, life in my cell dragged on as it had in the past. Little incidents kept popping up which did little to improve relations between me and the guards. One was the matter of toilet paper. Horseface took it upon himself to cut prison expenses by rationing the paper. My visits to the latrine had been cut to a maximum of one every two days, but I had always been given a decent amount of paper to use. Horseface decided this was too much, or maybe he thought the extra couple of wipes were giving me too much exercise. He cut my ration down to one piece of paper about two inches square. My calling him a "stingy son of a bitch" didn't get me any more paper, but it gave me a little satisfaction. I could usually talk the other guards out of more paper, but never Horseface.

I had been in prison over two months and my health was beginning to give me concern. I contracted colds, coughs, and a sore throat periodically. Gradually I had lost weight and become weak from lack of exercise. The long stands and the days of sitting caused pains and symptoms which were new to me. They were aggravated by the constant state of chill which I was forced to endure. My eyes hurt, and now and then I had dizzy spells. I could often feel my pulse throbbing in my head, legs, and hands. It seemed very irregular and at times I was certain that it stopped completely for seconds at a time. My right ear developed a peculiar sizzling sound which often reached a paralyzing pitch. The bloody phlegm I coughed up occasionally only added to my worries.

I knew the long periods of standing, the poor diet, and insufficient sleep were a terrible strain. The long hours of enforced idleness made my strange symptoms seem much worse. There were nights I went to sleep not expecting to wake up. Most of the time, however, I managed to control my fear of these unknown symptoms and view them more or less logically. They were just one more thing added to the physical and mental effect prison life was having on me. They made me try all the harder to keep my mind occupied.

I found new ways to while away many idle hours. After I designed, built, and lived in several houses, I started writing novels —mentally, of course. I would have given a fortune for a pencil and a pad. I sometimes used myself as the main character, mentally living the part as my imagination developed the plot. Other times I built novels around people I had known. When I grew tired of "writing," I played with numbers and tried to remember or develop various mathematical formulas. At other times I tried my hand at inventing. A portable ditch-digger was one of these projects. It worked, mentally, and I sold it for a fortune, mentally. I spent the fortune, of course, and then figured ways to make others. It all passed time; that was my primary concern.

Except for the interrogations, I lived a life comparatively void of sound. Like the other prisoners, I was forbidden to talk. The only breaks in the monotonous silence of the cell block came at chow-time and during guard changes. Guards banged on the doors and stormed into the cells, but otherwise everything was completely quiet. Sounds from life outside the prison were few. The thick walls and covered windows effectively blocked them. Now and then at night, when the corridor door was left open, noises filtered in. Sometimes I could hear babies crying or an occasional motor vehicle start up. More often these nocturnal sounds were screams and the shouts of interrogators, always in Chinese. Once in awhile, usually late in the evening, a few strains of Oriental music, created by some unfamiliar instrument and punctuated with the resounding tones of a gong, found their way to my ears. Music was one of the things I missed most and I listened intently every time a bit was wafted my way, even though it was strange and unfamiliar. Sometimes I thought I recognized western classics, but not often.

Each night as I went to bed, I wondered if I would be getting up shortly to make the usual trip to the Blue Room. At the end of each interrogation, I wondered how many more there would be. It was beginning to seem like an endless process and I longed for some kind of change. What would happen when the Communists finally got what they wanted from me? I asked myself this question many times. Would they put us together in some kind of camp or would they just leave us as we were—to rot and die? If I was of no further value to them after they finished interrogating me, perhaps they would shoot me. I didn't really believe this, but it was a possibility to be considered and sometimes I thought it the most logical one. My experiences had thoroughly convinced me that they were capable of far worse acts of inhumanity.

On the twenty-fourth of March, my wedding anniversary, they began their longest interrogation of me.

As usual, I glanced at the clock hanging in the rotunda as I walked through on my way to the Blue Room. It was a few minutes before eleven P.M.

The interrogation began with a question which I had been asked many times before. It concerned our operations in the Chinese Nationalist stronghold of Formosa, or Taiwan as the interrogators preferred to call it. This was a subject I knew very little about, but I realized even this little bit might be of great value and might also expose other members of the crew to severe questioning.

I had continually denied having any knowledge at all on the subject, but this time they followed the question with the statement that they knew beyond doubt that I was lying. I was not expected, they said, to know everything about the operations of my Wing on this island, but anything I did know would be of much use to them. This last statement was a complete departure from their usual interrogation methods. Normally they said that any information I had was of little value to them, and in many cases they claimed to know more on the subject than I. They were testing my Attitude.

This time my attitude did not enter into the picture. They said they had not been sure whether I knew anything on this subject or not, but now they were. This was my chance, they added, to make up to the "peace-loving Chinese People" for the crimes I had committed. If I told them everything I knew, my life and living conditions would change overnight and I would have a "bright future." On the other hand, if I still refused to believe them and continued to support the "American imperialist dogs" by holding back information, my fate would be worse than death. All this gave me ample indication of the importance they placed on this subject. It made me all the more determined not to answer.

They asked if I clearly heard all they had said to me. I replied that I had. Then they wanted to know my decision. I told them I had no choice; I could not tell them something I did not know. A few curses, more lectures and more denials followed. I could tell this was going to be another long-drawn-out session. I tried to prepare myself for hours of standing. Had I known just how many there were to be, I probably would not have had the will power to continue to resist.

But I did not know. The longest session so far had been sixteen hours and I considered that to be near the maximum of human endurance. During the next week I came to realize just how wrong I was. I never learned how much of this kind of torture the human body can endure—I am still alive.

The first couple of hours of interrogation passed and I was left standing with two guards to keep me at attention. Already the pain was beginning to creep in. When the interrogation team returned about two hours later, my hands and feet had already begun to swell. With each successive bout of standing, the pain and swelling took less time to make their appearance.

The questioning continued in the same vein.

"Who else of your crew has knowledge of this subject?"

I did not know. I doubted if any did. This was a lie and I knew they knew it, but I refused to implicate any of the crew in something which might conceivably result in their death.

"When did you first learn of this thing?"

"I first learned of it when you asked me about it."

"God damn you! You lie, you son of a bitch! In the face of facts you lie! You can lie until your dying breath, but you will tell the truth!"

The shouting and cursing subsided somewhat and the questioning continued.

"Who told you of this project?"

"You did."

"You stupid bastard! You have no wish to live! You will die because of your stubbornness, but we will hear you tell the truth first!"

I had grown impervious to their shouted curses. They no longer made me angry enough to protest. The pain, gradually spreading to every part of my body, drew more and more of my attention, helping me ignore my questioners. I wished only for something to help me ignore the pain. I tried to concentrate on one of my mental projects only to be abruptly jarred back to reality by a guard's foot when I did not answer a direct question. Automatically I replied, "I don't know."

"You don't know! What don't you know?"

Then I realized my reply did not fit the question, but I did not care. The results would have been the same anyway—more shouting, cursing, and threats. The team stormed out again, leaving me with dire warnings. As usual, the guards stayed behind to keep me standing.

Daylight was spreading over the world outside, changing the shade of the blue cloth nailed over the windows. Noises of an awakening world penetrated the room. Soldiers shouted, women talked, babies cried, and now and then a donkey's bray floated in. These and the sound of trucks, cars, and motorcycles seemed to come from outside the prison walls, along with the singsong shouting of peddlers hawking their wares. One peddler accompanied his shouts with a beating of sticks. I remembered reading somewhere that these sticks were the trade-mark of fuel-venders. The sounds occupied my mind for a while as I tried to visualize who made them and conjure up pictures of the outside world. I did my best to imagine I was somewhere else, away from the pain and misery.

Soon I heard a familiar step approaching down the hall and the female jailer from my cell block entered with my chow bucket. She seemed only mildly interested in me and my predicament, but the appearance of my breakfast meant, to me, more long hours of standing. I had never been given food during an interrogation before, although I had missed meals when the sessions lasted into the mornings. She gave the bucket to one of the guards, who put it in a chair taken from behind the interrogator's desk. He motioned me to squat by the chair and eat, but after I made several painful attempts, he saw that my swollen legs would not allow this. He left to return shortly with the stool I had been allowed to sit on during my first interrogations. Instead of placing it upright, he laid it on its side and made me sit on the narrow legs. I wondered if he thought it made any difference to my tired, aching body.

I ate as much of the rice starch as I could, which wasn't more than a couple of cupfuls. My appetite was not at its best. Afterwards, the remaining food was taken out and the stool removed. I was forced to resume my place, standing in back of the still-burning light bulb.

One of the guards held a cup of hot water to my lips. After a while this had its normal effect, and I asked to be taken to a latrine. No such luck. Instead, one of the guards went out and got a clay pot. The pot had a round snout and a handle and was clearly made for the purpose to which I put it. They made me urinate standing at attention. I wondered what kind of pot they would bring when I had to relieve myself the other way. When I finished, the guard set the pot in a corner by the door.

The interrogation team made its appearance shortly and got right down to business. They seemed to be certain that I was ready to answer their question. "Give us your answer and you can go back to your room and sleep," they said. I could have used some rest. My back felt as if it could not hold my head, arms, and shoulders upright much longer. My spine seemed to be arching inward and slowly collapsing. The rest of my body was seared with pain which grew more intense by the minute, but I knew I could give only one answer to their question—the one that would keep me standing until they decided to give up, if they ever did.

I gave it and it immediately spoiled the interrogator's early-morning good humor. He jumped up and cursed his way to the door, followed by the two interpreters. There he paused and, looking me over with hate and scorn showing plainly in his face, told he that I had tried their patience too far. "You will stand until you drop dead," he said in English, "but you will tell truth first." With that they stormed out.

Some hours later another team came in. There were two of them, both males, who spoke English. They made it quite clear that they intended to succeed where the others had failed. According to them I was a dead man. I had already lost the chance to save my life, now all I could do was try to make my death as easy as possible. The sooner the better, I thought, and for once I really meant it. I said no matter what they did, they could not force me to tell them something I did not know. I figured I was near death anyway and whatever I said would not change that. "I'm ready. Go ahead and shoot me," I said.

I was reminded that they had not mentioned shooting; I had lost that choice. That was too easy. Then they started on me again, trying several different approaches.

Threatening: "The Chinese People are a humane race, but they will suffer no criminal to go unpunished. Death is too easy for such as you! Our People demand that first you repent and see the error of your ways. Then you will be allowed to die. . . .

"We have dealt with many stubborn criminals. We have ways of getting what we want. We are a very patient people. You will see.

We will kill you, but not until you have confessed. . . .

"We will not allow you to die. Your life and your death are in our hands. We are the masters of your body. Your God cannot help you here. Your God is back in America! Here we are the god. . . ."

Ridiculing: "You are a stupid bastard! How can you say you do not know? Do you not realize that we have facts to the contrary? You lie in the face of truth! Did your mother teach you to tell lies? Look at you! Don't you wish your wife could see you now! Hair growing all over your face, filthy, smelly—all because you lie. . . ."

Reasoning: "We have told you we do not hold you responsible for your crimes. We know you only follow orders. A junior lieutenant is not very important. Why should you die for the crimes of others? You are a young man. You should not die so young. Do you not wish to see your family again? We do not have to kill you. We can send you back to your country immediately. Confess and you can be with your wife within hours. We have ways of doing this. Why do you try to protect others. . . ."

Bluffing: "Why do you deny what is common knowledge? Why do you refuse to admit something that has been printed in your newspapers? Do you think we are fools? Do you think you are the only one who knows this? Do you think we have only your crew to get information from? I can tell you we have many of your people, right here in this jail—more than your crew, more than twice the number of your crew, more than three times the number of your crew. They have talked. They are not so foolish as you. . . ."

For hours this continued. Finally their voices got hoarse and they left. My lunch was brought in and, as at breakfast, I was allowed to sit on the stool legs to eat.

That afternoon I broke my previous record of sixteen hours of constant standing. I couldn't guess how much longer it would last. I had no choice but to stand there until I collapsed or until they gave up. The guards, always one on each side, were pretty efficient at preventing a premature collapse. Their blows and kicks were not vicious, although they came more and more often. They made use of them only to keep me standing. A kick could be very painful, but it was minor compared to the pain that already existed. The only thing that kept me from collapsing as long as I had the strength to stand was my pride. To fall on the floor in front of my tormentors would have been like the cringing of a beaten dog. I would not admit defeat or beg for mercy. I could not fall until I fell unconscious. My pride did not prevent me from wishing that time would come soon. I would have induced unconsciousness if I could have.

There was another interrogation that afternoon, then another short break from standing when my evening meal was brought in. I asked to be taken to the latrine. They refused, nor did they bring a pot. The urine pot still sat in the corner and I was allowed to use it whenever the guards thought I needed to. I asked again. Again I was refused. I decided to go anyway. I started toward the door, but I got no further than half a step. My legs would not obey me. The normal step my brain ordered turned out to be a slight movement of one leg. This movement, slight as it was, brought an immediate reaction from the guards. They kicked my foot and leg back into place.

Although I could do nothing to resist, I felt compelled to protest. My mouth obeyed my brain's orders somewhat better than my leg. I cursed the guards, using some of the interrogator's favorite phrases. All the time I was talking, the guards shouted "*pu shih, pu shih*" and held my arms. Finally one of the guards left and when he returned a few minutes later, I was taken out to a latrine. When I tried to assume a squatting position, my knees bent only so far and my legs felt as if they were tearing apart at the joints. Convinced that I had used the latrine as an excuse to get relief from standing, the guards were impatient and angry as they took me back to the Blue Room. Their anger bothered me very little.

The interrogation teams came in regularly, every two to three hours. I was glad to see them return and just as glad, after a couple of hours, to see them leave. The interrogations helped to keep my mind off the pain in my body, but after a while their lectures and curses grew tiresome. I resorted to my past tricks of occupying myself with some mental project, but this was more and more difficult to do. My aching, burning, screaming body became harder and harder to ignore.

The night crept past and the second day of my interrogation began. During this second day the prison doctor came in and looked me over. He made the guards remove my brogans, which were in danger of bursting from my swollen feet. They also took off my socks and then put my bare feet into my overshoes. This brought a small measure of relief, but it was short-lived. My feet, no longer bound by the size nine shoes, began swelling again and soon filled the overshoes. The insides of the overshoes were made to conform to the bottom of a shoe and not a foot. This added considerably to my pain and discomfort. My heel expanded and filled the depression that was meant to contain the heel of a shoe. If the overshoes had been a box, I would have had square feet. I was amazed at the elasticity of my skin.

The following night the doctor returned and this time inspected my clothing. My B-15 flying jacket was beginning to feel rather snug, especially around the arms, and my long johns were definitely in danger of being ripped apart by my swelling limbs. The doctor told the guards to remove my underwear. To do this they had to strip me completely. This was the first time in two months that I had had my clothes off. My body from the waist down was swollen out of all proportion to its normal size. My arms and hands were almost as bad and my fingers were beyond bending. My skin was shiny and a light purplish color.

At the sight of all this distended flesh, I thought it couldn't be long before I died from a mass rupture of blood-vessels. The doctor checked my chest and pulse, then pressed his thumb into the flesh of my leg, leaving a deep depression when he removed it. I remembered reading somewhere that this was a sign of beriberi, but I didn't care. The guards dressed me again and put me back into position. They made sure my shoes were at a forty-five degree angle with heels together and that I was standing at attention or a semblance thereof. I passed my forty-eighth hour that night. They'll give up soon, I told myself.

Another day, another night, another day and yet another night, and still I occupied the spot on the floor in the Blue Room. Time, moving at a snail's pace at first, now seemed to have stopped. Each hour seemed like a month and every second was filled with pain. I now had three interrogation teams working on me, in shifts.

During one particularly interesting session, there were six people participating, not counting myself and the two guards. An additional desk and chairs had to be brought in to accommodate the extra people. My number one interrogator and his two female interpreters were there, along with the small, pallid "executioner." The other two were new to me. They all took turns lecturing and questioning, but one of the strangers, a comparatively tall, slender, and delicate-looking man, was the star of the show. He spoke only in Chinese and used one of the girl interpreters to translate. They worked together perfectly, and listening to them was almost a pleasure. I immediately labeled him "the preacher."

He paced back and forth behind the others, never looking at me, but staring first at one part of the ceiling and then another. As he walked he spoke in short, sing-song sentences with hardly a pause in between. The interpreter picked up in the middle of the first sentence and stayed half a sentence behind, never faltering or hesitating. It was something like listening to two radios at the same time, each tuned to a different station in different languages. It was obvious that these two had had much practice working together. The preacher performed over an hour, asking many questions but never waiting for an answer. Most of his speech concerned my "crimes," my "attitude," and my "future." Everyone appeared to be thoroughly disgusted with me and had many times consigned me and all my barbarian ancestors to the many Chinese devils.

That night I stood through my hundredth hour. Perhaps they were not bluffing when they said I would stand there until I died, I decided. I was surprised at having lasted so long. The guards had to make use of their hands and feet more and more often to keep me standing and awake. Their kicks and blows only made a dent in the terrible pain that unceasingly flowed from every part of my body. Some of the guards, tired of hitting me to keep me awake, devised even less pleasant methods. Taking a mouthful of water, they stood in front of me and spewed it into my face. After a spurt or two, the water was gone and saliva would follow. The first time this happened, I attempted to kick the guard, but my swollen limbs wouldn't obey. I spat back, but without success. My mouth was dry.

Another guard, who always carried a foot-long flashlight day or night, often held it a few inches from my eyes when he thought I looked sleepy. My eyes, already sorely punished by the light which hung just above them and by lack of sleep, revolted when this direct beam of light probed into them. My lids closed and for this I was hit. But even with them open it was several minutes before they could transmit a clear image to my brain.

I wondered how much longer I could last. I wished now that I had tried one of the desperate escape plans I had formulated. Even as I stood there, I contemplated trying to use the stool or the heavy pot in the corner as a weapon to bash in the guards' heads. These were futile and foolish thoughts. I could move no faster than a rheumatic old man.

The questioning still centered around the subject of Formosa, but it also spread out to include other topics. I had already answered some of their questions. Others I answered in an attempt to convince the interrogators that I was being truthful in denying knowledge of the more important ones. They continued to claim possession of proof that I was lying. I found myself fighting a battle of wits in addition to the terrible and constant pain.

The next day was a two-meal day—a Sunday—but food had

long since ceased to have any importance. I had no hunger and to eat only meant postponing my ultimate collapse and enduring a few more hours of pain. Still, with the help of the guards, I ate a little each time food was brought to me. Though I hardly cared, I clung to the slender hope that somehow I would come out alive. This hope deserted me now and then and was replaced by a desire for the opposite—for an end to the whole miserable nightmare. I knew it would end sooner or later, but it seemed increasingly unlikely that the Communists had any intentions of letting me live.

I tried to honor the Sabbath by praying. This was not my first attempt at prayer nor my last. Sometimes I thought it helped, but all too often my faith wavered and failed. Praying was a diversion; it was another way of occupying my mind, even though my prayers were seldom answered—or so it seemed at the time.

Sunday and the following Monday dragged by and the three interrogation teams paid me regular visits. Still I was able to stick to my denial of knowing what they wished to know. On Monday I discovered one of the guards slipping the contents of a small folded square of paper into my cup of drinking water. I refused the water. The guard cursed me, but set the cup aside until I wanted it. This action verified the fact that something had been put in the cup. Any other time they tossed the water I didn't drink on the floor without comment.

The water was still there when the guard changed, and the conversation between the new and the old guards assured me further that something had been added to it. Listening carefully to their talk, I was convinced that the stuff they put in the water was something to keep me awake. This seemed reasonable to me; I knew that I would soon pass out from lack of sleep if from nothing else.

The guards seemed determined to keep me awake, using their various and painful methods, so when next they offered me the cup of water I drank it. It seemed the easier of the two ways of staying awake. The bottom of the cup was covered with a whitish substance and, just in case it was not what I thought, I tried not to stir it up as the guard held the cup to my lips. I left an inch or so of water which the guard threw on the floor.

This was the first cup of cold water I had had since becoming a prisoner. The jailers and guards had always been careful to serve me nothing but steaming hot water. The taste of that cup of cold water was so different from the usual hot water that I could not be sure if I was tasting the contents of the paper or not. Nor could I detect any effects from drinking the water.

Each time I was given a cup of water I watched closely to see if the guards added anything to it. It was very easy to tell when they did. They attempted to keep the cup from my view when they inserted the powders or whatever the paper contained. This alone was enough to give them away. They were completely lacking in finesse. A hand would slip stealthily into a pocket and out again, the contents would be dumped into the cup and the paper put back into a pocket to be disposed of later by dropping it into the spittoon. The guards went through these proceedings about every six hours. No canary swallowing a cat ever looked more guilty.

Monday night I stood through my sixth full day. I knew that I would surely drop dead before many more hours passed. It must have been obvious to others that I had about reached the limits of human endurance. Shortly after midnight the doctor made another appearance and after looking me over told the guards to help me sit down. This they did in a corner of the room. I was not impressed, I had ceased to care. I immediately dropped off to sleep, exploding my theory that the powders were to keep me awake—I had just been given a doctored cup of water a few minutes before.

I was allowed to sleep less than an hour. When the interrogation team came in, they made the guards rouse me and stand me back in position. Remembering the doctored water, I began to worry again, wondering what its purpose was. A truth drug? I had heard that such a thing existed, but knew nothing about it. If that is what it was, I wondered why they had waited so long to use it. Were they experimenting with some such drug, using me as a guinea pig? Whatever they were doing, the drug seemed to have no effect on me.

This interrogation ended leaving me standing the rest of the night. About the middle of the next morning, I was interrogated again. This session was conducted by a particularly nasty and obnoxious officer who spoke fair English and never bothered to use an interpreter or take down what was said. He had just informed me that I would never again leave the room "except to be carried out dead" when my first interrogator walked in. He spoke a few words, in Chinese, to the presiding interrogator and they left together. A few minutes later a jailer appeared and I was taken, slowly and painfully, back to my cell.

I had been standing in the Blue Room for one hundred and fifty-four hours—more than six and a half days! I had been under interrogation over sixty hours. I had slept less than an hour in almost a week. My body was so swollen that it looked more like a dead stump than a human being. The pain I had endured was much greater than I ever dreamed the human body could bear.

Once I was back in my cell, the guards made me sit and stay awake until normal bedtime. This required constant effort on their part and brought the total time that I had gone on less than an hour's sleep up to one hundred and sixty-five hours.

During the next day the pain and swelling gradually left my body, but it had far from disappeared when the doctor paid me a visit that evening. He made the guard let me lie down with my feet and legs propped up. I imagined I could feel the blood draining back into my upper body. The guard made it quite clear that I could not go to sleep while lying there. Although the full night's sleep had far from satisfied my needs, I managed to stay awake the two or three hours I was allowed to lie flat on my back. This helped reduce the swelling considerably. It was several days, however, before all my limbs shrank back to anywhere near normal size.

CHAPTER

TWELVE

For the next week I sat in my cell and was content to do so. I didn't know whether my interrogations were finished or not, but as each day passed without one, I began to hope there would be no more. I didn't think I could possibly survive another week-long session.

Now that I was away from the torture of standing, I became a little more concerned about the powder that had been slipped into my drinking water. My first theory no longer seemed logical; the powder had not kept me awake. And I became aware that the guards were still putting the stuff in my water. From all appearances they gave me two doses per day. I tried in several ways to get out of drinking it. About half the time I refused the water, but they only saved it and gave it to me later. I also tried spilling it or drinking part of it, then emptying the rest in my urine bucket. For a day or so these ruses worked, but then the guards watched me closely and made me return all the water I did not drink. The water I received after the noon meal was not doctored. I could drink it or pour it out, the guard did not care.

After a while they changed their tactics and started putting the powder in the small cup of thin soup I got with my meals. It was a day or so before I realized they had switched. I thought at first they had stopped, but I noticed the guards opened my food bucket outside my cell instead of inside. This made me suspicious again, and by listening closely I could hear the paper wrapper being opened.

For the next two weeks I was sometimes sure and sometimes not sure that they were still trying to dope me. Most of the time I tried to avoid it, but often I just didn't care. I never found out why the powder was being given me, nor could I decide on any certain theory of my own. At times I thought perhaps it was medicine, given to counter the effects of the long interrogation. At other times I considered the truth-drug angle. Was it something to build my health or destroy it? Was it something to destroy my power to reason or was it a harmless sedative given to induce complacency, thus lowering my resistance to interrogation? I didn't know, but I do know that when they began interrogating me again, my resistance was not what it had been before. Among other things, my physical condition was at its lowest and the memory of my week of standing was still too fresh. All the pain had not left my body and I was still in somewhat of a daze. Was this alone enough to reduce my will to resist or did the powder have some subtle effect? I don't know.

My next interrogation came a week after my "long stand." When I heard the familiar steps of Big Stoop approaching, I expected to be taken back to the Blue Room. Instead he led me to a small room in a different part of the prison. Inside the room, behind a desk, sat my old friend, the number one interrogator.

He greeted me with a smile and motioned me into the chair facing him. He asked about my health and offered me a cup of tea from the pot on the desk. Not knowing why, I refused. I also refused the cigarette he offered me from the green-and-white pack he pushed across the desk. I don't know why; I wished later, while back in my cell thinking about the interrogation, that I had not.

The conversation that followed was of a casual and not unpleasant nature. He explained that there would be more interviews for me during the next few days or weeks. How many depended on me—on whether my "attitude" showed improvement. He said I would be asked questions, but the interviews were to test my attitude. I wondered if they would ever drop that line. He assured me that I would not be put under pressure to answer the questions. They already had all the information they wanted and could tell me much about my unit's operations that I didn't know. It seemed they would never give up trying to convince me that an interrogation was for things other than to get information. However, I did not argue with him.

He ended the chitchat by saying that the series of interviews to follow would be used to determine what my future would be. I must try to overcome my extremely poor attitude of the past so that the court would be lenient with me when my case came to trial. Once or twice before they had mentioned a case and trial, but to my knowledge, prisoners of war were not subject to trials. I said as much, but might as well have saved my breath. I got the same old line about having "invaded Chinese territorial air." The interview lasted about an hour.

This was the eighth of April—my eighty-sixth day in Communist hands. Throughout the rest of the month and most of May, the interviews came almost daily and lasted usually about ninety minutes. In June they came only intermittently. Although the interrogator quite often became impatient with me, he never attempted to get rough. He no longer cursed me, but often ridiculed me for being stupid and refusing to understand that he was trying to help me. My attitude was a constant subject; it was brought up each time I refused to answer questions.

Many of the questions I knew nothing about. Others I had already answered. The interrogator often asked me to "tell again" what I had said about such and such a thing, an obvious trick to make me think I had already given the information. He constantly explained that he was already in possession of all the information he wanted about my unit. Pointing to his red-backed notebook, he said, "This book contains everything we need to know about your Wing, and still you refuse to answer questions. You are being very, very foolish!"

Once I asked to see the red notebook, thinking he would never allow it. He did, however, open it at random and let me glance over a couple of pages. He probably did know a great deal about me, my fellow crew members, and our operations, but I was not stupid enough to fall for his line about not wanting more information. He did want one other thing, however—a confession of having flown into China for the purpose of conducting subversive activities. He twisted statements around to imply as much, but he never got what he really wanted.

At the end of each interview I was dismissed with instructions to think about certain things back in my cell. Sometimes instead of an interview the interrogator sent writing materials to my cell with a list of questions I was supposed to answer. Write all you know about such and such a thing, the note said, or, more often, write down what you told us about such and such. This was another obvious ruse, for in most cases I had not told them anything about such and such.

Although the interviews offered a welcome break in the sitting routine, they soon became boring. Once when paper and pen were sent to my cell, I used them to draw one of the houses I had mentally designed. The guard watched me, but since he could not read English, he did not know that I was not following the instructions of the note. When I completed my drawing I wrote on another sheet of paper that I did not know the answer to the questions. I gave this sheet to the guard, intending to keep the house drawings. The guard had other ideas. He knew how many sheets of paper he had given me and he insisted that I return the same number. Finally I gave up arguing and let him have the drawings.

It was only a matter of minutes before I was taken out of my cell to the interviewing room. The interrogator asked me to explain my drawings. I did so and was severely chastised for daring to play games with the Chinese People's representatives. My "extremely poor attitude" was mentioned again, along with other things concerning my doubtful "future."

Thereafter the guards took it upon themselves to see that I didn't draw pictures and they refused to accept a paper from me unless there was more than "I don't know" written on it. I didn't care.

Sooner or later they took it anyway. Once I filled a sheet with "I don't know" and gave it to the guard. He didn't notice that it was all repetitions and left with a big smile on his face, no doubt thinking that my attitude had taken a change for the better. The smile was gone when he returned a little later. He stood staring through the peephole muttering curses for several minutes. The interrogator never mentioned the incident.

The month of April saw the guards and jailers preparing for Chinese spring. One of the first signs showed up in the latrine, which was now clear of ice. With large buckets they dipped the cesspool dry and carried the full buckets through the patio outside. The smell was terrible. Next they removed the two coal stoves that were outside in the lofty, drafty corridor. They disassembled the stovepipes, and for hours the cell block resounded with the noise of sticks beating against metal as they cleaned the stoves and pipes before storing them in an empty cell.

This noise and activity were a godsend. The jailers used Chinese prisoners to help with some of the spring cleaning, and while any of them were in the corridor my peephole stayed closed for minutes at a time. I took fullest advantage of this wonderful opportunity. Although the guard still stood outside the door, the noise effectively screened my movements and, by keeping a constant watch on the guard's shadow against the flap cover, I was able to stand up and move my arms and legs with a freedom that had not been mine for over two months.

At first my movements were extremely cautious. I took a few seconds of the mildest exercise immediately after the guard looked in, and then I sat and waited until he looked in again before stretching any more stiff, aching muscles. Then I grew more and more bold and ventured some quick push-ups and deep knee-bends between peeps of the guard. A few of these were enough to tire me out and I soon contented myself with less strenuous exercise. Unfortunately, the stove removal only took a couple of days and then the guards resumed their almost constant watch.

Approaching spring was heralded in other ways, though somewhat prematurely, I thought. I was given a pair of straw sandals in exchange for my flying shoes. Not only did my feet suffer from the cold, but they also were in danger of becoming permanently deformed from having to wear shoes which were a good inch too short. When I showed the jailer that it was impossible to fit my feet into the new sandals, he solved the problem by folding in the back so that my heel extended beyond the back of the shoe. I protested daily, but was forced to wear my new sandals for nearly three weeks.

To add further to my discomfort, Horseface decided I was not getting enough fresh air. He proceeded to remove part of the paper which was pasted over the cell window. There was no glass behind it, so the temperature inside immediately dropped several degrees.

This was not all bad, however. I could now hear outside activities better. The prison public-address system which I had heard occasionally was now louder. It blared away several hours a day, giving out Oriental music and long-winded speeches. Now and then, but far too infrequently, Western classical music was broadcast. I occasionally recognized a Chopin Polonaise. Once I heard "Red Wing" from beginning to end, and decided I had never heard a more beautiful piece of music in all my life. Less musical, but only a little less enjoyable, was a harmonica played by some unseen guard or jailer just outside my window. The only tune he ever practiced was "Clementine." These brief interludes of familiar sounds were a priceless break in my dull life.

Each morning a few minutes after the bell roused the prison's occupants, the public-address system sent out a half hour of "music to exercise by." Though it was strictly oriental, its purpose was made obvious by the rhythm and by the vocal cadence that accompanied the music. The program appeared to be coming from a radio connected to the public-address system, and I presumed that good Communists all over China were doing their morning jerks in obedience to its command. Another early morning sound was the braying of donkeys. There appeared to be a dozen or so of these vociferous animals stabled somewhere near the prison.

Just as the donkeys greeted the mornings, the nights were ushered in by a flock of birds which apparently roosted in a tree near my cell. I caught occasional glimpses of them as they flew past the hole in the paper over my window. They were the size of American crows and looked like them except for white breasts and white stripes on their wings. The noise they made may have been that of a crow, but if it was, they cawed in Chinese. These jail-birds were a noisy bunch; they reminded me of my interrogators. They fought and scrapped and seemed unable to get to roost at a reasonable hour. The least disturbance set them off, flapping and squawking. I asked my interrogator the name of the birds, but he smiled and said, "Just birds."

Each evening, drill exercises were held not too far from my cell block. They lasted two to three hours and were accompanied by one of the least talented, but most persistent, drummers I have ever heard. The sound faded and grew, faded and grew as the marchers paraded back and forth. I somehow got the idea that they were a group of young kids, playing soldiers—Young Communists, probably.

The various noises outside my cell helped, somewhat, to fill the long, vacant hours. They furnished a small amount of entertainment to a life otherwise completely void of any pastime except that of a purely mental nature. I should not say completely void, for the normal and natural acts of eating, urinating, and occasionally defecating took on an unnatural importance. They offered the only breaks in my sitting and sleeping routine.

In the middle of April there was a new interruption. Just a few days after I could no longer detect any tampering with my food, I was visited by the doctor. He looked at my eyes and down my throat, listened to my chest with his stethoscope (U.S. Medical Corps brand), and pressed his thumb into my leg.

I had not asked for a doctor, and though I had plenty of aches and strange symptoms, I saw no particular need for one. He left after checking me over, and that afternoon I was visited by a trio of doctors. None of them spoke English and there was no interpreter present, so I couldn't ask the reason for all the attention.

The three of them looked me over, taking my pulse, blood pressure, and temperature. Several minutes were spent in consultation. Finally they left, but a little later a female nurse entered my cell armed with a small hypodermic syringe and another one considerably larger. She quickly and efficiently gave me a shot in the arm and an injection in a vein. The entire business was enough to give me a bad case of hypochondria, but I was too bewildered to protest.

Next morning, when the same nurse appeared, armed as before, I refused to submit. I indicated to the guard that I wanted an interpreter. He sent for one and shortly number one interrogator came in.

"What is you matter?" he asked.

When I told him my matter, he informed me that I was being given glucose and vitamin B to build up my health. He said the doctor told him that there was nothing seriously wrong with me—I was just in a run-down condition. That was the world's most understated understatement; I peacefully submitted to being shot, injected, pulsed, and temperatured. This routine continued twice a day for the next twenty days. After that the shots and injections stopped, but the nurse continued to take my pulse count and temperature for several more days.

I was never fully convinced that my run-down condition, which could have been easily treated by a bigger and more nutritious food ration, was the sole reason for the medical treatment. Dizzy spells, ringing ears, and palpitating heart made me wonder at times if there were not more serious things wrong with me—things purposely caused by drugs. But I soon learned to ignore all my symptoms just as I ignored all the other discomforts of prison life.

A few other welcome changes began to take place. Horseface entered my cell one day brandishing a rusty pair of hedge shears.

With these he proceeded to trim my fingernails while I sat in mortal fear of losing at least a finger if not a hand. He trimmed my nails closer than I would have dared with a pair of conventional nail scissors. He didn't stop with my fingernails—he did my toenails as well, and, contrary to my fears, he did so without drawing blood.

On the fourth of May the padded clothes and flying suits I had been wearing so many weeks were replaced by a new outfit. At the same time I was given a pan of hot water and allowed to bathe from head to foot. What a glorious feeling! It was my first bath in over three months. The cell was cold and the guard tried to hurry me, but I refused to be hurried. Clean clothes and a bath—what a holiday!

My new clothes consisted of a pair of coarse sack shorts and an undershirt, a pair of thin black cotton pants and a shirt of the same material and color. These outer garments would have passed for pajamas at home, but here they were my all-day clothes. On the seat of the shorts, on the front and back of the undershirt and top shirt, and on the left knee of the trousers was sewn the Chinese character for *prisoner*, which looked like a man standing in a square. The one on the seat of my shorts made sitting very uncomfortable. It was cut from a heavy piece of cloth, and I'm sure its imprint was still visible many weeks after the patch was removed some months later.

Just as my winter clothing had not kept me warm, my new issue of summer clothing did little more than keep me from turning blue. After seeing me shake and shiver for a couple of days, the jailer returned my padded coat. It was a big improvement, but my bottom half still suffered.

The abrupt switch from winter clothing to two thin layers of summer cottons brought on just what one would expect—a severe cold and cough. This was aided by Horseface, who suddenly decided I needed still more fresh air and proceeded to remove all the paper covering from my cell window. I was in grave danger of dying from exposure, so the nurse, on one of her visits, held a long discussion with the guard. Soon a jailer brought two glassed shutters and hinged them into place. Why they had been removed and paper put up instead was a mystery to me, but there was no doubt that the two shutters had been there before—the hinges, screws, and latches matched the window-casing perfectly.

My severe cough brought on another visit from a doctor, and this time I knew I needed one. I was sick with fever and chills and could hardly sit. An interpreter was present to help the doctor in his short examination. Before leaving he asked, "Have you ever had T.B. before?" The word "before" alarmed me, but he assured me that I did not have tuberculosis.

When the paper over the window was removed, I gained a cell mate—almost. "Stingie," a wasp, staked out a claim on the wooden blind that shielded the lower half of my window. Watching him, or her, lay the foundation for a nest and add to it each day furnished many hours of entertainment. I watched Stingie's home go up (or rather down, since it hung underneath a board) from the first daub of gray stuff until the last cell was completed. At first Stingie worked all alone, but as one of the cells neared completion, another wasp, presumably of the opposite sex, made an appearance. Things went along smoothly until a third wasp showed up—then there was trouble. The newcomer wasn't easily discouraged, however. He continued to show up for two or three days before he finally became convinced he wasn't wanted.

The nest construction was interesting to watch. The two wasps began work about an hour after sunrise and usually kept at it until nearly sunset, although on warm days they were not above taking off a few hours in the middle of the day. They made several trips for building material, gradually adding to the nest. Then one stayed at the nest, flying in rapid circles round and round the newly added part. At first I thought the circling wasp had gone off its rocker, but I soon decided he was speeding up the drying process of the paperlike building material by beating his wings. While this went on, the other wasp brought more material and added it to the edges of the nest. Slowly, day by day, the nest grew until finally the center cell was completed. From that point on, construction was a one-wasp job; the other wasp devoted all its time to filling the cell with pollen after depositing an egg in it. Sealing over the cell was also her job. Their coordination was such that the second cell was ready by the time the first was filled and sealed.

This process continued for several weeks until finally the nest had fourteen cells. Not all of the cells were filled, however. The female wasp failed to show up one morning. Her mate continued working for a few days and then he, too, left, never to return. I wondered if this was normal or if they had met with an accident. I had no way of knowing. I waited eagerly for the young to hatch out, but the nest, too, met with foul play. Horseface spotted it one day while inspecting the window and knocked it down. I felt like knocking him down, but I was glad the two wasps were not there to see the destruction of their weeks of labor.

The only other friends I had in the cell were mosquitoes, flies, and an occasional flat, crab-like spider. The spiders were extremely fast and seemed to take great pleasure in scurrying across the floor toward my feet. This usually caused an equally fast movement on my part which, in turn, angered the guard. I always took the blame, for fear the guard would kill the spider if I showed it to him. I didn't like it crawling across my feet, but I enjoyed watching it and considered the spider more of a friend than the guard.

May slowly passed and June made its appearance. It was warmer and the temperature in my cell was more comfortable. June had big things in store for me. I woke up one morning and there was no guard at my cell door! At first I could hardly believe it. The corridor guard who usually made steady rounds of all the cells in my cell block looked in and then went on to the next cell. Before, he always skipped my cell, leaving it entirely to my own private guard. As the minutes passed and he made regular rounds, I began to hope I would no longer have a private guard to hound me.

Breakfast came and after that Horseface showed up. He took his usual post at my door for a few minutes and then came into my cell. He informed me that I must continue to sit as I had been forced to do in the past, then he left. Throughout the rest of that day and for several days following, one of my private guards slipped up to my door every few hours, peeped in, and then departed. My time under constant observation was over! What a relief not to have someone staring at me twenty-four hours a day. By careful calculation I determined that the Chinese had used over a year and a half of eight-hour man-days in guarding me the four and one-half months I had been their prisoner!

Of course the corridor guard still looked in at me every one to two minutes, but the minute or so between his rounds gave me an opportunity for freedom of movement that I had not known for months. I took fullest advantage of it. I didn't want the corridor guard to catch me violating prison rules for fear the permanent guard would be put back, but this was easily avoided with the exercise of a little caution.

The first thing I did was make a thorough inspection of my seven-by-nine cell. I had occupied it four months and had not yet been able to check the walls for writing. Anything scratched in the chalk-plastered walls was not visible more than a couple of feet away, so I started a systematic search of one small area at a time. The nearest thing to a message I found was in the form of a calendar. It wasn't designed as English calendars are, although it had English numerals. The days were written out, but in a language I could not read. I later determined it to be Russian. Whoever drew it had occupied the cell at least forty-five days—that was the number of days crossed off.

I found other groups of marks where prisoners had kept tally of the days. The longest had sixty marks. My stay had already made that unknown prisoner a short-timer. I scratched in my own vital statistics. To make sure the cell's next occupant would find it, I put my name, date of capture, and current date in three different places. Each day I brought it up to date.

After spending a couple of days inspecting the cell, I began to concentrate on looking out the window. This was somewhat more difficult, since the lower half of the window was covered by a wooden blind. To get a view of anything except sky and the roof of another prison building, I had to stand on tiptoe on my bunk. There was not much to see, but even this brought a welcome change after looking at the wall opposite my bunk for so long.

Outside my window was a triangular patio walled in by another building and a brick wall. Two trees and several circular flower beds with paths winding around them filled the space. The trees were putting on new leaves and flowers were already filling in the beds. In one corner there were a few dozen young stalks of corn. Brief glimpses of all this greenery were well worth the risks I ran. I was starved for sight of anything outside my cell.

Now and then I had heard people walking just outside my window. The next time I heard them, I took advantage of my wonderful few seconds of freedom to peep out. The patio, I discovered, was used to exercise prisoners. Sometimes one, sometimes a group of five or so were taken out and allowed to walk around and around the paths. There was always a guard or two watching. These guards invariably stood just under my window and nearly caught me peeping out on several occasions, but I got a good look at the other prisoners. Although they were all Orientals, the sight of human beings other than my hated guards and jailers gave me a fair amount of pleasure. I kept hoping that sooner or later some of my fellow crew members would be taken out for exercise. They never were.

All these additional activities added a little excitement to my life, but I was still very much a prisoner and time continued to pass slowly. I still had plenty of spare time for the mental activities which I used to combat boredom. I would have given much for something to study or something to read. On the few occasions that I asked for reading material, I was told to use my time thinking of ways to "atone for my crimes." If the crimes I had committed warranted the kind of treatment I received, I wondered what happened to real criminals who fell into Communist hands! The blood-chilling screams which still haunted some of my nights gave me a fair indication.

For a few days following the removal of my permanent guard, Horseface returned after supper to escort me to the latrine. I could now go once a day whether I needed to or not. That was another big improvement over the months during which my bowels had to regulate themselves to whims of the guards. Horseface appeared to have received a promotion of some sort. He no longer wore the brown of the guards. Instead he wore the blue of a jailer. No doubt his promotion was a reward for his untiring, never-ceasing vigil at the door of the American Criminal Number 1003, in cell number five, block number one.

I discovered that 1003 was my number when written questions were sent to my cell. The paper always had that number at the top. I asked my interrogator if it meant they were holding over a thousand Americans. He took it for a big joke, but replied, "No, only a few."

Gradually the intervals between Horseface's visits became longer and longer. One of the female jailers took over the duty of checking my cell periodically as well as escorting me to the latrine each evening. I had long since grown used to the guards standing in front of me while I squatted over the chute, but I never enjoyed having a female jailer peep through the door at me. Whether they became ashamed or if they finally satisfied their curiosity I don't know, but I was much relieved when, after a few weeks, the female jailers stopped watching me while I was in the latrine.

June tenth was a big day in my prison life. It was my one hundred and forty-ninth day as a prisoner, and not once had I had a haircut or even a shave. My hair was long and filthy, but worse, my moustache and beard had grown to immense proportions and were a source of constant irritation. They got in my mouth when I ate,

I could not drink without having them dip in my cup, they collected food and dust, they itched, and my reflection when I bent over a pan of water was enough to make me feel like the criminal I was accused of being.

I tried pulling out the longest of the hairs in my moustache, but soon gave that up. When Horseface made his second appearance with the hedge shears, I tried to get him to let me trim my face, but he refused. I had to bear with it and do what little I could to keep the brush patch clean.

On June tenth, Horseface, the warden, and two guards entered my cell along with another man in a white wrap. I didn't have long to wonder about the purpose of their visit. They surrounded me and the barber got busy with his clippers. He made quick work of both the hair on my head and the hair on my face, clipping it all as close as possible. When he finished there was enough hair on the floor to stuff a fair-sized cushion.

I felt like a different person and no doubt looked like one. The four observers stood back, smiling and chatting among themselves, as they looked at my clipped head. The rest of the day I was a major attraction for the guards and jailers. They came by singly and in pairs to peer through the door at me. Some of them went so far as to take off their hats, showing me their clipped pates. Chubby, one of my female jailers, performed her first kind act and gave me a pan of hot water to wash my head. What a pleasure! So very kind of them to give a prisoner a haircut—after five months!

To take the place of the mat of hair that had covered my head, Horseface brought me a black skullcap. I couldn't help admitting that it was an improvement. My only regret was that I did not have a mirror so I could see better what I looked like before the clipping—I knew that if I had my choice I'd never look that way again.

Four days later, on June fourteenth, I got another pleasant surprise. I heard the familiar walk of Big Stoop approaching, but instead of taking me to an interrogation, he led me out a small side door into the triangular patio. Describing a circular motion with his arm, he pointed to the well-worn path. I needed no further encouragement. Round and round I walked. I had an unrestricted view of a large tree and a couple of smaller ones that were not visible from inside my cell. The flowers, the clouds, and the sky made these few minutes outside comparable to a week's vacation back home.

Although I thoroughly enjoyed my outing, I was far from being at ease. The unaccustomed freedom was almost too much for me. I found myself glancing at Big Stoop, expecting him to shout at me at each step. I must have looked like a caged animal which has suddenly been released. I felt like one. I was almost relieved when, after a few minutes, I was taken back to my cage. The rest of the day I sat recovering from the excitement of my walk. I felt tight and tense as I tried to guess the significance of this new event in my life.

Interrogations were coming less and less frequently now. I hoped they were nearing an end, but I had no idea what to expect when they finally realized they had all the information they could get from me. After the treatment I had received at their hands, it seemed doubtful that they would ever release me. The best I hoped for was to be put with the rest of the crew.

The last of June did see the end of my interrogations. I did not know it; I was not told that there would be no more; they just stopped. I figured the Chinese had spent over two hundred and fifty hours prying information from me—two hundred and fifty hours spread out over five and a half months. They got some information from me, but what they tried for hardest they did not get. I knew I had done my best.

Early in July I was given a physical examination. I was taken to an empty cell in another part of the prison where a doctor and nurse had set up an office. I didn't know if they were authentic medical personnel, just as I don't know whether any of the doctors and nurses I had seen before were really what they appeared to be. Maybe they were for show, maybe not. It made little difference; there was nothing I could do about it.

The examination they gave me appeared to be thorough, although it was evident that more pains were taken in filling out the report than in looking at me. They performed most of the usual checks, but only one meant anything to me—the weighing. The scales were graduated in kilograms, but by making a mental conversion, I found my weight to be about one hundred and twenty pounds—some twenty-five to thirty pounds below normal. And it had been lower than that a couple of months before. In spite of my below-normal weight, I could tell that my waist was at least two inches larger than it had ever been—the result of months of total inactivity which let my arm and leg muscles dwindle away to nothing and bloated my middle.

My trips to the patio continued at the rate of one to three a week. They usually lasted around twenty minutes and were always a source of the greatest enjoyment, especially after I grew accustomed to being let out of my cage. As the month of July slowly passed and August began creeping by, I began to wonder if I had been salted away for the rest of my life. Only once did I see anyone other than the guards, the jailers and the occasional prisoners I peeped at through my window. This one time was after a minor revolt at not being allowed to exercise in my cell.

A few weeks after my permanent guard had been removed, I decided to see what would happen if I openly moved around in my cell. I had grown impatient at having to slip around between rounds of the guard, so I got up and paced back and forth, purposely letting the guard see me. He stood peering through the peephole, dumbfounded that a prisoner would dare be so bold. Finally he tapped on the door and motioned me to sit down. When I ignored him he called another guard, and after a short confab I heard one of them leave the corridor.

As I expected, the warden returned with an interpreter and read me the riot act. "Unless you obey the guards," he said, "you will lose the privilege of exercising outside and be put back under severe guard." I didn't press the issue. As it was, I lost a week of trips to the patio.

August saw one other out-of-the-ordinary event which for awhile was a great boon to my dull life. The prison officials graciously gave me something to read—one magazine and one book, to be exact. The magazine was the same copy of *China Reconstructs* which I had refused to read during my first few days of imprisonment. I read it now—at least ten times. The book was a report titled "Economic Progress in New China, 1951–1952." It was a mass of impressive figures and statements. I read it twice, then read it again—this time in Morse code, saying the dits and dahs for each letter. I practiced speed-reading, then I tried reading backwards. When I grew tired of this I tried reading upside down.

Thinking some of the crew might have been given the book and magazine, I checked them thoroughly for marks. Finding none, I made a few, hoping they would be passed on to someone else. After about two weeks I gave the books to Chubby and was given a pictorial printed in the Soviet Union—in Russian. Although I couldn't read it, I spent many hours trying to figure out words and the Russian alphabet. I gave this one back after four days, hoping I would get another in exchange. I didn't and wished I had kept it a little longer.

On the twenty-second day August I got the happiest surprise of my prison life. I was taken into the interrogation room where I was informed that I was going to be put into a cell with another crew member. The interpreter said he did not know which one, but I didn't care. The prospect of seeing and talking to a fellow American after 222 days in solitary confinement was great indeed!

CHAPTER

THIRTEEN

I had seen the interpreter early in the morning, and back in my cell, I impatiently waited for the change. When my noon meal was served I was too excited to eat much of it. I didn't know what time the change was to take place and, as the hours crept by, I began to wonder if the prison authorities were telling the truth. I was a model prisoner that day. I didn't do a thing to offend the guard for fear that it might jeopardize my chances of being taken out of solitary.

Finally about five in the evening, Horseface and Big Stoop appeared. They gathered up my bedding, bedboards, and urine bucket and, with another guard bringing up the rear, they escorted me through the rotunda, down one long cell block, and into another. They left me, along with my furniture, in the first cell of the block. It was empty.

The cell was twice the size of my former one and had a window as well as a door opening into the corridor. The door was made of wood, but was heavy and solid. It was fastened on the outside by a crude but effective iron bolt. I noticed that there was no lock on the door. There was no need for one; it was impossible to open the bolt from inside the cell. The corridor window had iron bars instead of glass and the lower half was screened with a piece of heavy cloth. In one corner of the cloth was a hole about six inches square—the usual peephole. It was covered with a cloth flap. At the opposite end of the cell, there was another window which had glassed shutters inside and heavy wire mesh and a row of bars outside. Beyond the bars was a wooden blind which blocked the view through the lower half of the window, leaving only the top of an adjacent building, an electrified wire-capped wall and some sky visible through the top half of the window. In a hole in one wall, high up near the ceiling, burned an electric light. A heavy wire screen and a pane of glass sealed the hole. As in my last cell, there was no switch inside the cell. I wondered now that I was to have a roommate if I would still be required to sleep with a light on. I hoped not, thinking how great it would be to "see" darkness again after nearly eight months.

Soon I heard several people approaching. My cell door swung open to admit Big Stoop, Horseface, and Lieutenant John Buck, the bombardier from the crew. This was perhaps the happiest moment of my life. We shook hands, but could find no words. The guards set up his bunk along the wall opposite mine and for the next minute or so we just sat and looked at each other. After over seven months of solitary confinement we found each other's presence almost unbelievable. We didn't know how to begin a conversation or what to say. It was almost as if we were waiting for someone to tell us we could talk. But the guards and jailers had gone.

Finally we found our voices. We would say a few words and then laugh—at nothing at all. Everything we said seemed funny. The guard, walking up and down the corridor outside, must have thought we had lost our minds. The relief we found in each other's company, in no longer being alone, made us as light-hearted as kittens. I felt as if a heavy load had suddenly been removed from my shoulders. The sudden release of some of the nervous tension which had accumulated over the past months left us in a state approaching hysteria.

Our evening chow was brought in, and our talk and laughter was interrupted. For once we had little interest in eating—there was too much we wanted to say. The guard brought us back to reality by rapping on the bars of the corridor window. He indicated that we must not talk while eating. He wasn't concerned with our manners. It was the same old business of a prisoner eating as fast as possible. That had not changed with the change in our confinement.

We found it next to impossible to obey the guard's instructions. We did manage to speak lower when he was nearby, and this appeased him to some extent. That was the best we could do. Only after we began to lower our voices did we notice that there were other voices down the corridor, voices we could not recognize, but which were speaking English and bursting into laughter after every few words. The rest of our crew, we thought, but we were too busy talking ourselves to be very curious about them.

When the prison bell rang signaling bedtime, the guard again had to remind us to stop talking. We lay down, but sleep would not come. We whispered late into the night, often bursting into open and uncontrollable laughter. We were not alone. Low voices and not so low laughter could be heard coming from other cells. The guard busily ran back and forth, rapping on cell windows and growling ominous sounds, but he was up against more than human will. After all these months of silence except for the interrogations, we could not stop talking—not if our lives depended on it. Sleep came late, finally accomplishing what the guard could not do.

The next day was a continuation of the evening before. We talked and talked and everything seemed funny. During the morning we were visited by the warden and a girl interpreter who read us the prison rules as they applied to us now that we were no longer in solitary. They were the same as before, with the exception that we were allowed to talk. But they warned us against talking too loudly or trying to communicate with other prisoners—meaning, of course, other members of the crew in cells down the corridor.

The nearest crew members were only two cells away. It was about twenty feet from their cell door to ours, but the thick masonry walls and heavy doors made it impossible to understand words spoken at a normal voice level. Occasionally we could pick up snatches of conversation, but we were still not sure whose voices we were hearing, nor were we too concerned about it. Two weeks passed before our own conversation slowed down and we became curious about the occupants of the other cells.

Finally we decided to find out who of the crew was there and who was missing. When the guard was at the far end of the corridor, we raised our voices loud enough to be heard in the third cell and asked who was there. The talking suddenly stopped and we repeated our question. This time we received an immediate response—from two sources. One came from the third cell and the other from the guard in the corridor who rushed up to quiet us. While he stood looking in our cell, the crew members down the corridor raised their voices, gave their names and asked ours. When the guard rushed to their cell, we raised our voices again. This went on for several minutes—long enough for us to find out the identity of the occupants of the other cells. Finally we yielded to the guard's insistence that we lower our voices.

There were nine of us from the crew in the cells down the corridor. Across the corridor were cells containing three Chinese prisoners. All the other cells were empty. Five members of the crew were missing. Of these, two were known to have been captured and we presumed that they were somewhere nearby in another cell block. None of us had any information about the remaining three. We hoped that they had been picked up by rescue helicopters.

The guard was unhappy with us for the loud talking we had done and he speeded up his rounds from cell to cell, but apparently he was not sure that we had been talking between cells and did not report us. For the next several days we continued our conversations. Buck and I talked to our aircraft commander, Captain Vaadi, and the navigator, Captain Llewellyn, who occupied the third cell. They in turn talked to the other five who occupied two cells further down the corridor. In these two cells were the flight engineer, Sergeant Howard Brown, the radio operator, Airman Kiba, and three scanners, Airmen Schmidt, Thompson, and Benjamin. Missing but known to have been captured were our wing commander, Colonel John Arnold, and the instructor pilot, Major Baumer. Also missing and feared dead were the two radar observers and our tail-gunner. The guards finally put additional pressure on us to stop our loud talking, and we gave up for a few days, hoping they would grow lax.

Meanwhile Buck and I managed to get our first look at the other seven. The latrine for the cell block was in a cell directly across the corridor from us. Once a day a jailer escorted us to the latrine. When we were back in our cell, he did the same for the others, one cell at a time. Usually the corridor guard stood by the peephole at our cell window when the others were in the latrine. Occasionally he did not, and we took advantage of his absence to peep through the flap or, by standing on one of our bed platforms, over the cloth which covered the lower half of the window. These few brief glimpses of our friends were big events and afterwards we spent many minutes discussing their appearance. They looked quite different from the men who had been with us on "Stardust 40," but then we realized our own looks had not improved either. We tried to pass our comments down the corridor, usually joking about how ugly or how distinguished they looked. When we could, we made ourselves visible to them as they stepped out of the latrine into the corridor. But we had to be extremely careful that the jailer didn't see us.

For a while, time was no longer a burden. During the next few months, my cell-mate and I found much to talk about. We spent weeks telling each other everything that had happened to us since the night our B-29 was shot out of the sky. We passed as much of this as possible on to the other men in the cells down the corridor. In return we listened to their stories. This was done bit by bit, a few words at a time. Often a few words were the only contact we could make for several days—sometimes weeks. In this way I learned that the rest of the crew had been treated much the same as I had been.

When we were first taken out of solitary, we discussed the possibility of hidden microphones. Checking our cell over as much as we could, we found no evidence of any, but were careful to watch the subjects of our conversation anyway. We gave each other code names and assigned names to each of the cells. In addition to this, we passed on the bits of information each of us had been able to collect about the prison, its grounds and cell blocks. By pooling information and our geographical knowledge of China, we decided we were being held in Peking. Still we were not sure. All of us had asked our captors at one time or another the name of the place, but all had been refused an answer.

Periodically the guards and jailers got tough about our talking in violation of prison rules. If we pushed them too far they reported us and we received a visit from the warden. Sometimes he brought an interpreter and other times he berated us in Chinese. Either way his meaning was quite clear and we laid off for a few days. During one of these visits I asked the interpreter, just for kicks, the names of the men down the corridor. He refused to tell me and even refused to admit that they were Americans—in spite of the fact that he had just finished reading me the riot act for talking to them. This was typical of their attitude toward giving us information of any kind. After that, whenever the guards, jailers, or anyone else accused us of talking between cells, and even when we were caught in the act, we denied it emphatically.

To cut down on the amount of loud talking necessary to carry on a conversation with the men in the other cells, we developed, with the help of Kiba, the radio operator, a coughing code. This began by substituting a single cough for "no," two for "yes," and three for "I don't know." But soon we devised a more elaborate system. Using the standard Morse code which we all knew, we pretended to have a coughing spell and hacked out entire sentences in dits and dahs. We all developed sore throats for a while, but with a little practice after our windpipes toughened, this method of communication became highly effective. It carried through the entire cell block, letting every one of us hear what the sender was saying and eliminating the need to relay messages from cell to cell. Later when we were again partially separated, we were able to use this method of communication between cell blocks which were some distance apart.

The guards apparently had never heard of the Morse code, for it took them a surprisingly long time to get wise to us. In our favor was the fact that almost all the guards had chronic coughs, making our own hacking less noticeable. Also there was usually at least one of us with a real cough. It was easy to convert a legitimate cough into code, accomplishing two things at once. Few coughs were wasted, but whenever one of us was unable to control a fit of real coughing, the others were thrown into confusion trying to decipher what had not been said. After the guards finally caught on, some of them walked up and down the corridor coughing away, trying to imitate and confuse us. This was easily detected as fake, but sometimes we heard coughing which sounded artificial coming from other corridors. We listened for hours hoping it was one of the missing crew members, but it always turned out to be a Chinese prisoner or a guard with a real cough.

We had such success with our hacking that for a long time we relied almost entirely on it for intercell communication. Even after the guards figured out what was going on, most of them were hesitant to call us down for it. They could never be sure when it was real or when it was artificial. Whenever they did try to stop us, we went to great lengths to pretend it was necessary, coughing more, clearing our throats, and using the bucket in the corner. Captain Vaadi was so convincing that the guard sent for a doctor. Vaadi got a bottle of cough medicine, which did nothing to cure his cough. A second visit by the lady doctor and more medicine brought the same negative results, and I suppose she gave him up as incurable.

As effective as it was, the hacking code was slow and, in order to keep from sounding too obvious, we were forced to limit it to short periods. It far from filled the desire we all had to talk at length with each other. The ridiculous and unreasonable prison rules which prohibited us from openly seeing, visiting, or even conversing with anyone except our cellmates made us bitter toward the guards and jailers. They were aware of our hatred. As we became more accustomed to our new situation, we grew bolder and openly defied them at times. On several occasions each of us reached the point of bursting from pent-up anger. The guards bore the brunt of these explosions and then called for a jailer. Whenever this happened, the entire cell block, including the Chinese prisoners across the corridor, were perfectly quiet. But if the conflict sounded serious, the rest of the crew in the other cells became noisy to draw the guard's attention to themselves.

The result of this sort of thing was usually not too serious as long as we didn't take it too far. We usually calmed down by the time the jailer or warden arrived. We had little desire to force them to save face by carrying out their threats and putting us in handcuffs or returning us to solitary confinement. Occasionally we didn't stop in time, and some member of the crew found himself in cuffs for a few days.

Often we amused ourselves by teasing a guard. Choosing a time just after he looked in our cell, we made an unusual noise. He came rushing back to see what we were doing and found us sitting just as we had been when he last looked in. He stood and stared a few minutes and when he started toward the next cell we did the same thing again. After about the third or fourth time, the guard would be fuming. One particular guard checked very thoroughly every time he looked in, eyeing the walls, the window, the bunks, ceiling, and every item inside the cell. The normal guard round was still every two to three minutes and he did the same thing every time. During the short intervals that he was away, we changed the position of some article in the cell—usually the short window stick. Each time he looked in, it was on the opposite side of the window from where it had been the last time he saw it. He always noticed and tried time and again to catch us in the act of moving it. We were still supposed to sit on our bunks, and when the guard couldn't catch us moving the stick, he became slightly unhappy. He pointed to the shifted object and muttered curses, while we sat and pretended not to know what he was mad about.

The system of guarding us was the same as it had been just before we were taken out of solitary. We had one guard who walked up and down the corridor, looking in each cell as he passed. The corporal of the guard continued his half-hour rounds and a jailer brought our food and let us out of our cells when we went to the latrine. Neither the guards nor the jailers were armed. In peeping through the window, however, I had noted that the guards always kept one hand in their pocket. I wondered why. With more peeping during guard changes, I saw that some object was stealthily passed to the next guard. For a long time I was unable to see what it was, but finally one of the guards dropped it while giving it to his relief. I was peeping through the window flap at them, and I saw it was a police whistle—kept handy, no doubt, so that the guard could give an alarm in case of serious trouble. It was an effective method of guarding, since it was impossible for a prisoner to get anywhere near an armed guard, yet a blast of the whistle would bring plenty of armed guards to quell any trouble.

Some of our corridor guards appeared to be little more than boys. There were many short ones, some of whom must have been less than five feet tall. They had to stand on tiptoe to see through the peephole into the cells. One of these earned the name "Banty Rooster" by strutting up and down the corridor with his chest puffed out like a cock ready to fight. He made up for his size by his actions, however. He did his best to see that we obeyed all prison rules, and whenever he thought we were talking too loud he rushed up, raising his chin above the window sill, and growled something that sounded like *"walla walla, pu shih, walla walla, pu shih."* His voice and his facial expression were as tough as he could make them. His words obviously meant "loud talk is forbidden" or something similar, but we informed him that Walla Walla was a city in Washington. He couldn't understand, of course, and became even more angry.

We named another of the very short guards "The Great Expectorator." With almost every step, he cleared his throat and deposited the results on the corridor floor with a mighty splat that could be heard all through the cell block. This was an operation that continued throughout his entire two-hour guard tour, day or night. We credited his throat-clearing to nervousness.

Still another of our guards was so young and short that at first he wasn't allowed to walk a guard tour alone. For a week he followed in the footsteps of an older guard, making every move he made and staying a few steps behind him. The old hand would look through a peephole and move on to the next. A couple of seconds later, "Baby" snapped open the same flap, peered in, and then he, too, moved on to the next cell. The two seldom spoke to each other while on duty, but it was obvious that Baby was receiving on-the-job training. After a week he was allowed to take over the job all alone. He hastily made his rounds, stopping only when he found one of us breaking some prison rule. He was too timid to call us down, but he stood and stared at us. We stared back and this always got rid of him. He quietly closed the flap and eased away, muttering to himself words that he had heard the other guards use. We teased and picked on him for a few days, but soon grew rather fond of him. Feeling sorry for him, we stopped our teasing and tried to befriend him instead. We were careful never to let the corporal of the guard catch us violating any prison rules while Baby was on duty. This made it appear that he was doing his job well and had us properly subdued. In return he let us do as we pleased. We could talk between cells, sing, or even walk around inside our cells freely, which at this time was still forbidden.

There were few guards with whom we were able to work out such congenial relations, however. Most of them continued to do their best to make life miserable for us. Often we tried to talk to them, hoping to get information about the remainder of our crew or news of the war. They rarely responded to our offered friendship, and even if they did, they never told us anything we wanted to know.

There was one exception. For a week in November, 1953, we had a complete guard change. None of us had ever seen any of the guards around the prison before. Apparently a new bunch had arrived. All of them wore new uniforms, but they were quite obviously not rookies. They were young, but not as young as some of our past guards. Only a few would talk to us, but almost all of them were friendly. Those who did talk knew a few words of English. They had apparently had some contact with American soldiers somewhere. Either they had just returned from Korea, had been POW's, or had guarded captured Americans. Whatever the case, they had no hatred for us, and this was a very pleasant change. They had the carefree attitudes of combat soldiers on leave and could not have cared less what we did as long as we stayed in our cells.

This was our tenth month in the hands of the Communists; we were still kept completely in the dark about everything that was happening in the outside world. Naturally we clutched at every tiny straw of information, and often our imaginations filled in things we wanted to hear. We had several different theories about our new set of guards: the war was over and they were Volunteers returning home; they were released POW's, in which case we too would soon be going home. These were typical thoughts. The guards' skimpy knowledge of English and our even skimpier knowledge of Chinese gave us the freedom to assign any meaning we desired to the words that passed between us. For the first time we really felt as if we might be near release.

The week the new guards were on duty was almost a vacation, but we were soon faced with our old guards again. They immediately tried to stop our talking and our exercising. They were as sour as usual and life became pretty routine again—different, by far, from solitary confinement, but still dull and tiresome.

After a few months my cellmate and I had told each other our life stories over and over so many times that we knew each other as well as ourselves. We were at a loss for things to talk about. Every time we started to say something or ask a question, we realized that we had already said it or asked it, probably not many days before. We were out of anything new to offer each other in the way of entertaining conversation. For this reason we wanted badly to talk freely with the other men down the corridor. We asked to be changed from cell to cell now and then so we would have different cellmates to talk to. This was summarily refused. We asked for reading and studying material. They said they would see.

Two or three times each week, the jailers took us out of the cell block into the adjoining patio for short periods. Here we could exercise and walk around among the flower beds; it was the high spot in our lives. Every four to six weeks the barber set up shop in an empty cell and our heads and faces were clipped. Once a month we were given water for washing our clothes. Each morning we received a small pan of water and were allowed the time to use it. Finally during the winter of 1953–1954, nearly a year after our capture, we were permitted to walk around inside our cells for a few minutes each day. About the same time our food became slightly more plentiful, but still far from satisfying our constant hunger. The food also developed a welcome variety. Rice was still the staple, but it was not unusual to get millet-seed gruel for breakfast instead of rice starch, or to get corn bread, noodles, or wheat bread instead of steamed rice for one of the other meals. Once in a rare while we got fried rice. Whenever that happened, our spirits soared. We acted like kids at an icecream party.

Food was no longer served in mess buckets. It was brought into the cell block in one large bucket and each prisoner got his share served in a small bowl. These bowls, along with our few toilet articles, were kept on shelves under small tables which were set up in the corridor. The tables were probably meant for the prisoners' use inside the cells, but instead they were kept outside. Our green enamel drinking cups were the only article besides our urine bucket, bedding, and a window stick which we were allowed to keep inside our cells. The cups had to be kept in a position so the guards could see them at all times.

When the winter of 1953–1954 arrived, we were given the padded clothing which had been taken from us in the spring, along with a pair of heavier shoes. We got our winter clothing just in time. Our outside window had a northern exposure and several large cracks through which an icy wind found its way into the cell. As winter progressed, the contents of our bucket froze and any water spilt on the floor immediately turned to ice. Cold as it was, we fared far better than during the previous winter when we were not allowed to move around to keep our blood circulating.

Christmas of 1953 came, and we celebrated by wishing each other and our guards a merry one. On Christmas Eve we worked up a plan to greet each guard the following morning with the words "Merry Christmas" as he looked into the cells. We had some confused guards that day as they went from cell to cell and heard the same words come from the occupants. We greeted the jailer in the same way when he brought our breakfast. He became just as confused; he didn't know whether we were cursing him, complaining about something, or asking for something. After he made his rounds, the jailer came back to our cell to ask us what *"mer crismus"* meant, but we didn't help him out. Finally he left the cell block, muttering the words over and over to himself. When we saw him again, he had found out their meaning and was beaming from ear to ear. He put the guards wise and they, too, were visibly relieved.

Other than that, Christmas was no different for us than any other day. We did, however, decide that we would not spend another Christmas in prison. If we were still here when spring arrived, we would make some kind of an escape attempt. During the following week we formulated tentative plans.

I think we all realized that, unless there was a radical change in the way we were confined, there was no possibility of carrying out our plans. The system of guarding us made it impossible to make a break, either secretly or openly. Even if we could get out of our cells, the wall with the electric wires and the armed guards on top of the rotunda stood between us and freedom. And where would we go, once outside? None of us knew, but still we made plans. They helped us pass a few hours and gave us pleasure in thinking about the freedom we would have after we made an escape.

Our favorite topics of conversation, when we talked between cells, were the world situation and our chances of being released. We usually sounded optimistic. Each of us tried to keep the others cheered up. We did some fantastic reasoning to back up our opinion that we would soon be going home. Few, if any, really believed it, but it sounded good. Sometimes we faced the facts and admitted that we had no idea when, if ever, we would be parting company with our hosts. We simply had nothing on which to build our hopes. And the fact that we were in the Communist capital, as we supposed, seemed to indicate that we were considered important prisoners. We wondered if the Chinese intended to use us as pawns in a propaganda chess game, or maybe as hostages in political blackmail. If so, we felt that our situation might change at any time. On the other hand, it might never change.

During the winter we were given a few books to read. Some of these were novels by Chinese or Russian authors, written strictly along Communist Party lines. Most were war stories, both about World War II and Korea. They told of incredible feats of heroism performed by members of the various "people's armies."

A typical tale was about a member of the Chinese Communist Volunteers in Korea. This particular soldier, single-handed, charged an American machine-gun manned by four GI's. He killed one, wounded another, grabbed the two remaining "fear-crazed" soldiers, one under each arm, and returned to his lines. It was stated, significantly, that the machine-gun crew had "murdered" dozens of volunteers before it was knocked out. In all the stories the American soldiers murdered, but the Communists only killed. The Communist soldiers were credited with fantastic and impossible acts; the American soldiers were described as rapists, pillagers, torturers, and above all, cowards.

The books about World War II, both fictional and, supposedly, factual, twisted history beyond all recognition. The United States and its non-Communist allies got little credit for victory in Europe or in the Pacific. For instance, "The U.S.S.R. forced the Japanese to surrender in just six days after declaring war against them." Such is history as taught to school children behind the various curtains.

Other books had such titles as *Das Kapital*, *Problems of Leninism*, and *History of the Communist Party of the U.S.* We read these books for lack of anything else to do, and out of curiosity, but most of them made dull reading. One small travelogue diary by a British dean left us with exasperated and bitter anger. The author had just made a tour of Communist China and claimed to have visited and interviewed many prisoners, some of them American. He stated, among other things, that there could be no doubt that all the foreign prisoners held by the Communists were guilty. Their crimes ranged from germ-dropping to spying. To us, sitting in one of those prisons, this was a bitter pill to swallow. Could we have spoken to the dean, I think we might have convinced him of his errors.

During the many months that followed, we continued to receive reading material periodically. It averaged out, however, to be less than one book per month, which hardly made a dent in the long dull hours of idleness. We asked the jailers for chess or checker sets, but were refused. We could have made our own, but we had absolutely nothing in the way of materials. Playing cards were refused us also. A Bible, a dictionary, or any kind of textbook would have given us an opportunity to do something to improve our minds, but these, too, were refused. The Communists were afraid that prison life would not be miserable enough for us if they gave us these things. They wanted us to have time to sit and think about our "crimes."

In lieu of any other type of entertainment, we held quizzes and made up stories. We planned menus and voted to see which ones were the best. We made elaborate plans for our return home, and we told each other our life stories for the umpteenth time. But all of this filled only a small part of the hundred or so hours in each day—days intentionally made longer by the devilishly ingenious methods used by our jailers.

With the arrival of Spring in 1954, we celebrated our fifteenth month in jail. It came and went without our attempting to execute our escape plans—there was no possible chance. We received a summer issue of prison clothes and our first bath of the year. Sam, one of the jailers, put a large wooden tub in an empty cell and filled it with water. We all used the same water and my cellmate and I were among the last. We got wet all over, if not very clean.

We took the bath as an indication that we would soon be released; the Communists wouldn't want us to go home dirty and smelly, would they? But then we took every little unexpected pleasure as a sign that we were on our way out. But when Captains Llewellyn and Vaadi were suddenly separated and one of them moved to a distant cell block, we decided that we might not be as close to release as we thought. This happened one night just after supper. They were punished for being "disrespectful" to a guard and were put in solitary for one hundred days. So, for a hundred days our hopes for release were meager. We did not know that the Korean War was over. We thought the only way we would be released was if the American army invaded China and captured Peking. As far as we knew, the Third World War might already be under way.

Meanwhile, time continued to creep by and we oscillated between hope and despair. We learned to live with despair and joke about it. We wondered if the Chinese would pay us our retirement allotment when we became eligible, or if our families had collected our insurance yet. On the rare occasions when we were visited by interpreters, we asked about the war and the world situation in general. They either replied that they did not know or that we had no need to know—just one more expression of Chinese humanity, served up Communist style.

The quantity and quality of our food continued its gradual improvement, but spread over a period of months this was hardly noticeable. There was still plenty of room for further improvement. The thin soup we had received in solitary was replaced by a sort of stew or, sometimes, by a small bowl of vegetables. When we found meat in the stew, it was an occasion for much discussion. A piece as big as a thumbnail was rare. Cornbread replaced rice almost entirely for one meal of the day. This gave us a welcome change from the stones and snails we found in the rice. All we found in the bread were straws and sticks. Once or twice a month we were given vegetable pies—bread stuffed with chopped leeks. Summer or winter our only drink was steaming hot water, served after each meal and once or twice between meals.

One month after our bath in the wooden tub, Sam gave each of us a new towel and a cake of soap. Then clearing the way through the corridors, he escorted us to the opposite side of the rotunda and into a long low building. This was, wonder of wonders, the prison bath house. Inside we found a row of shower stalls, complete with hot and cold running water! I had almost forgotten that such things existed. The stall doors had latches on the *outside* and contained the usual flap-covered peepholes.

My cellmate and I quickly undressed and stepped into two of the stalls. A guard locked us in and Sam departed to bring another cell full of Americans to take a bath. Soon all nine of us were locked in shower stalls and, as the guards walked up and down looking through the peepholes, we could hear each other splashing around and enjoying the luxurious feeling of hot water pouring over our bodies. For once I didn't mind the peeping of the guard—I was far too engrossed in soaping and rinsing to notice. The showers raised our spirits considerably and caused much optimistic coughing back and forth through the cell block. We took them every four to ten weeks after that, and they remained a source of the greatest pleasure.

During the summer months we were taken outside to exercise in the patio almost daily—Sundays excepted. We stripped to our shorts and absorbed as much of the delicious sunshine as possible in the few minutes we were out. It took half the summer to get the chill left by the cold winter out of our bones.

In the summer of 1954, we were moved to another cell block, but it was no different from the previous one and life continued without change—without change, that is, until August ninth.

My cellmate and I were becoming more and more bored and had been giving the guards more and more trouble. Our nerves were on edge and our tempers short. We talked too much and too loudly and refused to sit when the guards told us to. If the guard cursed us, we cursed back; sometimes we shouted at them for merely peering into our cell. This happened only when we felt exceptionally low and were fed up to our hats with the guards. Usually we used more discretion, realizing that the guards were only obeying orders and that we were the Americans by which they judged all Americans. But something had to give, and that day we pushed them too far. We suddenly found ourselves in solitary confinement again.

This stint in solitary was not as bad as the last one, but it was far from pleasant. It was made easier by the fact that neither my ex-cellmate nor I were removed from the cell block. Instead of being together, we were put in two cells, side by side, with sixteen inches of brick and concrete between us.

Solitary confinement meant losing the privilege of talking, and the guards did their best to enforce our silence. I could hack, however, and the other men who were still together did their best to keep me entertained by talking to me. In addition to hacking code, I tapped on the walls. With members of the crew in the cells on either side of me, I could make my taps heard, even through the thick walls. But this was hard on my knuckles, and I used it only when I didn't dare cough.

By this time the guards had almost entirely given up trying to prevent us from moving around inside our cells. Much of my second tour in solitary was spent walking round and round like a caged animal or doing calisthenics. I set myself a schedule of exercises which I tried to increase each day. These included push-ups, sit-ups, deep knee-bends, and shadow-boxing. The guards didn't mind the others, but were sometimes disagreeable about the boxing. Maybe they knew what was in my mind.

After working at the various exercises for a few weeks, I was able to do calisthenics for three or four hours a day. In the course of a day, I did several hundred repetitions of each exercise. My favorite was sit-ups, probably because I could see more progress in the number I could do. My first attempt was a complete failure. I was not able to do a single sit-up, but I kept at it and soon I could do a dozen or so at a stretch. Within a few weeks this number increased to several hundred at one sitting, and once, in an attempt to set some kind of record, I did eleven hundred. I stopped then, not from lack of strength, but because I had rubbed the skin off a sensitive spot.

This sort of activity had both advantages and disadvantages. It helped pass the time and greatly improved my physical well-being. But on the other hand it created a ravenous appetite which I could not satisfy.

The other men up and down the cell block had started a similar program of exercise and they too felt the need for more food. We constantly badgered the jailer, and gradually we succeeded. Sam brought the food and we put this away and still asked for more. After each meal, when Sam left the corridor, we hacked out a chow report, cell by cell, telling how much rice or how many pieces of cornbread we had consumed that meal. This developed into a sort of competition that could well have had disastrous consequences if we had had unlimited food. Except that it was usually given in hacked code, a chow report sounded something like this: "Uncle, fourteen," "Whiskey, twelve," and so on down the corridor. This meant that the two occupants of "Uncle" cell had consumed fourteen pieces of bread that meal, and that "Whiskey" had consumed twelve. These amounts were not unusual because the pieces were very small, and more often than not it was a one-course meal. Whenever any cell gave an unusually low accounting in one of these reports, the rest of us were concerned and wondered if someone were sick. We encouraged the light eater to eat more and tried to draw him into conversation to cheer him up.

September 8, 1954, brought the best news we had had since becoming prisoners. We received mail from home! After nineteen months the Communists had notified the American Red Cross that we were alive. All these months our families had not known whether we were alive or dead. Our captors had kept the outside world completely in the dark about us. We had not known this, but had guessed as much. Now, after twenty-one months, we knew that our government and our families were aware that we were still alive. We had letters from home to prove it.

The letters came as a complete surprise. Without any forewarning of any kind, I was suddenly taken from my cell and escorted to one of the interrogation rooms. There sat the warden and an interpreter. They explained that the "kind-hearted" Chinese People's Government had contacted my family through the Chinese Red Cross and had allowed them to write me. I would be allowed to send them a letter in a day or two, he said, and I must try to show my appreciation for this kindness by obeying the guards.

With the letters from home came the first *real* hope that freedom might not be far off. The letters themselves brought no news which indicated this. If there had been any, it had been carefully clipped out by the prison censor. The fact that Uncle Sam knew I was alive gave me this assurance.

The next day the jailer brought me a pen and paper and I was faced with one of the most difficult tasks I have ever attempted. It had been twenty-one months since I had seen my wife, but my captors had mastered the art of expanding time. I had lived many years during those months—years more real than reality itself, and this gulf of time was hard to cross by letter. There was so much to say and yet so little. What could I tell my wife? That I was in solitary confinement? That according to my captors I was a criminal? That I had no idea when I might see her again? I could not say these things. I couldn't write about my daily life because this, too, might cause unnecessary worry and concern. Finally I wrote that I was in good health and hoped to see her soon. After that I asked questions. Sam had given me two sheets of paper and I found these more than adequate. There was nothing to say except things I knew the censor would never let pass.

On the thirteenth of September, I was again given paper and pen. This time I could only fill one page—nothing had happened in the four days since my first letter. In fact, nothing had happened in the twenty-one months since I had seen my wife—at least, nothing I could write about.

For weeks our mail was the main topic of conversation in the cell block. Those of us who were allowed to talk talked, and the rest coughed. We exchanged and compared news. We discussed, at length, the significance of this new and unexpected improvement in our situation. We all agreed that we would soon be leaving China, but we could not agree on just how soon. Some thought a few days and some a few months; all of us were guessing.

October 9 brought another encouraging development. During the morning several comparatively well-dressed and important-

looking strangers roamed through our cell block, talking to Sam
and peering through the peepholes at us. This alone was enough to
start us speculating; no one other than the jailers and guards
had paid us any attention for nearly a year. Soon after their departure, the prison barber came in and set up shop. This would
not have been unusual except that we weren't due for a clipping.
Our head and face stubble was only two weeks old, and it had
never been clipped more often than every four to six weeks. When
all our heads and faces had been shorn and the cell block had
settled back to normal, we began to pass around our ideas about
what was up. This was cut short by the entry of a couple of jailers
carrying bundles of new clothes.

In spite of the fact that my old clothing had not yet worn out,
I was given two new outfits. Furthermore, Sam took great pains
to see that they were fairly close to being the correct size. Soon
the warden entered my cell and checked the fit of my new clothing. When a shirt didn't fit to suit him, he had it exchanged. This
sort of treatment was completely unheard-of in the entire history
of my prison life. No one had ever worried about the fit of my
clothing. It had always been thrown into my cell, and if I could
get into it I had to wear it. Sometimes my undergarments were
twice the size of my outer clothing, but no one except me had
seen anything wrong with that.

While I was being outfitted, I could tell, by the opening of cell
doors, that the other men were getting the same treatment. We
couldn't communicate between cells with the jailers and the
warden in the cell block, but as soon as they left we started our
discussion. All nine of us had received new clothes and a few had
been given new cloth shoes. The new clothing was the same
pajama cut as the old had been, but there was one big difference
—none of it had the prison insignia sewn on it.

By carefully analyzing all these recent happenings, and no
doubt influenced by a lot of wishful thinking, we were pretty
much in agreement that our prison life would soon be over. Those

of us who were in solitary at the time, myself included, were slightly less optimistic, but certainly something was in the wind.

When our noon rice was served, one of the crew asked Sam if we were going to be released. The report that circulated through the cell block was that Sam had nodded "yes." We knew from past experience that he nodded yes to anything we said, but this did not keep us from believing what we wanted to believe—that within a matter of hours we would be free men. The remainder of the day passed slowly and speculation ran wild. Bets were laid about the place, day, and hour that we would cross the border on our way out of China. Plans were made for the trip home and we decided what we would eat first. Our menus varied greatly, but all had one thing in common—no rice, no cornbread, no water, in any form.

When the prison bell rang signaling bedtime, Sam visited each cell, telling us not to remove our clothes. Clearly he wanted us ready to depart on short notice. This was enough to chase sleep away completely and there was little done that night. We were forced to stop talking, but we continued to hack out occasional messages. One by one, in the early hours of the morning, we quieted down and fell asleep.

CHAPTER
FOURTEEN

Next morning our spirits were still high as we hacked out our call sign and a dah-dah-dit, dah-dah—Morse for G.M., which was short for good morning. Things were normal in the cell block until midmorning when, one by one, we were taken from our cells and out of the cell block. My turn came about ten A.M. and I was led to my old interrogation room. The attitude of the jailer and guard who escorted me dispelled any hope I had of being near release. Yet I still was not prepared for what came next.

Sitting behind a desk in the interrogation room was a man in an officer's uniform. He growled a question, "What you name?" These were obviously the only English words he knew and these not too well. He shoved some papers toward me, then handed me a pen, pointing to a place on another sheet of paper. Apparently he wanted me to sign for the papers I had been given. I wasn't anxious to sign for something I didn't know anything about, so I started to look them over. The officer grew impatient and, pointing again to the paper I was to sign, he recited, "You name, you name!"

I only got a glance at the papers I held, but that glance was enough to dishearten me completely. I could tell they meant nothing good for me. The guards and the officer were becoming more insistent, so I took the pen and printed my name in the space indicated. This was not what they wanted, but the officer allowed the guards to hustle me out.

Instead of taking me back to the cell I had just left, my escort led me into the cell block where I had spent so many months in solitary. The cell block was not in use and I was shoved into an empty cell. The jailer locked the door behind me and left a guard standing outside to keep watch over me. I was back where I had started twenty months before.

I remembered the papers I had just received, and while my guard watched closely through the cloth flap, I looked them over. I was holding an indictment and a charge sheet—two copies of each, one in Chinese and one in English. The indictment mentioned a trial to be held in the near future, but gave no date. The other listed the "crimes" that my crew mates and I had committed. According to the charge sheet we had sneaked into the territorial air of Communist China by plane to conduct espionage activities. We were accused of dropping supplies to spies and saboteurs.

They were the same crimes that I had been accused of hundreds of times during my interrogations, but I thought that they were part of the interrogation method, used to try to scare me into talking. The interrogators had also mentioned a trial, but that had been over a year ago, and I never thought they were serious. I knew I had not committed any crimes and I knew the Chinese Communists knew it. Coming close on the heels of our recently soaring hopes of release, the indictment gave me quite a shock, so much of a shock that I could not find an appetite for the bread that was handed in at noon. I forced myself to eat a few mouthfuls, but found it even more tasteless than usual.

I sat reading the charge sheet over and over, hoping to find something that I had overlooked which would make it sound less serious. But with each reading I became more discouraged. I knew I was not alone, however, for listed on the indictment were ten more members of the crew—the eight who had been in the same cell block with me and two more who I knew had been captured, but whom none of us had seen. The remaining three men of the crew, it stated, had met death in the crash of our B-29. This, too, was a blow; I had hoped that somehow those missing three had lived.

The indictment stated that the investigation of our case had been completed and the results were to be brought before the "Chinese People's Military Tribunal." I tried to convince myself that, after keeping us in prison so long, the Communists had to hold some sort of trial to justify their actions; that after the trial all of us would be released. I had little successs; the charges sounded much too serious.

During the afternoon I was taken to another small room where a man in civilian clothes and an interpreter sat. The civilian, I was told, was to be my defense counsel at the forthcoming trial. This worthy legal personage, or whatever he was, immediately told me that my only hope was to plead guilty. He stated further, through the interpreter, that the Chinese People's Court required all criminals to plead guilty before leniency would be considered. No mercy would be shown the criminal who refused to confess his guilt. Some defense counsel. I had no intentions of pleading guilty to nonexistent crimes and stated as much, but even as the words left my mouth I knew it was useless. The interpreter was visibly annoyed by my answer, but he did not lose his temper. Instead, he told me that I would learn, and then turned to his companion. I don't know if he gave him a truthful translation of my reply, but I doubt if it made any difference anyway. My defense counsel said a few more words about the advantages of pleading guilty, after which I was dismissed.

The guard, who had waited outside during the interview with my defense counsel, escorted me back to the cell I had just left and once again locked the door behind me. As I sat on the wooden bed platform, I could hear other cells at the far end of the corridor being opened, and I reasoned that the rest of the crew were being taken to meet their "defense." By counting the number of times doors were opened, I could tell that three other men had been brought into the cell block. I got a small measure of comfort in knowing that I had not been isolated completely. A few short hacked messages were exchanged before the guards made it clear this would not be condoned.

About midafternoon, two guards dressed in new uniforms and armed with pistols entered my cell. They snapped a pair of handcuffs around my wrists and escorted me through a number of long corridors and across a patio toward several waiting vehicles. One of these was a bus; I was pushed into it. Inside, sitting in a row on the floor between the seats, were seven of the crew. I took my place on the floor with them, and then Capt. Vaadi was led up and shoved in. Occupying the seats on either side of us were armed soldiers, all holding one hand on the wooden-holstered pistols strapped to their waists. There were two for each of us, plus a few extra in the front and back of the bus. They all wore new uniforms which were in sharp contrast to the faded and shabby ones worn by our corridor guards.

After a few minutes I could hear other vehicles starting up and soon our bus joined them, moving slowly through the prison gate into the street outside. The nine of us were closer together than at any time since bailing out of our burning plane, but we could not talk or look around. When we tried, we received an immediate cuff from a guard. Sitting as we were, with our backs between the knees of the person behind us, all nine had continuous body contact so we could still communicate with each other. By slight pressures, applied in longs and shorts, we were able to pass a few words of encouragement back and forth without the guards knowing it.

As the bus moved along we saw the tops of buildings and massive walls. Colorful temples with sweeping curves in their roofs and modern concrete structures were visible from where we sat on the floor of the bus. The guards, however, took a dim view of our looking around; they made it clearly understood that we were not on a sight-seeing tour.

The ride lasted close to half an hour and ended in front of a large three-story building which was one of several surrounded by a wall and spacious grounds. We were quickly hustled off the bus and through the large doors of the building. Here we were split into groups. I was led, along with Captain Llewellyn and Buck, to a room down a hallway.

Once inside the room our handcuffs were removed, and we were told to sit on the floor along one wall. The guards stood opposite us and made sure we didn't sit too close or communicate in any way. After sitting there several minutes we were escorted, a guard on each side, back to the center of the building and up a set of wide red-carpeted stairs. In a broad hallway at the top of the stairs we were lined up side by side with the rest of the crew. A guard took up a position directly in front of each of us.

First in this line of black-clad prisoners were the two members of our crew who had been kept completely apart from the rest of us. They were the ranking members—Colonel John Arnold and Major William Baumer. All of us were lined up by rank and crew position. Around us, hurrying back and forth and stopping to give instructions to the guards, were several Chinese dressed in brown woolen officer's uniform or the blue cottons of the prison officials.

A minor uproar was created when Colonel Arnold, our commanding officer, spoke to the man standing next to him. He was only trying to pass a greeting down the line to the crew he had not seen for so long, but even this cheering word was not allowed. Guards and officials hopped all about, and the guard standing in front of Colonel Arnold grabbed his arm and jerked him around to face the front. At this the airmen on the opposite end of the line started a commotion by grunting loudly, clearing their throats and stamping their feet. This immediately brought attention their way and it was some minutes before the guards and officials calmed down. The guards were easily rattled, it seemed—probably because of the presence of so much Communist brass. Even the brass were not very calm. It was becoming painfully obvious that the trial was going to be serious business—so serious that the accused were not even allowed to speak to each other. It was also plain that these representatives of the "peace-loving Chinese People" were not here to make friends with us.

As soon as things had quieted, we were faced about by the guards and marched into the courtroom. As we entered the large room, flash bulbs went off all around and batteries of floodlamps blinded us. There were cameramen with still cameras and cameramen with movie cameras. One end of the room was filled with spectators. At the other end, three impressive-looking officers sat on a platform in three large chairs behind three tall pulpits—the judges. We were halted in front of this platform, several feet back. The guards jerked us around to face the judges, then took up positions behind us.

To our left, there were four desks; behind one sat my defense counsel. Three other civilians were sitting near him, and I guessed they were the counsels for the rest of the crew. To our right, there were two other desks with officers occupying the chairs behind them—the prosecution, we soon discovered. Each desk had a microphone; two more were standing on the floor in front of us. Two armed soldiers stood near the judges, and others were spotted at strategic points about the room. Through an open door, to the right and behind the judges' platform, I could see a table full of recording equipment. Next to the door through which we had entered, there was a large table on which were laid out various articles of our survival equipment, the forty-five automatics each of us had carried, and pieces of flying gear that had been taken from us. Hanging on the wall behind the table were the orange-and-white nylon canopies of our parachutes.

As soon as the cameras stopped clicking and whirring, the proceedings got underway. A blue-uniformed interpreter stepped up to one of the microphones and called the court to order, first in Chinese, then in English. He asked each of us our names and rank, translating the replies for the benefit of the court. After this he read our case histories in Chinese and in English. He was careful to point out that we had been shot down and arrested after violating "Chinese territorial air."

Each of us knew this to be false, but months of protesting had done no good and we doubted if it would now. I suspected that only the few Chinese who were responsible for carting us across the Yalu actually knew the truth. No doubt most of the court firmly believed the charge to be true. I, along with the rest of the crew, waited and hoped that somewhere along the way we would get a chance to speak for ourselves.

The opening scene of our trial took more than half an hour. Obviously it was a show, a well-prepared propaganda production with a written script and all. Probably all the participants had rehearsed their parts—all but the eleven prisoners.

During the English reading of our case histories, Colonel Arnold made a comment which threw the court into confusion. Quite obviously this was not part of the script. One of the judges, silent until then, asked what had been said and, when he was told, uttered a few words not very becoming to so dignified a personage. When the court had quieted down, that part of the show was rerun.

Next we were marched out of the room and escorted back to our various waiting rooms. Three of us—Captain Llewellyn, Buck, and myself—sat on the floor for the better part of an hour, and I began to wonder if the trial was already over. Finally Captain Llewellyn and I were led out, up the stairs, and into the courtroom. Capt. Vaadi was already standing there in front of the judges. We were lined up beside him and again asked our names and rank. More pictures were taken as we stood there.

The interpreter read the charges as they applied to the three of us specifically. They were the same as before, but in more detail. We were accused of navigating and piloting our B-29 into Chinese territorial air to carry out espionage and to aid counter-revolutionaries. We had brought arms and radios with us to support the enemies of the "peace-loving Chinese People." Then the prosecutor went into his act, expanding on the crimes we had supposedly committed. He pointed out the things on the table by the door, saying they were undeniable proof of our guilt. The "evidence" was there for all to see, he said, referring to our parachutes and various other articles—articles that are standard flying gear for American airmen flying anywhere in the world. In his words, our emergency radios and survival kits became articles of espionage and our forty-five pistols were arms to aid counter-revolutionaries. Photographers flocked around the tables, snapping pictures of the evidence.

When the prosecutor finished, we were jerked around by the guards and taken back to our waiting rooms. As Captain Llewellyn and I resumed our places on the floor, Buck was taken out. He returned several minutes later, after having been indicted with the remainder of the crew.

For some reason the trial was being held in stages. We were taken singly or in small groups before the court. Maybe they were afraid things would not go smoothly if they tried us all at once, or maybe they were accusing us of different crimes, according to our rank and crew position. The latter seemed more likely.

We continued to sit, wondering if we would be allowed to say anything in our defense and wondering what good it would do if we did. After several minutes Captain Llewellyn and I were once again escorted to the courtroom and, as before, took our place beside Captain Vaadi, who had preceded us. Names and rank again —in both languages—after which our defense counsel was introduced. He was the same man who had instructed me to plead guilty back at the prison.

He began his speech in our behalf by apologizing to the court for having to defend such reactionary criminals. He stated that he had been appointed to serve as our defense by the Chinese People because "Chinese humanity" dictated that even the worst of criminals must be given a "fair and just" trial. Then he told the court that we, the accused, had been born and educated under the imperialist system, which bred nothing but vermin and criminals. This we could not help, he said, but since we were grown men and officers we must bear full responsibility for our actions. We must accept whatever punishment the Chinese People dictated. With that our counsel rested his "defense."

To us this seemed worse than no defense at all. It was clear he knew which side his bread was buttered on. Before we could fully absorb what had been said or try to say anything ourselves, we were hustled back to the downstairs waiting room. We sat and waited while the remainder of the crew were "defended."

At this stage of the trial I was so tired and bewildered I could hardly think straight. We were being railroaded, I knew, but what difference did it make. With or without a trial, we were in prison and we knew the court would not allow anything to be said that was not in the script. A glance at Captain Llewellyn told me that he felt as weary and helpless as I did. This had been a trying day, mentally as well as physically. Night had already closed in outside, and the temperature inside the building had dropped considerably. We sat and shivered.

Buck soon returned to join us on the floor. The three of us waited in silence for the next move. Finally Captain Llewellyn was taken out alone. When he returned a few minutes later, I was taken out. I was the only prisoner in the courtroom this time. I stood with guards on each side and slightly behind me while they asked my name and rank for the fourth time. After this the interpreter asked one question.

"Do you realize the seriousness of the charges against you?"

I said yes, and the interpreter snapped, "That's all," and I was hustled out of the courtroom. I was thoroughly puzzled by this last move. Why had they gone to so much trouble to ask me that one question? Why couldn't they have done it when we were all in a group? As I entered the waiting room, Buck was led out. He was back in a few minutes, and the look on his face told me that he was as puzzled as I.

We remained in the waiting room perhaps half an hour longer, then all three of us were led back up the stairs. Just outside the courtroom we halted to wait until all eleven of us were lined up. Then we were taken into the courtrom. We stood there while a review of the trial proceedings was read to the court. This was a rather lengthy process of which I could make little sense. In the summary it was casually mentioned that we had all pleaded guilty. I had not and I felt sure none of the others had, but it was obviously part of the script. I knew it would be futile to protest. Apparently the other ten felt the same way, since they all remained quiet. I think they wanted only one thing, for the trial to be over as soon as possible. I know I did. I could see little point in prolonging something that could only go their way in the end.

With this summary, the trial ended and handcuffs were snapped back around our wrists before we boarded the bus. We made little attempt at any kind of communication during the ride back to the prison. We were tired and stunned by the events of the day. We just sat, lost in our own unhappy thoughts.

Back at the prison we were hustled off the bus and back through the several corridors to our own cells. In lieu of the supper we had missed, the jailer brought us each a cup of water. As he passed it out, I noticed he did not open all the cell doors. The cell which had contained Vaadi and Captain Llewellyn had not been opened. I hacked out their code name, but got no reply. They had not been brought back into the same cell block. This added to the despondency I already felt. A few more hacks and everyone in the cell block knew that "Uncle" was missing.

When things quieted down, we heard hacking coming from another part of the prison. "Uncle" was checking in, letting us know where they were and that they were OK. I hacked out a G.N. and gradually dropped off into troubled sleep.

The morning following our trial saw a change in our prison life. During the night the guard had been doubled and they seemed determined to stop all forms of communication between cells. About the only thing we were able to get through was a G.N. or a G.M., which sounded out whenever the prison bell sent us to bed or got us up. No amount of pressure put on by the guards and jailers could make us give up this small expression of comradeship.

We wanted to exchange our opinions of the trial, but we were not given the chance. When Airman Danny Schmidt tapped on my wall saying, "We've had it," I replied, "No sweat, the trial was a big farce." Others expressed the same opinion, but we were far from being fully convinced.

The more I thought of it, the surer I became that I had been tricked into pleading guilty when I answered "yes" to that one innocent-sounding question. (Later I discovered that most, if not all, of the crew had been asked the same question and had answered it the same way.) The question in Chinese could have been an entirely different one, such as "Do you plead guilty?" The English part of the recording of the trial would have been easy to change. It seemed childish to think that they would resort to such subterfuge, but they had gone to great lengths to stage the trial and had planned it in great detail. It was a master propaganda production, and no doubt it would seem authenic to the millions in Communist countries who would view the pictures and hear the recorded proceedings.

For two weeks following the trial the double guard made their rounds from cell to cell, looking in each one at least once every thirty seconds. One checked a cell and thirty seconds later the other came by. I wondered again if they felt a little silly, but if their purpose was to keep us under constant observation, they were successful. It was impossible to ignore the steady clicking of the flaps as they were jerked open and then released. It was almost as bad as having a private guard.

As soon as the double guard was reduced to the usual single one, we increased our intercell communications. We discussed the trial and the opinions we expressed were many and varied. For the most part, they were on the optimistic side. Things slowly settled back to normal. We received a few more letters from home and were allowed to write again. I didn't mention the trial. Winter was near —our third in China—and our summer clothing was exchanged for the winter paddeds.

The next big change in routine came on the seventeenth of November. Exactly one hundred days after being put into solitary confinement, I was put back into the cell with my former cell mate, Buck. This was a welcome change, for I had grown terribly tired of my own company. To further brighten our life, "Uncle" was returned to our cell block and all nine of us were moved into cells across the corridor. We were still divided as before, but these accommodations were far better. We were now on the south side of the cell block, and the temperature was a good ten degrees warmer. It made us bitter to think that we had needlessly and purposely been kept on the cold side of the cell block during the last winter.

The same day the *jailer* asked *us* if we wanted more food. He even went so far as to give us larger chow bowls. For the first time we ate all we could hold, which was a great deal more than we should have. A full stomach after nearly two years! And that was not the end of the day's good news. The guard didn't seem to mind our talking between cells and we were soon conversing freely, discussing the significance of all the changes. Things really seemed to be looking up. This continued, and five days later, on the twenty-third of November, when we were given a new issue of winter uniforms, our morale was at a new high. In spite of the fact that the memory of our last disappointment was still fresh in our minds, we began to speculate about going home.

Early in the afternoon our hopes were once again crushed. Handcuffs were brought in and snapped on. We were taken out of our cells, through the prison, and back to a waiting bus. The ride that followed was a duplication of the last one, with the same destination.

It had occurred to none of us that after a trial there would be a sentence. That's what followed, however. Again we found ourselves in the courtroom—this time with only one judge presiding. There was somewhat less fanfare this time, fewer lights, fewer photographers, and fewer spectators.

The proceedings were short and to the point. After names and ranks had been given, the record of our trial was read. Next came the sentences. It was obvious that the criteria used to assign us prison terms were rank and crew position. Col. Arnold was to serve ten years, Major Baumer eight, Capt. Vaadi six, Capt. Llewellyn and I five years each, and the remainder of the crew drew terms of four years each. The twenty-two months we had already been in prison was not to count against these terms.

At last we were faced with the cold facts. The uncertainty of our situation had been dispelled, but yet I could not believe it. Knowing the charges were false and knowing that our government was aware of our predicament, I could not believe I would have to spend another five years in China.

As soon as the sentences were read, we were taken out of the courtroom. Colonel Arnold and Major Baumer were separated from us, and we were taken downstairs to a small room, where we were forced to sit on the floor while half a dozen soldiers watched us. They tried to keep us from talking, but had little success. Everyone seemed to be in a humorous mood, which was rather strange considering we had just been given prison sentences. We joked and laughed and expressed the opinion that it was all a big joke. When the guards tried to quiet one of us, someone across the room started rattling handcuffs or tapping the floor. This kept the guards in a state of anger and confusion.

When I rattled my cuffs, one clamp accidentally popped open. They were a well-worn pair, no doubt having seen much use in Communist China, and the spring inside the clamp had broken or grown weak. I knew that the guards would soon spot the open clamp, so with a few quick jerks I slipped my hand through the other clamp. Then I handed the cuffs to the nearest guard. My fellow crew members roared with laughter. It was not so funny to the humorless guards, however. They rushed around in confusion, reaching for their pistols, grabbing hold of me, and trying to quiet the others. I tried to assure them that I had no intention of running away, but they didn't seem to understand. Finally they reapplied the handcuffs, and when one of the guards who had dashed out the door returned with another pair, I found myself wearing two sets. It was several minutes before our laughter stopped and the guards reached a reasonable state of calm.

It was nearly dark outside when we were again loaded into the bus and taken back to prison. Now that we had been tried and sentenced, we expected some kind of change to take place in our confinement. We hoped we would all be put together and allowed more freedom. One of the men mentioned the possibility of our being sent to a prison farm. No doubt he was longing for the outdoors, as was I. We also hoped that Colonel Arnold and Major Baumer would soon join us. We could not believe that the Communists really intended to make us serve out our sentences. Still, we did not know. They had certainly been known to do worse things.

Our food continued to be plentiful, although the quality remained poor. We hoped that this abundance meant we were being fattened up for release. We cooperated wholeheartedly. Nothing pleased us more than to see a little meat cover our bones and our muscles slowly build.

Saturday, December 4, brought a pleasant surprise. When they learned that we were alive, our families had sent packages of food, clothing, and various other articles which the gracious prison officials were keeping for us. That Saturday, for the first time, we were allowed to see the packages and even take a few of the articles back to our cells. The underclothing, handkerchiefs, and toilet articles were a dream to see. There were also magazines, novels and textbooks, but these, along with the canned food, candy, cigarettes and medicines were not allowed us.

On December 7, another big change took place. The nine of us were taken, along with our belongings, to another cell block. This was the same cell block I had walked through so many nights on my way to and from interrogations. Now it was empty of prisoners. Two of the end cells were fairly large, about sixteen by nine feet.

Our bunks and bedding were deposited here and we moved in. Later we were joined by Major Baumer. At last we were to be together! For the first time in twenty-three months we could see each other plainly, shake hands, and carry on unrestricted conversation. It was a great reunion, especially for Major Baumer who had been held in solitary confinement for twenty-three months.

We were still one man short, not counting the three the Chinese said were dead. Our commander, Colonel Arnold, was still in solitary. That was the only thing that blighted our happiness as we sat around talking, laughing, and smoking the cigarettes we had just been given—the first since our capture.

Although this new arrangement was a pleasant one, we all agreed that the Communists deserved no thanks. As far as we were concerned they had violated international law as well as human morality by their treatment of us. The weeks that followed were spent in relative comfort. There were always two guards present in the cell block. An interpreter, whom we called "Bugs Bunny," set up an office in one of the empty cells. He was usually nosing around and it was several days before we learned why. He said he was there to see that our needs were taken care of. All the other cells in the block were empty, and during the day we were allowed the run of our two cells and the corridor. At night we were locked in, but we didn't mind the crowded conditions—we reveled in them. To make matters better yet, we were given a few more articles from the packages from home and we continued to receive mail every two or three weeks.

On Christmas day of 1954, we were given a special meal. To the jailers it may have been something great, but we would have preferred our normal food. Baked chicken was the main dish, but somehow the sight of the heads with empty eye sockets and bills still attached dulled our appetite. The numerous feathers didn't help either, and most of the meat had ben stripped off the bones. We doubted that there had been much there to begin with. Someone remarked that the number of the black and white birds that nestled around the prison had shown a decrease that day. "Bugs Bunny" was disappointed in our failure to do justice to the special meal, but we weren't as hungry as we had been a few months before.

We finally persuaded the prison officials to let us have a Bible from one of the packages from home, and on Sundays we held simple religious services. The guards at first were curious, but after we had the interpreter explain, they did not interfere.

In spite of the severe cold that winter, we were often taken outside to a courtyard for exercise. The guards even gave us a volleyball and net, which we strung up between two trees that stood about fifteen feet apart. We tried to organize a few games, but usually we just passed the ball around. Once a week we were taken to the prison bath house and allowed to scrub down. This remained a high spot in our lives. In addition to a weekly hot shower, we bathed daily, taking water from a large urn which sat in our cell block and which Sam kept filled. He grumbled and complained at our "wasting" so much water which he had to carry by bucket from a hand pump some distance away, but we ignored him.

The generous Chinese finally gave us some bridge cards which helped, more than anything, to pass the time away. Those of us who could not play were soon taught. Tournaments followed, but Bugs Bunny soon decided we were wasting too much time. He drew up a schedule which included several hours a day for study. We agreed to this on the condition that he give us the math, English, and Spanish textbooks which were in one of my packages. He finally did and we held classes in each subject—Maj. Baumer, the best-qualified man, was instructor. From then on we referred to the prison as Peking Tech.

We settled down to the new routine and lived fairly comfortably compared to our recent past. In letters from home our families hinted that negotiations were being made to obtain our release. We all felt sure we would soon go home. We just had to make the best of things until the time came.

CHAPTER
FIFTEEN

Things began to happen on the ninth of January, 1955, which, for a short while, made us again sure release was not far off. The warden and a group of jailers came into our cell block carrying bundles of new clothing. We remembered that a new clothing issue had twice raised our hopes in vain, but this was it. Why else would we be given new clothing when our old clothing was still good? And this clothing was of the same cut and color that all the jailers wore, instead of the pocketless blacks which we had worn until then.

Bugs Bunny soon explained the reason for the new clothing. The prison authorities were giving us a party. Some pictures would be taken to be sent to our families so they could see how we were living. Even after we heard this, we still thought we were on our way home.

Before putting on the new clothes we were given an unscheduled shower, and wonder of wonders, we were shaved with a real razor—the first real shave any of us had had in two years minus three days! We were not allowed to handle the razor. The prison barber did the job, and while this was going on, a photographer appeared and started snapping pictures—pictures of the "everyday" life of American prisoners in China. Pictures were also taken inside our cells while we read letters and played cards.

Then three more prisoners were brought in. One was our commanding officer, Colonel Arnold. The other two were American civilians who had been in Communist hands since late 1952. We were the first Americans they had seen in all this time. It was an incomparable experience for them as well as for Colonel Arnold.

The presence of these three made us all the more certain we were being prepared for release.

The next thing on the agenda for the day was a game of volleyball. We were taken out of our cell block and down a long covered walk, through a hallway, and into a large yard surrounded by walls and buildings. In the center of the bare yard was a full-size volleyball court. Pictures were snapped as we batted the ball over the net a few times, but the icy, biting wind that blew across the yard soon drove the guards, jailers, and photographers back inside. We, of course, were taken along.

Next we were shown into a large dining room. There, sitting on two of the tables, were bowls of steaming Chinese food. Small eating bowls and sets of chopsticks were passed out and we were told to sit and eat. This was by far the best food we had seen in China and we sat down to try it. More pictures were made of this "typical" prisoner's dinner. We were told not to eat too much because we were going to have some American food also. That was all we needed to spoil our appetite for Chinese food.

Baked buns, sausages, sliced meats, eggs, butter, and canned foods of all kinds sent by our families were brought in and placed on another table. We needed no encouragement to move to this table and start opening cans. Good American canned meats! The Chinese food was ignored as we dug into the food from home— the first we had been allowed to have. The photographer clicked away, taking pictures of more "typical" scenes in our daily life, proof that we had received the food our families sent.

We knew the pictures would be used for propaganda purposes, but we were more concerned with what we believed to be preparation for our release and with being all together for the first time. We felt also that the pictures would be a boon to our families—if the Chinese kept their word and sent them. We knew that we could counter any favorable Communist propaganda as soon as we crossed the border into freedom.

After our American-style meal, we moved to the other end of

the dining hall where more tables sat waiting, loaded with bowls of fruit, candy, cigarettes, and pots of tea. A table-tennis set was brought in along with checker and chess games. We hardly touched them; we were much more interested in talking about our departure theories and in comparing stories with Colonel Arnold and the two civilians. We occupied the next couple of hours in this manner, then we were interrupted by the prison officials and told to go with them to another room nearby.

We were led down a short hallway and into a room that had been soldiers' quarters during my interrogation days. Here a group of doctors, nurses, and technicians had set up their equipment and we were given a thorough and lengthy physical examination. I have no reason to believe that the people behind the gauze masks were not what they were supposed to be. They may have been serious about the examinations, but these examinations were for propaganda and not for the prisoners—the clicking camera attested to that.

The physical examination brought the end of our party, and we were escorted back to our cell block—that is, all but three of the group. Along the way, Colonel Arnold and the two civilians were hustled off down another corridor and back to their respective cells. It was a terrible blow for everyone when we realized that they were not going to be left with us. The airmen of the crew— younger and perhaps bolder and less cautious than the rest of us— set up a loud and unruly chorus in protest, but it was hopeless. Bugs Bunny said we were displaying a very poor attitude and little appreciation for the nice party we had been given. For the next few days, we met the interpreters, guards and jailers with sullen looks and uncomplimentary remarks. Finally the warden paid us a visit and let us know that he was in charge, not we. We were a little surprised that nothing more was done, though he made it quite clear that if our poor attitude continued, we would find ourselves back in solitary.

The novelty of our new situation gradually wore off, but not the pleasure derived from having so many cell mates to talk to. Food was plentiful, and after the party the prison officials began handing out some of the food from home. Each time one of us received a new package, we were taken into the interpreter's office where we could inspect its contents and where we were graciously allowed to pick out a few articles to use. The other things would be given to us later, we were told. The jailers and guards must have become convinced we were all capitalist millionaires when they saw the contents of our packages. Our families were sparing nothing in their efforts to supply us with every possible need. We were thankful they did not know we weren't allowed to have most of it.

A few days after the party, the warden paid us another visit. He told us that the Chinese government had invited our families to come to China. He said that we should write letters home encouraging them to make the trip. When he finished and left, we were given writing materials.

It only took a short discussion to decide what we would do. We all wrote letters, but none of us mentioned the proposed trip. We knew that if we told our families not to come over, the letters would never be sent. Most of us felt it would be perfectly safe for them to make the trip. We believed they would be treated royally, and thought it likely that the Chinese planned to make a bid for world good-will by releasing us so that we could accompany our families home after their visit. Still, we did not want them to make the trip. The propaganda value to the Communists would be far too great.

After reading the letters we had written, the interpreter interviewed each of us and wanted to know why we had not asked our families to visit us. Some gave honest answers and some made other excuses, but he was visibly disappointed. Later we were told that the U.S. State Department had refused passports to our families and again we were encouraged to write favorably of the proposal. None of us did.

In February, Bugs Bunny told us we were to begin supervised

study sessions. They would last six hours each day during the week. Saturday mornings would be used in open discussions of what had been learned during the week, and Saturday evening and Sundays we would be free to do as we liked. Study materials—books, pamphlets, newspapers—would be furnished. This sounded fine—for the Communists. To us it smelled of political indoctrination and we wanted none of it. They insisted, however, so we agreed to bide our time and see what the study sessions turned out to be.

Chairs and tables were brought in and an empty cell became a study. Bugs Bunny appeared with reading material and we sat down to look it over. Bugs sat at the table with us to make sure we didn't waste our time playing cards or talking.

The reading material consisted of various magazines, a few political pamphlets, and a few novels. Some were interesting and worthwhile; some were dull and boring. We read them, looked at the pictures, and passed them around. As students, however, we were pretty much of a disappointment. One or two of the group were always up getting water or going to the latrine. Others were whispering or laughing.

When Saturday morning came, Bugs opened the discussion. It was a complete flop. At first no one would do any talking so Bugs asked questions. The answers he got were not to his liking, so we wound up getting a long lecture on the evils of capitalism versus the good of Communism. We let him finish his speech, the sooner to be rid of him, but thereafter during the Saturday morning discussions, we steered things our way so we didn't have to listen to lectures. The discussions rapidly deteriorated into little more than bull sessions, and after a few weeks the interpreter dropped them altogether and absented himself from many of our study periods.

They continued to make us sit in the study room a few hours each day, but we used the time to write letters, write short stories, draw house plans, and shoot the breeze. A minimum of time was spent reading the various magazines and pamphlets, although we looked them over out of curiosity. Most of them were strictly propaganda. We did, however, receive several novels by well-known American and English authors. These we read with relish.

In March we were given our first newspaper. It was a small English-language tabloid published by the Hsinhua News Agency. Of course it presented everything from the Communist point of view, but it was a newspaper and the first look at current events we had had in over two years. We were news-starved and welcomed even a one-sided presentation of current happenings. The paper was a daily, but we received them in batches, once or twice each week.

From articles in the paper, we were able to determine definitely that the Korean War had been over for several months. Confronted with this, Bugs Bunny had to admit that there had been a truce. He would not say why the prison officials had denied for so long that the fighting had stopped. Nor would he tell us when it had ended. From then on he censored the paper more carefully, cutting out many entire articles and keeping whole papers now and then.

Our letters from home continued to mention negotiations, although most such news also was censored. Each time we got a paper with articles missing, we decided it had probably contained something about us. When we asked Bugs Bunny about our release, he said that he thought there was nothing our government could do. It depended on us, he said, adding that we must study hard and show our good will toward the People's Republic of China. He never gave us any hope of being released before our four-to-ten-year sentences were up.

We didn't need any encouraging hints from him. In things concerning our release, our imaginations knew no bounds. We took every tiny improvement in our daily life, every break in the normal routine as an indication of our imminent departure. Only in moments of despondency did we seriously consider the possibility that we would have to serve out our sentences. Nor did we seriously believe that our attitude toward our studies would have any effect on our date of departure. If our release depended on good will toward the Chinese People's Republic, then there was little chance we'd ever be sent home. On the other hand, there seemed little advantage in pushing our jailers to the point of returning us to solitary confinement. Except in rare cases of temperamental outbursts, we always tried to show our jailers and guards that we were well-disciplined American soldiers.

In May of 1955 we were moved to another cell block some distance from our former one. This was a part of the prison that none of us had been in before. As far as we were able to determine, there were no other prisoners in any of the cell blocks in the area. Some cells were empty and some were living quarters for the jailers, guards, and their families. We were given much more freedom of movement in our new quarters, and the guards no longer tried to make us keep our voices down. Our food showed a sudden marked improvement and more things from our packages were handed out, including some of the many cartons of cigarettes our families had thoughtfully sent. Even the cigarettes that had been stored in the prison for many months tasted better than the brand rationed out by the Communists.

We took all this to mean that we were one step closer to release. Some of us even wrote our families that we would be seeing them soon. They, of course, expressed the same opinion in their letters to us. We felt they knew more about our impending release than we, and in order to look less like jailbirds when the time came, we refused the next scheduled hair-clipping. The jailers had no objections, and so we became even more certain our release was near. Our hair had plenty of time to grow before that happened, however.

We settled back into the usual routine after our move. We glued pictures of our wives, mothers, and fathers on the walls of our cells with paste made from rice. Then we wrote home for more snapshots. Some of us saved labels from candy and canned goods and tinfoil from cigarette and chewing-gum wrappers and used them to make designs on the whitewashed cell walls—anything to decorate the drab walls we had to stare at so many months. Here our cells were smaller; there was room for only two wooden bunks in each one. We were paired off again, although we had the run of all the cells except at night. One of these cells—Captain Vaadi's, I believe—was very close to being completely wall-papered with labels by the time the prison authorities got around to moving us again. It looked quite impressive.

In our letters home we asked for the latest automobile literature. It came, in due time, in the form of colorful folders collected from automobile dealers. The folders joined the pictures and labels to cover large areas of our cell walls. They were a source of never-ending curiosity and amazement to our guards and jailers. When we told them we owned automobiles—that almost every family in Capitalist United States owned an automobile—and pointed out, on the folders, the picture of the car each of us intended to buy when we got home, they were even more amazed. They could not understand how it was possible for even the lowest-ranking member of our crew to own an automobile. That probably did more to damage their faith in Communism than anything else we could do.

Automobile folders and candy wrappers did not provide our only occupation. They took up some of our time, but there were many long hours left in every prison day. We continued to get a few worthwhile books now and then, and we played bridge, but we had to be constantly on the lookout for new ways to pass the time. Major Baumer received a couple of books of beginner's piano music in one of his packages, and he conceived the idea of constructing a replica of a piano keyboard from cardboard. In due time this was accomplished—four octaves of black and white keys. With this and the music books we were able to pass many hours, banging away on the silent keys. We got pitying stares from our guards and not a few from other members of the crew. I suppose the guards finally figured out what we were doing.

The move to the new cell block brought other improvements to our daily life. In the patio outside there was a basketball court which we were allowed to use an hour or so each day. It seemed as if the Chinese were really out to make our prison life easier—after so many months of making it as torturous and miserable as possible. We accepted these improvements as long overdue and knew that there was room left for many more.

In June we read of four American fliers who had just been released. Until then we had not known of their existence, nor did we know the circumstance surrounding their capture and imprisonment. The article said that they had been shot down after invading Chinese territorial air and that the Chinese government had deported them. Deported! That was a nice, blame-shifting word. We wished the Communists would do as much for us! After seeing that article, we were sure we would be released in only a matter of days. Our interpreter said our case had nothing to do with theirs and that we should stop thinking of going home. This didn't mar our hopes the least bit—we knew him to be capable of lying in the face of the truth.

Also in June I was taken sick—not seriously, the doctor said, but I was told to stay in bed a few days. I could hardly have done otherwise. I was too weak to sit or stand for very long. When I was able to stay up, I was called in to see the interpreter, who told me I was going to be taken into town to see a dentist. It was about time; I had had a toothache for months. Soon I found myself sitting in the back of a closed truck with a jailer and a guard. There were no handcuffs this trip.

The truck effectively screened me from the local populace and kept me from seeing much along the way. I was able to get glimpses of numerous donkey carts as our driver honked his way past them. He made liberal use of the horn, but we came up behind one vehicle at which he didn't honk—a light tank. The tank appeared to be on a street patrol. A helmeted gunner was in position beside a machine-gun mounted on the open turret hatch. I wondered why. We followed the tank a few blocks then turned into a side street. We soon pulled up to a large brick building which was still partially under construction. It was the hospital, five or six stories high and of a modern, practical design. There were no Oriental carvings or curving gables. The wing we entered appeared to be completed and in use, although there was no one in sight except the receptionist. She directed us to a waiting-room where we took seats on bare wooden benches. For so modern a building, the simple furnishings seemed crude and out of place.

After we had waited several minutes, two people wearing white wraps, caps, and masks walked up. We followed them into a room nearby where a dental unit was set up. The unit was far from modern, but the room was clean and tidy. After seating me in the chair, the dentist discovered that the electricity was not turned on. His assistant departed, but returned from his mission unsuccessful. A flashlight was located and I was soon minus a tooth.

The ride back to prison was uneventful. My nine cell-block mates, who had no idea where I had been taken, became highly optimistic about our release when they learned the prison authorities had taken the trouble to have my tooth pulled.

During the last of June we moved again, this time to a cell block in the same area. The apparent reason for the move was to get us nearer the prison well. We had gradually increased our consumption of water until now we used several buckets full each day. Every time we came in from exercising we insisted on having a bath, plus one at night and a good wash-up each morning. We also insisted on keeping our clothes reasonably clean. This meant washing almost every day.

The jailers had griped and protested, but we griped louder and they brought us the water. This was a lot of extra work for Sam. Soon he was unable to keep up with our needs, so he started letting us take turns fetching it. This arrangement was fine with us, but required extra guards. Finally they moved us to the cell block opening onto the patio that contained the well and pump. Our water consumption became even greater, but we didn't have to transport our bath water into the cell block. Outside in the patio by the pump, there was a large round reservoir which we used as a bathtub.

The guards and jailers could not understand our desire to bathe so often, but they did nothing about it. To us the chance to stay clean was a luxury and we took full advantage of it. With soaps, shampoos, wash cloths and large, colorful, fluffy towels sent from home, we tried to wash away the memory of our long bathless months. We had lived in filth and worn filthy, smelly clothes for two years and we did our best to make up for them.

Not only did we have more water in our new quarters, we had more freedom. At one end of the cell block there was a small, walled patio in which to take sunbaths. We were allowed out into the large patio only once or twice a day, but we could go into the small one any time we wished, except at night. There we spent several hours a day, stripped to our shorts, absorbing the sun's rays.

The interpreter had completely given up his attempts to hold study sessions. Much to our gratification, he found business elsewhere most of the time and paid us visits only when he had new reading material to give us. We usually ignored everything he gave us, with the exception of newspapers and novels. The prison officials finally decided to let us have the magazines which had been sent from home, and these we read over and over again.

While the interpreter left us alone much of the time, the guards still stayed close by, watching our every move. They seldom interfered more than by just being present, however. On the other hand, Sam, the jailer who had been with us the longest, began to spend much more time with us. He was being downright friendly. Though none of us wanted his friendship, we were civil to him, but we did not forget the many months he had not been so genial.

In our new quarters, we used two large cells as sleeping rooms and another even larger one for a dining room. Sam set up shop in a small cell near the end of the cell block and even spent some nights there. As before, we were locked in at night. The electric bulb that lit our new quarters was in a socket in the center of the ceiling. The first night there we unscrewed the bulb. Darkness! For the first time in over two years we could sleep in the dark! It didn't last long, however. As soon as the guard discovered what had happened, he started banging on the door. We ignored him at first, but he persisted and finally called the jailer. We were forced to replace the light bulb, but we didn't give up completely. Those few minutes of darkness had been too delicious. We took a black sock and stretched it over the bulb. The guard's view of this procedure was as dim as the sock-covered light, but we ignored him completely, hoping he'd go away. He did, finally, but only to fetch the jailer again.

We argued with the jailer and talked him into letting us leave the sock over the light. Of course, we ruined a good pair of American socks; by morning the heat from the bulb had scorched it to cinders, but the relative darkness had been more than worth it. Next day we made some rice paste and built a paper shade. Sam looked it over and approved after a little griping, and for the rest of our stay in China we slept in almost total darkness.

CHAPTER

SIXTEEN

Sunday, July 31, 1955 was a day I'll remember all my life. When a couple of unusual events occurred that morning, I started taking notes:

Sunday, July 31, Peking Tech.

9 A.M.—Showers! And on Sunday! Something fishy—we're not due until tomorrow. Oh well, it's probably of no significance. They just don't want the workers who are rebuilding part of the prison to see us tomorrow.

10 A.M.—Who just walked into Sam's office? My gosh, the barber! Two of them. Let's see, the last time we got a shave out of schedule we had a party. Yeah, party! Propaganda photos. Could this be a repeat? Or could it possibly be . . . no, I'm afraid to think about it. We've been disappointed so many times before.

6 P.M.—Well, we got a shave and a haircut. That barber sure took a lot of pains, too. He didn't go to all that trouble for no reason. Something *is* up! What's more, supper was due ten minutes ago and it's never late. These Chinks wouldn't dare get fouled up or they'd be in the next cell. Howard Brown just asked about chow, so the interpreter came in and said we were getting a special meal tonight. Why? He said because it is Sunday. Now let's see, how many Sundays have we been in this institution? About 133, and we've never had a special meal yet. Oh well, must be more propaganda photos.

7 P.M.—Everyone sitting around in shorts (been pretty hot). What's up? Four jailers just came in. Let's go, they say. Like this? No, put on clothes. Well, now we're in black pants and T-shirts and here we go toward the same room where we had our last spe-

cial meal.

There my notes ended. What happened next made me lose all interest in them. We were taken into a small room, and after a few minutes wait we were informed that a representative of the People's Government wanted to talk to us. About then our commander, Colonel Arnold, was brought up and we all were taken into another room nearby.

Here behind a desk sat the warden and a stranger. We stood in two ranks as the stranger began to speak. Then I recognized him. He had been the prosecutor at our trial. I felt sure I knew what he was going to say, but I was afraid to let my hopes get too high. I stood and prayed. He had quite a lot to say. He went into the entire history of our case. Finally he read out each of our names— eleven of us—and said because of our good behavior we were being pardoned.

Although we had been telling ourselves for months that this would happen, it was still hard to believe. There was no shouting as we were dismissed. We turned and walked out of the room as sober as when we entered. Gradually we overcame our shock and began to talk excitedly. We were taken to the room where the propaganda party had been given. A sumptuous Chinese meal was waiting on a table. We sat, but we ate very little. We lost our appetites as our excitement grew.

The warden, the interpreter, and several of our jailers were present and seemed disappointed at the injustice we were doing the food. For awhile they encouraged us to eat, all smiles and friendliness, but finally they gave up and we were taken back to our cells where we were each given a net sack and told to pack our belongings.

I stuck the few notes I'd made into a letter from my wife, but I tore up stories I had written and house plans I had drawn in an effort to keep busy. I was sure I would not be allowed to keep them. I was right.

Our packing took only a few minutes. Then we were taken to

the far side of the prison to what appeared to be the warden's office. Here we were given new clothes—not the prison style, but regular street clothes. Here also we received the rest of the things our families had sent. We were given Red Cross parcels—about half a dozen each—which the American Red Cross had started sending us many months before and which we now saw for the first time.

All our belongings were collected and searched by the prison authorities. Articles of prison clothing were thrown aside, along with poems and stories some of the crew had written and wished to keep. Our letters from home, the contents of the packages and our new clothes were all that was allowed us.

About ten P.M. a bus drove up and we were loaded in with only half a dozen guards this time. About twenty minutes later we were in a train station and soon were on a train. At ten-fifty we left Peking, but under quite different circumstances than we had arrived thirty months earlier.

The three-day train ride that followed was pleasant and interesting. We had sleepers, but we did little sleeping. We were too excited. An interpreter and six yellow-clad security guards accompanied us in the coach, but they left us alone. The meals served aboard the train were relatively good, but we ate the food left over from our packages, mostly. The people we encountered on the train and during the stops seemed only mildly curious, if they took notice of us at all.

At Hankow we crossed the Yangtse River on a ferry. Our next train continued south and on August 3, 1955, more than two and a half years after we were taken into Red China at the northern city of Antung, we arrived in the southern Chinese city of Canton. We were quartered in a hotel overnight, and the next morning we boarded another train which took us, slowly, to the border station at Kowloon. There we went through Chinese customs, and shortly after one P.M., we walked across the Lo Wu bridge. We were met by British customs officers and American Air Force officers and I drew my first easy breath. I knew now that it was too late for the Communists to change their minds about our release. I was free! After nine hundred and thirty-five days I was free!

For many days following our release, I was almost afraid to go to sleep at night. I thought I might wake up and find that my freedom was only a dream.

But it was not a dream. I was free, and I was on my way home.

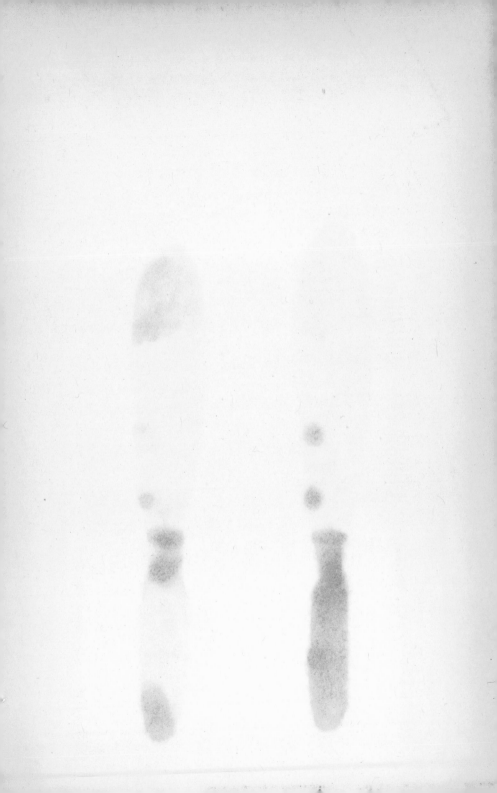